DATE DUE

MARKETPLACE COMMUNICATION

MARKETPLACE COMMUNICATION

MERRIE SPAETH

MASTERMEDIA LIMITED
NEW YORK

ISBN # 1-57-101-032-7

Designed by Michael Woyton
Manufactured in the United States of America
10 9 8 7 6 5 4 3 2 1

CONTENTS

Acknowledgments   xiii

Introduction   xv

Part I: QUICK CASE STUDIES

This section examines a number of case studies, positive and negative, where communication helped or hindered a company or organization in dealing with a crisis, and why a set of events turned into a crisis.

Mickey Loses Manassas   3

The Disney Corporation thought it had a win-win situation with its theme park located on a site near a Civil War battlefield. But the press ended up being the real battlefield, and Disney surrendered.

Can Your Cellular Telephone Really Cause Cancer?   6

This stupid rumor, first heard on a talk show, cost cellular phone companies a lot of time and money. But the Cellular Phone Association's long-term strategy buried the negative news with positive images. Also: a cautionary word for those who write manuals.

When Your Accuser is Inside   9

The Food Lion grocery chain got a raw deal from the media, but their own actions made it worse.

What Response is In-Line?   12

When the Consumer Product Safety Commission issued a warning about in-line skates the same week a child was killed in an accident, the industry's response was not "in-line."

A New Brand of Health Care   15

Memphis-based Baptist Memorial Health Care System, Inc., the nation's largest private system, set about to capitalize on its stature as a premier provider so that it can dominate the market in the future and deliver the best care.

Is Anything Secret?   18

A cautionary tale from insurers of how documents written for internal use look very different to other eyes.

Romance   21
*A romantic job description turns out to characterize a
traditional company. Personal research and replication of
author's conclusion are a must.*

When Your Industry is Under Attack   23
*The story of the image portrayed by the pharmaceutical compa-
nies and how it carried the day in public perception against
President and Mrs. Clinton's charges of "greedy, profiteering"
businesses.*

What's in a Name?   26
Job description titles can mean a lot.

Oil Companies Screw Up   30
The oil companies can make things worse for themselves.

Pepsi Tampering Scare   33
*A model of how to perform under stress. A company doesn't
have to do a perfect job to do a good job.*

Sandoz Pharmaceuticals—"Shame on You?"   36
*Sandoz Pharmaceuticals, makers of the popular and effective
children's cough medicine Triaminic, shoots itself in the foot
in a CBS interview, but the "shame on you" really is on CBS.*

The Car Dealers Launch an Ethics Program   40
*Congratulations to the New Car Dealers for an innovative
and much needed program.*

The Strikes and Strife at Caterpillar   42
Nyah. Nyah. Did too. Did not. Are these adults?

We Messed Up   44
*When software maker Intuit's popular TurboTax and
MacinTax were discovered to have problems, and then the
company waited to announce it, they were just about to suffer
the same fate as Intel for the problems with the Pentium Chip.*

Lowering (the Perception of) Doctors' Salaries   48
*Will it work to decree that physicians don't make as much as
you think they do?*

They Protest Too Much   51
*Example where protesting a less-than-favorable book about
your company confirms the writer's thesis.*

New Cheerios?   54
Don't mess with my kid's favorite cereal.

The Tower of Babel   57
*An unusually good example of how Sky Chefs forged a
team environment with minimum-wage employees who*

speak 38 languages and live in different countries.
Ma'hlo.

More Examples 59
The power of example is the best teacher.

Part II: THE CEO AS LEADER
The CEO sets the tone and others imitate his behavior. A few comments and examples.

Superb Honesty 65
Mike Walsh, CEO of Tenneco, demonstrated leadership in death as well as life.

CEOs and Speeches 68
How good are you at giving a speech?

Stupid, Stupid, Stupid 70
So you made a fool of yourself. Don't worry.

CEO Salaries 74
Are CEO salaries out of line? How do you explain them to someone who makes, according to a 1991 business survey, 1/150th of what the CEO makes?

Should a Company President Do His Own Ads? 77
When can a tough man sell a tender chicken?

The Embarrassment in Your Industry 79
Should you ignore the ignorant, biased, insulting comments of someone from another company? (If you answer "yes," go to jail. Do not pass Go.)

What Does the Board Know? 81
And who should tell them? Boards are demanding to know more these days and more from their CEO.

Vision 84
Do you need the "vision thing"?

What We Learned From NAFTA 87
We learned that companies need to take an interest in what employees know before the company needs to know they know it.

Part III: COMMUNICATION AS PART OF OTHER THINGS
Analysis of communication topics as one part of something else going on.

Just What is Sexual Harassment? 93
Sleep with me or else? A look? A glance? What does this say about the ability to communicate a standard?

New, Casual Clothes 96
Loosening up dress codes can loosen up creativity.

Should a Company Publicize Good Deeds? 98
When it's appropriate and when it's not.

What Manners Tell Us 101
Good manners say a lot. Bad manners — slurp, slurp — also say a lot.

Creating a Culture of Good Manners 104
People imitate others' good manners.

Use Humor 107
Are you funny . . . enough?

Empowerment 110
How you get it and keep it.

False and Deceptive 112
A publishing trend that misleads says a lot about publishing today.

Direct Marketing 115
Technology evens the playing field.

General Motors 118
Virtually every problem has a communication component.

Does Business Want Good News? 120
Not all reporters are Sam Donaldson, but some companies behave as if they are.

The Re-engineering Rhythm 122
He says "restructuring," you say ????

Somebody's Listening 126
Analysts love layoffs. Employees hear something different.

The Case of the Bleeding Messages 129
One group loves the message; another panics.

Business Messages 132
More on how what we say sounds different to certain listeners.

Being Included 134
What's missing from this picture? Who notices and what does it say?

Diversity Training 136
Too diverse.

School Days 139
Your second grader is joining Toastmasters.

Customer Satisfaction 142
Examples. What encourages "above and beyond" performance and what discourages it?

Acquisition 146
Routinely mouthed words during takeovers can compromise credibility.

Part IV: COMMUNICATION TOPICS EVERYONE UNDERSTANDS
Writing, videotaping, newsletters — everyone understands these topics involve communication.

Communication and Strategy 151
Where the proverbial ounce of prevention would have made a difference.

Where to Place the Communication Person 155
For maximum effectiveness, to whom should the communication person in a corporation report?

Corporate Video 158
A great tool, frequently misused.

Do Women Communicate Differently From Men? 161
This has spawned several best-sellers. The answer is both yes and no. Relevant to human resources departments struggling with gender issues.

E-Mail 164
This communication tool has great potential.

Newsletters I: Old Hat 167
This communication tool, which had great potential, has lost most of it.

Newsletters II: Old Hat but a Vital Tool 170
And how to get the zing back.

Quarterly Reports 173
What's happened to some quarterly reports is a great example of what Hammer and Champy meant by the famous definition of "re-engineering" — start all over again.

Resume Writing to Sell 175
With so many people looking for a job, one would think resumes would be better written.

Model Memos 177
Although schools no longer teach writing, can a book really give us a set of "models" to follow which will make everything work?

Communication Training: I 180
Another hot word, "training," has some pluses.

Communication Training: II 184
But do it right or it's not money well spent.

I Am Not a Crook   187
Why what we say sometimes has the opposite effect of what we mean.

A Company's Greatest Untapped Resource: I   190
Are people really your most important asset?

Untapped Resource: II   193
Again, are people really your most important asset?

Dealing with the Difficult Employee   196
Can communication help deal with the difficult colleague?

The Difficult Boss   199
What about the impossible boss?

Part V: TIPS FOR THE OUTSTANDING SPEAKER
Ideas and benchmarks for those who want to differentiate themselves.

The Introduction   205
The introduction should be just what the chapter title says; learn how to do this right.

Tell an Anecdote   208
Facts have their place, but we live in the age of anecdotes.

But I Can't Talk Without Overheads!   211
The executive says, "Of course I'm ready for my presentation, I have 100 overheads." Is he ready?

The Perfect Speech   214
Not a perfect speaker, but a model of how to prepare and be effective.

You Don't Have to be Perfect   218
In fact, we don't want you to be perfect today.

Let a Smile Be Your Umbrella   221
The first rule of communication.

Interaction: Today's Key Speakers' Tool   223
The most exciting, demanding tool for speakers.

How Numbers Lie   227
Don't think you're being persuasive because you're armed with statistics.

More on How Numbers Lie   229
More traps with numbers.

The Panel   233
How to make the most of being on a panel.

Part VI: WHEN YOU HAVE TO SAY IT YOURSELF
In my experience, the three toughest things when you have to say them yourself.

I'm Sorry   239
It's important.

I was Fired   242
More options than traditionally thought.

I Quit   245
Should be a great moment but is frequently very difficult.

Part VII: DEALING WITH THE MEDIA
A few words of advice about working with a powerful route of communication internally and externally.

No Comment   251
Don't.

Confirm or Deny   255
You just did.

What Did You Really Say?   258
In our surveys, most executives say they fear being misquoted. Here's why.

Reporting — Just the Facts   260
When the reporter says he only wants the facts, don't laugh in his face.

No Fair   263
Reporters are unfair. You aren't powerless.

What Do Reporters Think of PR?   266
A plea for mutual respect and civility.

Part VIII: BEGINNING THOUGHTS ON COMMUNICATION, GOVERNMENT, AND PUBLIC POLICY ISSUES
The government tells us much more than it thinks we hear ... and Abe Lincoln was right.

Use Good Judgment   273
Why birds of a feather flock together.

Should Business Communication Involve Economics?   275
Why business shares the blame for the widespread misunderstanding of how a market economy works.

Bankers' Confusion   277
Lack of clarity from regulators has grave consequences for real people.

Law Abiding   280
   *Passing laws is only one part of communicating what society
   expects, not a very convincing part either.*

The Budget Agreements   282
   What Congress is really telling us . . . if we listen hard.

Disclosure? Disclosing What?   285
   *Regulatory zeal accomplishes the opposite of what is intended
   and claimed.*

Disclosure, Disclosing Nothing   288
   Information that's less than useful.

ACKNOWLEDGMENTS

This collection exists because of the interest and encouragement of many people.

Communication today is a hot topic, and every article on re-engineering or changing corporate culture or customer satisfaction uses the word communication frequently. But — what does it mean?

Several years ago *Marketplace*, a daily business show produced by Public Radio International from the University of Southern California, decided to explore the topic and devote a regular forum to the topic of communication. *Marketplace* airs on more than 200 national public radio stations across the country. My first expression of thanks goes to the group there for their interest in the subject, their open-mindedness, their encouragement, and their keen editing abilities. These include J. J. Yore, Jim Russell, Penny Dennis, Debra Baer, and their colleagues at KERA in Dallas, my home station that actually does the work which gets my material from Dallas to Los Angeles. These individuals are generous with their insights and improvements and give me the opportunity to hammer home the idea that communication takes some thought and is worth learning, and to do so helps all other business goals and not to do so puts them at risk.

I owe a great deal to Columbia Business School, which nursed me through the master's program, particularly to Professor Ian MacMillan (now head of the Center for Enterprising at the Wharton School) and Tom Ference, as well as to the Business Leadership Center at the Cox School of Business at Southern Methodist University. The latter has given me a forum to influence future business leaders.

Additional thanks goes to our clients. We have prospered because of them and are living proof of the importance and success of forming long-term relationships. A special and heartfelt note of appreciation to Dallas-based Baylor Health Care System, which funded our first lecture series nine years ago. Baylor continues as a reminder that good communication and strategic communication is about good judgment, competence, integrity, and approaching life with a sense of mission and humility. I am deeply grateful to Boone Powell, Sr., and his son, Boone Powell, Jr., for their support and for being role models as CEOs.

At various points in life, certain individuals take time to perform a "mitzvah," a good deed, to point the way or to offer advice at a crucial time. These individuals have included Sheldon Zalaznick, former editor of *Forbes*, who as editor of *New York* magazine, told me to go "write my brains out"; Av Westin, former executive producer at ABC's *20/20*; James Miller, former chairman of the Federal Trade Commission, who gave me the opportunity to use communication to help the Commission enforce crucial laws, to show lawyers how communication skills could improve the Commission's effectiveness, and who said, "I think you approach this in a way totally different from anyone else"; and President Ronald Reagan, who gave me the chance to build the media office at the White House and bring it "into the space age," in the words of *The Washington Times*.

Every author who is also a decent human being always notes those whose day-to-day assistance makes achievement possible, for virtually everything today is a product of teamwork. At our company that includes Rebecca Shaw, my toughest critic; Marci Borders Johnson, our chief administrative officer who handles all the details and technical aspects of running a vigorous consulting company so I don't have to; and the assistants who have helped organize material, particularly Jennifer Enlow.

A special note of thanks to Thomas Cole and my friend Lisette McSoud.

My family has supported the amount of time it takes to start, build, and run a company as well as to act as a missionary for deeply held beliefs. My parents, Nancy and Phil Spaeth, have consistently stressed that opportunity is there for those willing to work hard. I am grateful to them for being living examples of the importance of doing the right thing for the right reason.

INTRODUCTION

This book is for CEOs, senior executives, those who hope to be senior executives, and anyone else who functions in today's competitive, volatile business environment. This is a book about how to use communication as an effective tool to accomplish *other* business objectives.

Communication is one of the business buzzwords of the 1990s. You can't find anyone who wants bad communication. Like "quality" and other buzzwords, communication risks being all things to all people and so, in the end, nothing at all and not at all useful.

The reader will quickly see that this is not a textbook or a book of learned essays and lengthy case studies. My publisher Susan Stautberg, like me a former White House Fellow, tells a story about a book publishing chain which put a $50 gift certificate at page 150 of best-selling but lengthy tomes by major business writers. They did not have to redeem one certificate.

This book is designed to be read by the busy executive. I gratefully tip my hat to the contribution of *USA Today*, which self-styled serious journalists called "McNews" when it premiered a decade ago. The readability of *USA Today* has influenced countless other publications, even those as important as the *Wall Street Journal.*

This book should be fun to read, and the reader should be able to read it quickly or read parts of it quickly. The *Journal* is usually a model of how information should be put together. (Think of the *Journal* in its multimedia form, including the Dow Jones newswire and their effort to use the paper as a teaching tool in schools. The *Journal* is far more than the three sections of text which arrive on your desk every weekday.) Peter Kann, publisher of the *Journal*, says their average reader spends 47 minutes reading the paper.

Communication today needs to be customer focused. Like virtually all business practices, one must look at communication from the viewpoint of what the *customer*, or target audience, needs. This means abandoning the mind-set of "what I want to say," or the equally prevalent "what I think you need to know" approach. Both are natural and traditional, but both hinder rather than help communication.

My father, a retired ophthalmologist, says it's better to be lucky than smart, but the trick is knowing the difference. Our firm has clearly been lucky. We became entrepreneurs as so many other Texans did — by necessity, caught up in the throes of Texas banking's sinking ship. My father also says that I am living proof that Columbia Business School will help anyone graduate. Columbia taught me many useful things, including how to sit down with a target client and assess needs. On our first day in business, we sat down with the president of the Texas Division of Southwestern Bell Telephone who said, "We're training our customer representatives. They go talk to the customer. Someone else goes and talks to the customer, but we find the customer *remembers* something very different from what we told him."

It was an epiphany, and I realized I had spent my entire life, through an appointment as a White House Fellow, through a stint at the FBI and Federal Trade Commission, on to being Ronald Reagan's Director of Media Relations, and through a varied career in journalism, with the state of mind described above. I approached communication thinking, "What do I want to say?" As regulators, our approach was definitely, "What do those we regulate need to know?" Yet in the nine years we have been in business, whenever we turn to a group or client and ask, "How much does a listener remember? A lot or a little?" they invariably respond "a little."

Our initial clients, Arthur Andersen LLP, Baylor University Medical Center in Dallas and Ward Howell International, gave us the go-ahead to investigate the dynamics that drive the memory of the listener and to develop a model and approach for business to apply the concept to day-to-day business dealings.

The concept that you drive communication *by what you want a target listener to remember* became our mission. We call it analyzing communication based on how a person or audience *hears* certain things; what makes him a *believer,* and what makes him *remember* certain things (and not others).

The concept has implications for your personal communication skills and for how your company handles day-to-day affairs and crises. Most of all, I hope it will affect how business people *think* about communication. Typically, communication has been regarded as a soft skill and an afterthought, not what a company really did as its main line of work.

Communication as a strategy has also been an afterthought. I call it the "quick, we need a brochure" way of thinking. Rather than thinking of the target customer or audience, and what avenues are available to reach them, or how good the skills are of the people involved — a company tends to have the knee-jerk reaction "we need a brochure." Many brochures are, of course, very useful, but a brochure is simply one of many ways to communicate.

Most of us learn most easily from mistakes. "How do you get good judgment? From the times you used bad judgment." So there is a section with quick case studies. These are not meant to be fully fleshed out expositions, but rather examples that will cause the reader to think a bit, or to reflect *before* doing something.

This collection of essays grew out of my regular commentaries on business communication on *Marketplace*, the daily business show produced at the University of Southern California (USC) and aired on more than 200 public radio stations around the country. Three years ago, *Marketplace* producers J. J. Yore and Jim Russell heard one of my commentaries locally on KERA in Dallas and asked me to be a regular participant in their lineup. "We want to make sure it's useful," said J. J. "Just keep it short," dictated Jim Russell. We tried to follow that instruction, and many of the "quick cases" discuss well-publicized situations. A number of the "quick cases" that are good examples were less publicized. Some of the "quick cases" — "Does your Cellular Phone *Really* Cause Cancer?" — discuss well-publicized cases but examine the thinking behind how an organization or company responded to a controversy.

Communication, like quality, flows from the top down in an organization, so Part II of the book is for the company's leadership. You will note that it does *not* deal with how the CEO stands, sits or buttons his shirt. Issues of style are not irrelevant, but they are far less relevant than most people realize. Someone can communicate effectively but still be mediocre according to the arbiters of style and presentation skills. Someone can be very good, according to the traditional benchmarks of analysis, but not very effective by our standards. Again, effectiveness means whether the right message gets to the right person or audience.

In my experience, CEOs and other business leaders lose their perspective because they fail to understand how information is modified *for them.* One of my earliest teachers on communication was former FBI Director William Webster. A former Federal judge, Webster maintained a system which ensured multiple sources of information and multiple ways to analyze information.

Webster would have agreed with the advice, "Don't believe your own press releases." Producer Jerome Hellman uttered that chestnut to me on the first day of filming *The World of Henry Orient* with Peter Sellers and Angela Lansbury back in 1963. Despite being a starstruck 14-year-old, I sensed that Hellman's words had the ring of truth, and more people should print them on a little wallet card and carry them around. In the corporate setting, the idea of continuing to question your past successes and re-examining why one does something well is called "re-engineering," a powerful force with its own communication challenges. We have seen many efforts fail to achieve their full potential because the leaders did not understand how to analyze and drive communication properly. The result was messages or information which were incomplete, occasionally inaccurate, inconsistent, and more often than one would like, contradictory.

Let me give you a quick example: many cost-cutting efforts start with great internal fanfare; they seek to involve all employees, and they are promoted internally with the message of what they will do for corporate competitiveness, etc. All this information is actually true. The problem comes when corporate executives decline to give up or put on the table for consideration their own salaries, perks, special offices, and so on. Employees are not dumb, and they quickly recognize that cost-cutting is important — but not apparently important enough to require the leadership to wound themselves. The articulated messages were absolutely correct, but other information affected how people received or believed it. The words weren't enough, and in some cases, they achieve exactly the opposite affect of what's desired.

"Words, words, words, I'm so sick of words. Is that all you blighters can do?" sings Eliza angrily in *My Fair Lady*. But words are, we believe strongly, the foundation of communication. They are the main lever of memory. That is, most of us listen to a presentation or to what went on at a meeting, and when we see someone else, we seize on certain words and form our recollections around them. So there are some comments about the relevance of spoken communication, mostly in the "Tips" section but scattered throughout the text. For example, "Tell an Anecdote" mentions a lesson learned from working for President Reagan, who deserved his title "The Great Communicator," although people misclassified him as merely a performer. (He certainly understood the need to rehearse.) Reagan was foremost a person who tried to find a way to make a bond with his listeners. He genuinely liked people, but he was not plagued by the incapacitating need of many politicians to have his listener like him. He received adulation graciously, but his communication skills were an outgrowth of his respect for his listeners. Anecdotes about some of the other things we have to say appear in "When You Have to Say it Yourself," and three of the hardest things to say: "I'm Sorry," "I was Fired," and "I Quit."

One of the worst things to say, "No comment," appears in "Dealing with the Media." The press is a crucial method of communication today for both external and internal communication, so every businessperson should glance at this section to avoid some of the most common and easily avoided mistakes. Get your lawyers to read the chapter "Confirm or Deny" to understand that just because he or she wants you to say it for legal reasons doesn't mean you necessarily should.

Similarly, give your lawyers the chapter "Disclosure, Disclosing Nothing," which appears in the final section and begins to examine how government has mangled communication and forced business to do the same. I'm arguing that we shouldn't go down without a fight.

The first chapter in this section takes another cue from Judge Webster. When I was assigned as a White House Fellow to the FBI, my first reaction was panic. At ABC's *20/20*, I hadn't been awake at 7:30 a.m., let alone dressed, at the office, coherent (well, sort of coherent), and prepared to discuss the day's events. There's hardly been a sharper clash of cultures than going from *20/20* to the FBI. I was the first White House Fellow and (arriving simultaneously with another woman) the first woman on the Director's staff. Everyone else was a lawyer. I stuck out like a sore thumb. After several weeks, I asked Judge Webster if we could put together a job description so I could tell people what I was doing at the Bureau. (It would, of course, also tell me what I was supposed to be doing.) He said, "Good idea," put on his half glasses and jotted something on a piece of paper. He handed it over to me. It said "Duties as needed." I gulped and asked if we could flesh it out a little. "Certainly," he replied. He wrote something else and handed the paper back to me. He had added the phrase "Use good judgment."

This book is about good judgment. What's in here should be common sense and second nature, but it rarely is. You, my reader, don't have much time. You are already good at what you do. I hope these short chapters will give you food for thought, insight, and, ultimately, good judgment.

Thank you for taking the time to pick up the book. We hope you find it useful and fun, and I personally welcome your comments, criticism, and your own stories about what doesn't work and what does.

Part I

QUICK CASE STUDIES

"In a crass, poorly articulated way, Michael Eisner was right. Our populace doesn't know who lives at Mount Vernon, and who has the track record of attracting people? Disney."
— MERRIE SPAETH

MICKEY LOSES MANASSAS

Never underestimate old battles, battlefields, and battle axes. Like vampires, they never die. This is not Serbia. This is a lesson learned by the Disney Company, which planned to build a theme park near the Civil War battlefields in Northern Virginia.

What went wrong? In hindsight, it's clear. And a lose-lose situation was created. The battlefield has not been protected from future development. The community lost 17,000 jobs. Disney lost a new project as well as enough face to erase the ears, pointed noses, and painted cheeks of its well-known characters.

The proposal — to build a theme park and related businesses near a Civil War battleground — was rolled out with much fanfare. At first, the rumblings of discontent were dismissed as unimportant. Then, a rage as strong as Stonewall Jackson's charges welled up and ultimately caused the Disney Company to slink away. What went wrong and what lessons can be learned?

First, never underestimate history. The Civil War plays a unique role in our heritage. People still "live" the Civil War, whether it's re-enacting battles (mud and original cooking included) or tramping around green hills like Gettysburg. My husband and I returned to Gettysburg one afternoon years ago to look for the name of his great-great-grandfather, a drummer boy in a Pennsylvania regiment. We found his name on a monument and, like the other visitors paying tribute to kin, buffed away the grime obscuring his name with my emery board. Emotions like these make a powerful foe.

Second, CEOs need media training. The media will behave predictably, quoting the sensational and outrageous over the reasonable and appropriate. Disney Chairman Michael Eisner was quoted in numerous papers saying that he "sat through many history classes where I read some of their stuff and I didn't learn anything," which needlessly infuriated every history teacher in the country. Candor has limits. Mr. Eisner's comment, "I never heard of Middleburg," or the company's assertion that they owned it so it was theirs, helped the opposition rally. Left out were his other comments that, "most kids don't know who lived at Monticello, Montpelier and Mount Vernon." (This is a test. Do you know? See the next page for answers.)

Third, in a battle there's usually a loser. Rallying the local community with the argument that the theme park would create jobs and economic development was the right move at the wrong time, creating a "win-lose" equation.

Next, money doesn't buy everything. Disney belatedly hired experts to guide them and put their stamp of approval on the development plans, but hiring them late in the game and the question of pay tainted the appearance of objectivity. It shouldn't have, but it did. Most press stories described the Disney advisors as "paid consultants," or some other phrase implying that they were less than honest.

Another lesson: Great writing is still important, even in the MTV age. Historian C. Vann Woodward, allied with the anti-Disney forces, wrote, "This part of Northern Virginia has soaked up more of the blood, sweat, and tears of American history than any other area of the country. It has bred more founding fathers, inspired more soaring hopes and ideals, and witnessed more triumphs and failures, victories, and lost causes than any other place in the country. If such a past can render a soil 'sacred,' this sliver is the perfect venue." M–I–C–K–E–Y–M–O–U–S–E was ill equipped to compete with this eloquence.

Opinion leaders are a separate constituency. When planning a campaign, targeting the audience and tailoring the message and the vehicle are important. The Disney people apparently used too broad a brush.

Build coalitions early in the game. This is part of the "win-lose" problem.

Time and trust are crucial. We see this frequently. The out-of-towners blow in with their Gucci shoes and well-fitting suits accompanied by prosperous-looking lawyers only to run afoul of locals who make much less money but control the zoning regulations. Today's publicly held American corporations, driven by the God of Quarterly Earnings, are ill equipped to invest time, which is as valuable a commodity as money.

And so Professor Woodward calls it right again: triumphs, failures, victories, and lost causes. American business loses big at Manassas. But that's not the only loss. In a crass, poorly articulated way, Michael Eisner was right. Our populace doesn't know who lives at Mount Vernon, and who has the track record of attracting people? Disney. And the American people will never get a chance to see if Disney could have married its skills with American history.

(**Answer:** Jefferson lived at Monticello, Madison at Montpelier, and Washington at Mount Vernon.)

> *"... the people in the cellular telephone industry believe passionately that they have a mission. The power of this conviction and excitement jump through their industry and corporate messages."* — MERRIE SPAETH

CAN YOUR CELLULAR TELEPHONE REALLY CAUSE CANCER?

You've heard the saying that everything good is either illegal, immoral, or fattening. The modern version adds, "or causes cancer." One cautionary example of what a company has to face today are the allegations against Motorola and NEC that their cellular phones cause brain cancer.

Naturally, this started on the *Larry King Show*. A man is sure his wife's cellular phone caused her brain cancer. How could he get such an insane idea? Easy. From the operating manual. It advises users to avoid contact with the phone antenna during "high radiation periods." Radiation? Three Mile Island in your portable phone? Who wrote that? I'll bet it was technical people or lawyers — or both.

First problem: The so-called disclosure statement is full of gobbledygook and jargon. What is 0.6 watts and why do I care? Technicians write like this because it shows their power over us. Lawyers write like this in the vain hope of avoiding litigation.

Second problem: The word "radiation" is what I call a "high velocity" word. It travels fast. It scares people. Like "layoff" and "bankruptcy." Most people think (wrongly) that there's no such thing as a little radiation. Or no such thing as good radiation.

That's absurd, of course. We get radiation just walking around on earth, riding in airplanes, and even from toasters (I think). But we've encouraged people to think they can, and should, avoid all risks. So a word like "radiation" is just waiting to fall on receptive, paranoid ears. Disclosures and manuals should be written in simple, clear language. Period.

6

Once these ridiculous charges were aired (literally), what did Motorola and NEC do? They fought back, defending their product. And not with a wishy-washy, "our product meets all safety standards." Ask the lawn-mower makers if that protected them from plaintiffs' lawyers. For example, one company had to pay a huge amount to a family that let their four-year-old drive the mower and feel around under the blade while the engine was running.

There were admittedly glitches along the way. Initially, *USA Today* and the *Wall Street Journal* reported that NEC's spokesman was "unavailable for comment." This was almost certainly the advice he received from the company's attorneys. But this was the time to mount an offensive campaign.

At a press conference for Motorola, the executive briefing the press made a strong start by saying, "Our products are safe," and by pointing out that many studies showed this. However, when a reporter asked him to describe some of those studies, the executive blanked out. What seemed like hours of silence (probably only a few seconds) changed the tenor of the press conference.

This happens to all of us. We know we should know the information. We may even actually know it, but it won't come out. Fortunately, this is just a performance technique which involves handling unexpected questions or handling your own delivery skills. (Unfortunately, training for such situations and practicing is something that few executives do.) Just as the Boy Scouts taught us, the time to prepare is before you actually need it. When you realize you need it, there's not time.

In a crisis, the best strategy is not a defensive one. And the test isn't perfection. Although Motorola suffered a temporary setback, there are plenty of people in the press who realize that defendants and lawyers have played all of us for patsies. NEC and Motorola are among the nation's leaders in providing high-quality products.

The longer-range strategy of the cellular phone industry has apparently been the sophisticated strategy of substitution. That is, although "cancer" is a scary word, and some people will always be convinced that cellular phones cause cancer, saving lives is an even more compelling message. The Cellular Telecommunications Industry Association (CTIA) has made sure that we hear numerous examples of how cellular phones save lives. In one dramatic example, a bus filled with Girl Scouts slipped off a steep highway in California. A following motorist had — you guessed it — a cellular phone and called for help. It arrived in time.

The message from this ongoing battle: Check your own material so you aren't the one suggesting the problem. Your material should be written by people, not lawyers, engineers or accountants. Next, the best defense is a good offense. Aggressively promoting the benefits of your products and services is the best way to reach the public.

It's interesting to note that the people in the cellular telephone industry believe passionately that they have a mission. They are convinced that having a cellular telephone will increase safety, business success, and the convenience of daily personal life. The power of this conviction and excitement jump through their industry and corporate messages. Other companies and other industries should take note.

Postscript to top management: Support tort reform, especially the principle (common in other countries) that the loser pays the legal fees. That will go a long way in discouraging these nutty lawsuits.

WHEN YOUR ACCUSER IS INSIDE

It's every company's worst nightmare. In many ways, it's worse than the plane that crashes or the product tainted by some nut. It's the crisis caused when your own employee publicly charges you with wrongdoing. What do you do when the enemy is inside? Food Lion, the giant supermarket chain, found itself under attack from its own people — and the media — for a number of alleged practices. The media joined with the employees making the charges. They successfully enlisted the press on their side.

This is not a situation to take lightly. Some Food Lion employees charged publicly on ABC's *PrimeTIME Live* that Food Lion sold spoiled meat camouflaged with lemon juice or Clorox, removed manufacturers' dates from packages to sell them past their prime, took food from trash dumpsters and sold it, and required employees to work overtime without pay.

Food Lion got wind of the ABC "investigation," threatened legal action, and actually delayed the airing of the show. Then they began an aggressive advertising campaign denying the charges.

Is this how to handle the situation? No. First, some history. This is actually a bitter labor dispute, and ABC got in the middle of it, attracted by the inflammatory charges of tainted meat. By stonewalling ABC, Food Lion convinced them the charges were true.

"Investigative" stories like this start out one-sided. That's because the producer gets an idea or a lead, researches it, and takes it up with the executive producer of the show, who then approves the resources to film it. Frequently, the "research" phase is too short, and the company that is the unhappy target of the "investigation" may learn of the story at the last minute. The ideal way to meet this challenge is to totally open up your shop. Issue a blanket invitation to the skeptical media that they can go anywhere, anytime. Occasionally, this works, and the story actually changes. This was the case years ago when *60 Minutes* "investigated" labor practices at Coors Beer. Advised by media experts Ken Fairchild and Lisa LeMaster, Coors opened its doors. Researchers and producers reached the conclusion that the pro-labor employees who had contacted them had misrepresented the company's attitude, working conditions, and the attitude of most employees. When the *60 Minutes* story went on the air, the *entire* story was reported: namely, that those attempting to organize the company had contacted the show, and made certain representations that the investigation did not bear those out. That's *real* investigatory work.

Companies perceive this as risky because it requires allowing the reporter to talk to employees who will be critical of the company. Unlike an investigation launched by an outside force, the allegations and complaints of employees have special credibility. Coors was lucky.

Far more frequent is the experience of Fort Sanders Alliance Hospital in Knoxville, Tennessee. A disgruntled donor to the hospital's cancer center set in motion a chain of events which included a *New York Times* investigation and a hearing in front of Congressman John Dingell, well-known for terrorizing witnesses in order to make headlines. Next, *Dateline* arrived. Despite the open-door policy, *Dateline* had no intention of truly investigating. Blatant untruths were broadcast as fact, and the obvious bias of the instigating party and those who supported his side were ignored. One "expert" witness had been paid by the annoyed donor to write a "report" analyzing and criticizing the hospital and cancer center's practices. He did so without ever visiting the center, talking to the staff, or even showing them the report so they could respond to it! These facts never made it on the air. The hospital was held up as an example of greed, mismanagement, and callous disregard for patient needs.

Still, the hospital did the right thing by participating with *Dateline.* At least the quote of the CEO got on the air. "Our concern has always been the care of the patients, always has, always will," he says earnestly to the camera. The staff of the center and the board of directors were infuriated by *Dateline*'s obvious bias, and they rallied around the hospital.

By contrast, Food Lion did not participate in ABC's show. They were convinced that they would not get a fair shake, and they were right. However, they participated anyway. They were saying, "We won't participate," "No comment," and "You would just edit our comments out."

Food Lion should have had a top executive or the CEO sit down in front of that camera and say, (1) "This is a labor dispute;" (2) "We have the highest quality products and practices;" and (3) "Please judge for yourself. Go into our stores and look — and here's my number if you find something."

Would *PrimeTIME Live* have edited that out? Maybe, maybe not. But the CEO needs to do it anyway. Food Lion's own camera crew should have filmed him saying it. The company should have circulated their video to crucial audiences such as employees. They are the ones who interact with customers, and they're the ones who have to maintain those high standards. It should have been sent to Wall Street analysts, to buttress the contention of adherence to regulatory standards, and probably to health inspectors and regulators. They read the papers, too, and get many ideas from the media. After the show, papers quoted inspectors as saying they would look harder at Food Lion stores.

Moving the press to a position of neutrality is important and sometimes possible. The print headlines read, "Food Lion Denies Selling Spoiled Goods." This is the wrong topic. It's the topic put forth by the pro-labor employees. By repeating this negative image, many people simply pick up the image of spoiled food. Food Lion needed to try to change the battle cry to "Food Lion Insists It Maintains Top Standards," or "Food Lion Commits to Fair Treatment of Employees." The story would contain statements of disbelief from the pro-union side, but at least Food Lion would have competing issues.

The irony of the Food Lion case is that well after the dispute and headlines Food Lion did open up its stores to reporters. They were clean; food was fresh; employees looked confident; customers looked pleased. By then, of course, the damage had been done to the company's image; expansion plans had been affected because of the negative effects.

As of this writing, Food Lion's litigation against ABC continues, but the communication posture does not appear to have changed. When we called for an update so our analysis would be correct, our researcher was treated with suspicion and given no information. The company used aggressive litigation as a strategy. It would have been improved by the addition of an aggressive communication strategy.

WHAT RESPONSE IS "IN-LINE"?

"Boy's Death Follows Warnings" — a headline (from the *Dallas Morning News* and other papers around the country) designed to strike terror into any manufacturer.

The story should have been a positive one for the in-line skating industry, whose popular product has swept the country by storm in the last few years. This is an example of how an industry missed an opportunity to turn a predictable problem into positive publicity for the sport.

The child, 11-year-old Carlos Mack, adored skating and would seem to be an advertisement for the industry. Indeed, the paper leads the story about his death saying, "[Carlos] could go fast, do cartwheels without falling over and stop sideways like a snow skier. [He] spent so much time practicing the nation's hottest sport on wheels that he gave lessons to the other kids."

In the next paragraph, he's dead.

Accidental deaths, particularly of a child, always make news. Only the week before, the Consumer Product Safety Commission (CPSC) had issued a warning on the sport's hazards and making a prediction (another sure news item) that injuries would double from the previous year.

The industry's response was a case study of poor communication. First, they argued defensively that the sport is statistically less dangerous than bicycling. That is like American Airlines defending the fact that they lost your luggage by telling you that they lose less than United. Or, after you've been mugged, a policeman telling you that your community had fewer robberies than elsewhere.

The industry used statistics from their point of view, saying that 99.3 percent of people who use skates use them without injuries. To the industry, that's a great record (and it is). But how would you feel if the chemical plant next to your house told you that the smokestack emissions

12

Reprinted by permission: Tribune Media Services

were 99.7 percent lead free? Would it make you feel safe or nervous? This is the common mistake of organizing information from the speaker's point of view rather than the listeners'. The obvious message should have been "skating is safe."

It is apparent the industry had a numbers strategy because they went on to say that less than 1 percent of 12.6 million skaters would be seriously injured. So 126,000 people are at risk. This got more and more confusing, because 0.07 percent is 37,800 people. Less than 126,000 but not an insubstantial number. And the CPSC estimated that there would be 83,000 injuries in 1994, more than double the documented 37,000 in 1993. Notice the confusion possible between the 37,000 (the documented 1993 injuries) and the 37,800 (the dummies who don't use the skates properly). Is there an exact correlation between those who don't use the skates properly and those who are injured? Do some people skate correctly, but are still injured?

The industry also fails to realize how we hear certain words. A "serious" injury could be a badly sprained arm, or it could mean lying in a bloody pool. Local news carries almost daily accident reports, which always contain the information that the person involved is at some hospital and is in "satisfactory," "serious," or "critical" condition.

Finally, the industry spokesman says, "There's no cause for alarm," repeating the negative — "alarm." Throughout, the industry adopted a defensive posture, never once expressing sympathy or concern about the injured child.

What should they have done? Their verbal response, of course, needed to be rethought. But there was a greater opportunity. The CPSC warning was issued only a week before. This guaranteed that any problem would be connected to the warning, so a proactive response should have been structured around the CPSC circular. The first question to ask is whether the industry could have worked with the CPSC so that the commission's warning was issued concurrently with a safety advisory from the industry. (Many papers reprinted a short "tips" box issued from the CPSC. Where was the industry's tip sheet or free brochure?) Perhaps the industry could have cosponsored safety seminars, like the ones run by many sporting goods stores, with grocery chains or other large companies.

There is precedent for this approach. The FTC issued the redrafted Care Labeling Rule, which governs the working on the little tags in clothing, jointly with a flyer from the Clorox company. Clorox put the flyer into millions of shoppers' bags in grocery stores during the week the Rule was released. The chairman of Clorox appeared with the chairman of the FTC on *Good Morning America* to discuss the Rule and what consumers needed to know. Clorox's interest was clear; in the first issuance of the Rule, they discovered manufacturers simply stuck in tags saying "Use no bleach." Many fabrics today need certain types of color-fast bleach to maintain brightness, and bleaches are safe on many fabrics that look flimsy.

Imagine the impact if the head of the in-line skating industry and the CPSC appeared together on *Good Morning America* to demonstrate the safe use of in-line skates.

We are talking about several topics. One is how to increase safe usage of skates. Publicity helps. The other is how to insulate the industry from regulation at local, state, and federal levels. Nothing brings regulation faster than a single accident (a bad anecdote) and the perception that an industry is arrogant and uncaring. The head of the industry is right. Skating is reasonably safe, and most people do it correctly. But perception drives reality, and both strategic and tactical response need to be designed with that in mind.

A NEW BRAND OF HEALTH CARE

Health care "reform" sank like a stone, done in by its grandiose views, its unfathomable plans for bureaucracy, and its spirit of self-aggrandizement. The "reform" movement, however, is alive and well in the marketplace. Contrary to what one might believe reading the headlines, health care reform isn't driven by cost reduction, although some large health care providers certainly talk about that all the time. It's driven by new ways of thinking at large health care providers, and correspondingly new requirements for communicating to important groups. A leader in this effort is the low-key, low-profile Baptist Memorial Hospital and Health Care System, headquartered in Memphis, Tennessee. The program that this company developed to realize their vision of the future is a model for the nation. It has also proved good business for Baptist, turning the system into one of the largest providers of managed care networks in the nation. Baptist is also in the running to become one of the first "branded" providers of care. That is, when you buy a Cadillac, although you buy from a local dealer, you have certain expectations about performance and service. You wouldn't have these expectations if you bought a Yugo. Baptist services and managed health care plans are achieving the same name recognition.

Baptist started by reevaluating its own mission. Large providers positioned themselves as "cure" agents for "illness." Their self-image, as well as the image of components ranging from physicians to pharmacists, were firmly in this mind-set. Baptist says you can fiddle with prices all you want, but if you don't understand the philosophical thought processes which define your mission, you will not be successful. Their energizing mission for almost a century has been to be a "leader in world medicine," to provide "teaching and research," to be a "healing force," and to do it within a "Christian environment." Joseph Powell, longtime

15

chairman of the system and currently head of the Baptist Foundation, points out that those words of so many decades ago proved eminently adaptable to today's needs. The result is a mind-set that begins with the consumer's (not the "patient's") needs (in this case, insurance) and follows through preventive medicine, regular care, highly specialized care, home health care, and finally hospice care.

This is quite different from simply figuring out how to shovel as much surgery as possible into the outpatient setting and how to cut down hospital stays.

"Wellness" is right in the middle of the spectrum from insurance to hospice rather than at the start of the process, where it is in other providers' thinking. The intellectual framework is stunningly simple, but the challenge is significant. It means rethinking and reeducating virtually every group in the health care system — physicians, nurses, administrators, staff, affiliate hospitals, primary care physicians, referral centers, and, of course, the customer or patient. It means reeducating them as partners, not as lecture recipients. Baptist was an early leader in this area, working with large Memphis businesses that comprise the Memphis Business Group on Health. At its inception, it was the first such plan in the nation and the subject of national attention from the press. The media focused on the cost reductions, as large as 50 percent, but missed the true significance of the plan. It was a true partnership of thinking about how to provide for people. Over seven years, the Business Group has awarded three successive contracts to Baptist.

In an environment of change this significant, every piece of material is on the table for rethinking, even in the face of confusion in the overall environment of health care services. Why not wait? Baptist's Director of Marketing Services, Michael Calhoun, calls it "snooze and lose." The system that acts first will be the viable plan. Those who wait to test the waters, or are nervous about antagonizing important groups like physicians by asking them to think and behave differently, will end up as subcontractors.

Despite the nonprofit status and sometimes excessively wholesome attitude of the people involved, the leaders shaping Baptist's future understand what made Microsoft dominant, why so many people eat Kellogg's Corn Flakes, and why "Coke Is It." They understand and are committed to the principles of branding.

Ad Age magazine writes, "Brands in Demand; Superstars Emerge." They discuss that just because a product is "new" and "good," it doesn't ensure its success. Nor does being a household name like Kraft or Del Monte guarantee your new product will survive, let alone be a hit. However, the best bets for investors: familiar names with well-capitalized market positions which produce products consumers want and test consumer reactions, and to expand what consumers value and quickly adapting to what they don't. Baptist's own market position is a familiar, respected name, with a well capitalized position. It understands and has a track record for innovation (women's services, new facilities which followed demographic patterns), and it knows how to expand what consumers value. They say they're not good enough yet at "flexibly adapting." (Do we really need a sleep center? A kidney specialist? An exercise center?)

Tracking what consumers value requires new processes to collect, process, and analyze information. However, reengineering every process, from how drugs are delivered to patients to how patients are admitted, is guaranteed to cause turmoil.

All this turmoil and change isn't painless, and people part slowly with old ways of doing things. However, market position enhances an organization's ability to bring about change. When Baptist decided the region needed to rethink how nurses were trained and accredited, it could bring this change about in the relatively short period of a year.

A key step in this repositioning is the public claim of being a leader. "We're Not Waiting for Washington," said the ads. Powell and CEO Steve Reynolds note that a public claim to be a leader sends an important message to everyone involved with the System directly or indirectly. "It puts us on notice to perform and creates a benchmark for us to be accountable to everyone," says Reynolds, a past president of the Tennessee Hospital Association.

Can you imagine a 2005 issue of *Ad Age* rating health care providers the way the 1994 issue rated cereals (Post, Kellogg, Nabisco, Ralston)? Baptist can. They are mindful of a 1964 survey of the top 20 retailers in the U.S. The 1994 version of the survey shows half the names from the 1964 list are gone. New names are in their place. A long heritage gives a great base, not a guarantee for future survival. Baptist thinks the 2005 analysis is right around the corner, and they can picture the list of leaders and survivors. You won't be surprised to know the name "Baptist Memorial" is on the list.

IS ANYTHING SECRET?

Is anything confidential anymore?

It doesn't seem so to American business. For example, the *Dallas Morning News* covered a bankruptcy hearing concerning the Zale Corporation, the nation's largest retail jeweler, during their stint in Chapter 11. The article reported on topics raised in a "confidential meeting in the Judge's chambers." Confidential? Right on the front of the business page?

Remember Dow Corning? They developed the now-controversial silicone breast implant. They find themselves responding to excerpts of old scientific memos appearing in the press, which seem to indicate that the company knew the product caused problems.

What's fair game for reporters and what, if anything, can be considered confidential? Answer, everything (is fair game) and nothing (is confidential). Jack Carley, former general counsel for the Federal Trade Commission and former managing partner for the New York law firm Donovan and Leisure, used to say, "How would you feel if you read about it on the front page of the *Washington Post?*" I'm not saying I agree with this, but it is a fact and companies should plan and act accordingly. Don't count on anything being or staying confidential.

The solution is to apply the "front page" test, and to teach your employees to use it. This means several things: forget trying to keep "secrets." There are too many interested parties today. And sooner or later it will be in the interest of one of them to communicate with another constituency — frequently via the press.

Jerry Jones, owner of the Dallas Cowboys, was trying to persuade the city of Irving, where the Cowboy's stadium is located, to allow him to sell beer. Only one other stadium in the NFL prohibits the sale of beer, and Jones's analysis showed that prohibiting the sale of beer didn't stop people from drinking it. On the contrary, it seemed to encourage people to drink more! At stadiums where beer was sold by concessionaires, about 45,000 cans were cleaned up after a game. At Texas Stadium, about 70,000 cans were cleaned up. Apparently people brought in six packs and felt that they had to drink all of it. So the sale of beer would mean more revenues for Texas Stadium, local merchants, and the city. This looked like a winning argument. Unfortunately, the Irving City Council had turned down the proposal for 10 years.

Jones put together an impressive and effective lobbying and public relations campaign. They gained the support of the business, citizen, and handicapped groups. The proposal passed the Zoning Commission. But Jones couldn't wait. He was suckered by state legislators who told him they could pass a "secret" bill to exempt the company from a certain regulation. It stayed "secret" for about 10 seconds. And it turned out that there were a number of other "secret" deals too — for liquor lobbyists and other business interests. Reporters, who got the story from legislative staff, opposed the exemption and started calling Jones. It was front page news, and the "secret" deal infuriated the City Council, the business interests who had been supporting the overall campaign, and just about everyone else. The only people who were delighted were those who opposed the sale of beer, because now they could point to the Cowboys' owner and depict him as someone who tried to short-circuit the democratic process.

To a reporter, labeling anything "secret" or "confidential" is like waving red meat in front of a wild animal.

The "front page" test scares companies because they think it means they can't discuss or consider options. That's not true, but it does mean you need to train people how to record those discussions. Make clear you are examining options. State your overall mission clearly and repeatedly. This could have saved Dow's memos, which are, from a scientific standpoint, clearly just a recounting of risks and benefits. But enumerating the known risks a decade later sure looks terrible to the layman.

For information that is truly "confidential," as defined by powerful regulatory agencies such as the SEC — information that would affect a stock price, advance or inside information on key events — precautions include minimizing paper handed out, reminding people at the start of a meeting that there are severe penalties for release of information, and asking people for an articulation of their agreement to maintain confidentiality. And, although it pains me to endorse the lawyer's right to veto information, for matters like this, the lawyers simply must be in charge. (Of course, it's helpful to have those rare lawyers who understand communication, who have had communication training, and who do not automatically ignore anyone who is not a lawyer.)

An elaboration on the idea of having people formally articulate their commitment to maintain information: Most people live up to what they say they will do. Emphasizing the changing nature of discussions or negotiations and asking at the start of a meeting "Is everyone here on board keeping the information to this working group?" is appropriate. When heads nod "yes," it has an effect on behavior. The phrasing of the articulation is important. Asking "Does everyone understand that this information is confidential?" is patronizing and ineffective. Everyone usually understands that perfectly well, and the mere understanding does not stop people from sharing it or blabbing it. Lawyers and physicians tend to ask "Do you understand?" because they think we're not as smart or well educated as they are. They take silence, or "yes," as assent. It's not. It translates into "Get lost."

For information which isn't regulated by an agency, but which is of vital interest to a key group, the best advice is to be open and honest as soon as possible. That preserves the presumption of truth telling, and that's a valuable position.

So — psst. Here's a secret. There aren't any.

ROMANCE

The ad was an attention grabber. A classified ad announced that a company was looking for a "Director of Romance." The main qualification: a romantic nature. The responsibilities turned out to involve "light-hearted romantic surveys," researching the latest news in romance, and being a resource for the would-be romantic.

This was obviously every woman's dream job. I kept it posted on my bulletin board for two years — just in case. But when I finally got around to checking it out, it turned out the person chosen for the position two years prior was leaving to devote more time to her own life. And I needn't bother applying for her spot, as it had been folded into the division of Weddings and Entertainment.

Korbel, the makers of fine champagne, was the company, and it turns out Korbel loves romance, but their real watchword is "quality." "Quality" became a business buzzword, but the overuse of the word shouldn't obscure its importance. Quality refers to the manufacturing and management trend that is supposed to eliminate defects, restore American competitiveness, and so on. Korbel insists that "while short-term glitz can be romantic, real romance is real quality," which they define as being the very best and having a long-term commitment.

The following list may explain the mix of people on Korbel's "Most Romantic People" list: Kevin Costner (before *Dances with Wolves*), actress Julia Roberts, the late Jessica Tandy and Hume Cronyn, and all the American military men and women in the Gulf, who were chosen for showing "unselfish love of country."

People magazine's latest list has *some* romantic people, such as Maxwell Caufield and Juliet Mills, married for 14 years. They still apparently adore and respect each other. There are far too many actors and celebrities on *People*'s list. Aren't there other romantic "people?" What about ordinary people? What about people who did the traditional thing without any fanfare and celebrity status?

Romance is rather traditional. The company discovered we tend to meet the people we become romantically involved with at parties (20 percent), school (19 percent), or work (13 percent). Men still take the initiative, but whatever the occasion, when champagne is part of it, Korbel thinks we want to tell the other person that he or she is special and will be forever.

As is always the case in good corporate communication, you find that the philosophy inside is just as good on the outside. Most employees have been at the company for life, and when employees suffer a personal tragedy, the company has a tradition of continuing their pay and jobs. There have only been two owners in the century Korbel has been making premium champagne. Incidentally, premium champagne is made using a complicated process, but take it from me, it's a great deal of fun to personally, ah, um, investigate.

Anyway, romance for Korbel turns out to be a serious message — wonderful, fun, and exciting, but much more than an advertising slogan. It's a way of life.

WHEN YOUR INDUSTRY IS UNDER ATTACK

How should you respond when your industry is attacked? Senator David Pryor (D-Arkansas) made headlines for years attacking U.S. pharmaceutical companies. He was egged on by a coalition of self-appointed consumer groups. These forces alone were sufficient to command attention from the media, but the Senator struck publicity pay dirt when his accusation of "profiteering" — a word I hadn't heard in years — was picked up by the President of the United States and the First Lady as they looked for villains and scapegoats in the debate on health care reform.

What do you do when you're attacked on that scale? The drug companies' response is an excellent case study. Predictably, the industry fought back. They made some initial missteps but ultimately came up with a winning communication campaign.

First, they did not shortchange the space or money needed to reach the public. Full-page ads appeared in local papers and national press like *USA Today*. They were positioned as a "people-to-people" message: "To the American People from the People Who Work in Pharmaceutical Companies." This was a good start, but the ads were seriously flawed.

First, the ads were too full of copy. Whoever designed them didn't understand that you can't bury people with a full page of copy.

Second, there were too many numbers. Was it meaningful that Americans work 14.4 hours to pay for drugs compared to 22.5 hours for Germans and 22.1 hours for Japanese? Is that how we measure what we buy? Do you think, "Hmm, I need to work 130 hours to pay for that new dining room set?"

23

Next, the ads had a confused strategy. Although they start as "people to people," there are no people in the ad. No one signed it, and there are no photos of anyone from the industry. We need to meet the lady who inspects pills for safety and the researcher working night and day to ease cancer pain.

The ad and the strategy make the familiar mistake of trying to counter an image of big companies ripping off consumers with information. Forget it. You cannot expect people to learn a lot about a topic. And the image they need to combat *is* compelling. Predictably, Senator Pryor and his side seized on anecdotes, describing the "old people who will skimp on food or not pay the electric bill in order to have their prescriptions filled." They actually produced real live people to tell their sad stories about how they were going to have to forgo buying drugs if they became more expensive.

Finally, the ads used too much jargon. The poet William Butler Yeats advised, "Talk the language of the people." Do you buy pharmaceutical prescriptions at the pharmaceutical store? Most of us buy drugs at the drugstore.

The results were predictable. "Our reputation has suffered greatly," said Jeff Hoyak, director of public affairs for Lederle Laboratories. "The industry has a very poor image right now," according to Carolyn Glenn, associate vice president and director for public policy and communications at Hoffmann-La Roche.

That changed, and the drug companies took a lesson from the other side. The health care and medical communities are slowly learning this general lesson. For example, scientists are finally making headway against the so-called Animal Rights activists. For years, medical researchers responded to pictures of stitched up or dead animals with technical research information. Then they got smart.

Major research centers like Baylor University Medical Center acquainted the public with such actual research physicians as Dr. Goran Klintmalm, a transplant surgeon from Baylor Medical Center, whose dedicated research allows transplant patients to lead normal lives. We met Dr. Steve Harms, whose research on animals has allowed the development of new surgical techniques. And we see and learn about the real people who have been helped by these efforts: a policeman, a 10-year-old, and a mother of two. We see them at work and play. The mother is holding and reading to her child; the policeman looks very official and tough; the 10-year-old is playing Little League baseball. The message is very compelling. Here are real people, real individuals who have been helped. Now the equation has been changed from "would you hurt this adorable kitty?" and "adorable kitty versus hard, cold sterile lab technician" to a new equation: "adorable kitty but still a kitty versus a 10-year-old child just like my son."

The drug companies profiled people whose lives have been changed by drugs. We meet Phyllis, and the ad shows an attractive, middle-aged African-American woman. "Ask Phyllis her opinion of the anti-stroke drug that lets her hold on to her independence and life savings," says the headline. The copy continues, "When medicines can help people like Phyllis avoid a stroke, that's obviously a good thing."

Another ad shows an adorable young girl. The headline announces, "Ask Katie's parents what they think of the asthma drug that's saving her trips to the emergency room." The copy adds, "When asthma medicine can save Katie and her parents from anxious races to the hospital, it's obviously a good thing."

All the ads go on to explain that the drugs not only improve the quality of life but decrease the costs of overall medical care dramatically.

The drug companies adjusted their communication. Now they need to expand their communication strategy. A major national public opinion campaign must be run at the local level with area spokesmen speaking to local groups and press. Advertising alone won't do it. The drug companies started with the right idea. People to people is convincing. Now, they just need to carry it out.

WHAT'S IN A NAME?

Gertrude Stein created one of the 20th century's most famous and enduring quotes when she said, "A rose is a rose is a rose," updating Shakespeare's line, "A rose by any other name would smell as sweet." All by way of asking whether a name *does* mean anything. What if the name is the title of a job? The Borden company thinks names matter, and they are making a public statement by giving an unusual name to a perfunctory job.

Most large companies have somebody responsible for interacting with local communities, handling tricky issues, or making corporate donations. These jobs are usually held by someone in charge of "public affairs," "community relations," or "corporate philanthropy." Sometimes this function falls under "public information" or "public relations." Today, there may be a "diversity" manager.

At the Borden Company, however, they have taken pieces of these traditional functions and vested them in Judy Barker. For a decade, Ms. Barker has been director of social responsibility for Borden. Recently, she was promoted to vice president of the same function.

This is the only large company I've ever found with a job title like this. It makes a statement, a claim that the company has many constituencies which have an important influence on what the company does and how it does it.

Barker's official job responsibilities are to monitor the company's performance on key social issues, suggest improvements, review proposed company actions from a social and community perspective, and to alert the CEO to any issues or actions which require an operational or policy response. In other words, she's an official gadfly or "minister-without-portfolio."

She reports directly to the chairman, a position which warns the rest of the corporation not to dismiss her. She can always have a quiet chat about you with the guy at the top.

This public commitment actually carries a risk for Borden. If they don't listen to Ms. Barker or make good on their commitments, we'll be more disappointed than if they hadn't made this statement in the first place. In standard economic terms, a company creating a "supply" of social responsibility is likely to find that it has created or strengthened the "demand" for the product. Failing to supply it will leave a lot of disappointed and disgruntled "buyers." It calls attention to their record, and my first question was about the level of corporate contributions. Barker is also president of the Borden Foundation, which together with the company gives about $5 million a year in grants. That's certainly worthy, but Borden is an $8 billion company. Given that the limit on corporate contributions is 5 percent of company profits, this is more than paper clip money but hardly the stuff of major social change.

Borden has also construed the definition of "social responsibility" far beyond contributions or workplace issues like child care. It means how they manufacture their products. Their Wise potato chip factory in Pennsylvania recovers starch, which used to be discarded after the manufacturing process. They sell the starch and reuse the water. In their annual report, they are justifiably proud of this operation, and report that they even make some money off what used to be a waste by-product while being sensitive to our environment. Great tasting potato chips aren't enough anymore. They think their public wants corporate policies that are as palatable.

The company reports that this required adapting the plant and installing a new and expensive treatment system. The system pays for itself by eliminating effluent treatment charges and lowering the intake of fresh water for the plant.

One of the interesting battles in "responsibility" is this assigning of cost. I learned long before the Columbia Business School taught me that a company can analyze costs in lots of ways. The *New York Times* subsidized student subscriptions for years and fought off the internal bean counters who wanted to cancel the program by claiming it cost too much. The defenders produced numbers showing they "broke even." The real fact is that they were doing something they believed was right, so they decided which costs to count and which to allocate elsewhere, so that the result would be that they "broke even."

Borden undoubtedly could have loaded the Berwick, Pennsylvania, potato chip factory with all sorts of overhead costs that would show it loses money. But they didn't; they are doing something they think is right.

Interestingly, in light of current events, the *New York Daily News*, which was embroiled in a bitter strike, examined whether to subsidize student subscriptions several times during the decades of the 1950s and 1960s. They always rejected the idea as being "too costly." While the *New York Times* grew its own next generation of readers, the *Daily News* never looked beyond the most narrowly focused and immediate version of its bottom line.

One of the most interesting aspects of Barker's job is the freedom and support Borden has given her to stimulate change outside the company. She spends a lot of time involved in other activities, including chairing a group of large companies that wish to encourage minority suppliers. Borden was one of the first companies to establish a minority purchasing program, and the company is big enough that she can gently encourage those who might not take this as seriously as she wants.

Barker has an assistant, a decent travel budget, and enough access so she has a few hours a week with the CEO. The key question is what happens to this commitment if the price of Borden's stock drops?

The tyranny of the Wall Street analysts and their pals, the takeover artists, dictate that social responsibility is a "frill" to be cut back. Borden's former chairman, R. J. Ventres, says it's not that "corporate responsibility has become a bottom-line issue." Borden says they are queried weekly by large institutional investors about their record on health, workplace, and environmental issues.

Again, if Borden is queried weekly, it must be because they invite queries or hear things other large companies don't. A random survey of a few other *Fortune* 500 companies with the same question, "Do you get regular queries from large institutional investors about your record on social responsibility?" produced chortles and disavowals. Now, everyone has learned not to pooh-pooh these things publicly, so all the investor relations types quickly added disclaimers to the effect that, of course, they all took corporate responsibility seriously, and so on and so forth. One comes away with the impression that it is strictly a secondary priority.

Borden is number one in U.S. dairy products. They are a world leader in other areas. By staking their claim with something as simple as a job title, they are announcing that they hope Americans care that they are a leader in social responsibility, and not just how good the cheese slices taste.

I hope they're right. They got my attention.

OIL COMPANIES SCREW UP

What would we do without the oil companies as bad examples? It's not enough that Exxon provided a case study with *Valdez*, of how not to handle the media and the public. The oil companies have contributed frequently to the stock of corporate examples of how to communicate and how not to communicate with the American public.

First, the problem. When gas prices rise, the American consumer, who has been raised to consider low prices a birthright, gets annoyed. "America's Fuming," read one headline in the *Washington Post*, with a subhead, "Oil Companies Battle Tarnished Image." Public opinion polls show the public has a low opinion of oil companies, rating them last or ahead of tobacco and chemicals. (And, as my mother used to say, you're known by the company you keep.)

Why? The first (and easy) answer is probably not correct. That is, we buy gas frequently. The price appears to jump quickly, and the average American does have a grasp of what "replacement cost" means, although he might not be able to give a lecture on it. The public has enough of an understanding of the federal deficit to act.

News reports when gas prices rise are predictable. The reporter finds someone who's annoyed. "It's greed with a capital 'G,'" says consumer Paul Evantoff in Los Angeles. In Scottsdale, Arizona, Howard Greenlee, filling up his car at the pump, is equally displeased. "The petroleum dealers of the United States have placed themselves at the top of the list of rip-off artists by their irresponsible actions in raising gasoline prices." He thinks the oil companies are "no different from the Iraqi government."

Whew! But are we mad as hell and not going to take it anymore? Do the prices at the pump mean that much? They're visible, that's for sure.

But how dumb are Americans? Reporters are not just out to stick it to the oil companies, and these stories may include Howard and Paul (or whatever their names are in the articles this time), but the press is doing a good job getting other comments.

Writes Bill Murchison in the *Dallas Morning News*, "The 1970s taught us better, and today the whole world knows the power of the market forces."

The *Chicago Tribune* notes that the Americans upset over price increases are "the same Americans who believe in the divine right of bargains." Oil has been a bargain for the last decade, and the prices have been rising because of uncertainty.

No matter what you paid for your raw material last month, if you think it's going to cost more to replace it, you raise your current prices to reflect what it costs to replace it, so that you can afford to buy more of the product. And it's astonishing how many Americans understand this. They may not be wildly happy, but they understand.

Plus, the increases are manageable. The *New York Times* points out that a recent increase in pump prices is about $7 a month, noting that it is a little less than what people spend on a bottle of suntan oil.

If things are different from the 1970s, if the press is smarter and doing a better job, if Americans are (remarkably) better educated about economics, why are the oil companies faring poorly in our estimation?

The answer: They continue to communicate by paying someone else to do it. That is, by the traditional methods of advertising. In fact, a few years ago, Mobil actually bought some ads to combat the charges of price gouging. The ads said, "Where's the rip-off?" (This is exactly the wrong thing to do, of course, because it raises the topic of "rip-off" and plants it firmly in your mind.)

The 1960s, 1970s, and 1980s brought new demands in communication. You've heard the comments about information clutter. It's true. What's called "paid" advertising, no matter how creative or how big the buy, can't manage negative news. The business explanation has to be part of the news package to gain the credibility needed.

Years ago, Ralph Bunche, one of the first international black diplomats, said, "If you want to get across an idea, wrap it up in a person." As more people get more of their news from television, that's truer than ever.

The oil companies experimented briefly years ago by training their people and sending them around the country, but they abandoned the effort. Too bad.

The rise of so-called public information groups or consumer groups makes it so much more important for American businesses, like the oil companies, to involve their own people and take their case directly — via the media — to every town and city in America.

The consumer groups went this route because they didn't have any ad budgets and because they did have enormous conviction. (My concern with all those groups is what they frequently *don't* have are the facts, but that never seems to bother them — or the media.)

They have become adept at this "person-to-person" communication. The oil companies actually miss a golden opportunity when prices rise or other bad news catches our attention. The reason is that public attention is focused on them. They probably wish it weren't, but it's exactly the moment to reach out.

The risk of not doing so? They turn the most credible routes of information over to their enemies. And the naysayers, the grandstanding consumer types, and politicians from both parties are only too happy to jump into the vacuum. During Desert Storm, Senator Larry Pressler (R-South Dakota) said, "I don't want the oil companies using Iraq's international crime as an excuse to gouge the working American public."

Not to be outdone, Senator Joseph Lieberman (D-Connecticut) added, "The oil industry in this country is plundering us just as Saddam Hussein is plundering Kuwait."

And there are many more sound bites designed for easy transmission through papers and TV news. The press must report statements like this, but an analysis of this topic over the years shows that reporters are looking for counterweights to offer other points of view. Many members of the press are skeptical of the public's complaints in wanting to help educate them by including positive and explanatory quotes and comments from the oil companies and other experts.

If the American public distrusts the oil companies, it's not wholly the fault of the press. But the oil companies will have no one to blame but themselves if they fail to exploit opportunities for aggressive communication.

PEPSI TAMPERING SCARE

Today's definitions of "crisis" for corporations include the concepts of volatility (will events get out of control quickly?); unpredictability (can we anticipate this?); mimicry (will the mere existence of one problem create many others?); validation (who will speak on behalf of the company to defuse criticism or build support?); and customer focus (where does a target audience best receive news or information?). An excellent case study of these concepts was the Pepsi company's bout with people claiming to find syringes and screws and who knows what else in their cans of Pepsi.

Some criticized Pepsi for not responding more quickly. In hindsight, that's not fair. Many crises should be anticipated — like a plane crash for an airline — and a company should have a plan that's triggered instantly. Product tampering can be anticipated (although I cannot imagine anticipating the inclusion of syringes), and Pepsi had an aggressive response. In contrast to Exxon's behavior in the *Valdez* spill, Pepsi's American CEO was personally involved, visible, and widely interviewed. He was credible. He was not perfect, but he was good, and he was sincere and obviously trying hard. He genuinely appeared concerned.

Pepsi's response was highly visual. They either had ready or produced in record time a video which showed the workings of a bottling plant. Americans now know that cans are upside down before the liquid goes into them. In fact, one woman asked me how Pepsi could get soda into the can if it was upside down. Pepsi's cooperation with the Food and Drug Administration (FDA) was an excellent example of sophisticated use of third-party, objective spokesmen. The combination of Pepsi and the FDA Administrator, Dr. Ron Kessler, went a long way in convincing the public that tampering during the bottling process was impossible. Working with the FDA was excellent "validation" of Pepsi's stature as a responsible corporate citizen, and the FDA is to be commended for a public-private partnership on the effort.

There's always room for improvement. The CEO was on the front page of *USA Today* saying "Pepsi is 99.98 percent safe." He meant, of course, that Pepsi was safe, but the use of the statistic conveyed that it was *possible* that there were some problem cans. This is the difference between perception and reality. Given the billions of soft drink cans of all types, there probably are some defective ones. That's truthful. However, we drink soda one can at a time. As *listeners*, we think "maybe it's my can." It's similar to the manufacturing company that insists "our smokestack emissions are 99.98 percent free of lead." We hear the word "lead" and it conveys contamination.

We are not entirely reassured by statistics. For example, an airline passenger doesn't care that a company has a good record if it's his bag which gets lost.

Learning from Pepsi's crisis and its response, the message may be that the concepts of mimicry, validation, and where target audiences receive information need more attention, preplanning, and strategy in the future.

National companies need a *local* presence. All the response came from national headquarters. Fine, but not enough. People will hear about the product tamperings through the national news, but overall, they get more information from local news than from national news. *Local* spokespeople should explain how the bottling process works, the company's commitment to quality control, etc. *Local* company folks involved in the community can point out the numerous sporting events and community and charitable efforts Pepsi makes. Viewers and readers are familiar with these and are more likely to remember them. A company's best defense is an aggressive local offense.

Although companies have made great strides in preparing for crises *that can be anticipated,* the next, crucial step is to prepare beforehand for a local media and response strategy.

I'm concerned about how people think of business in the "big picture" sense. The Pepsi tampering was the work of people with diseased minds or who were out for personal gain. A reputable, leading American company suffered. Although the head of the FDA validated Pepsi's quality control procedures, there were no cries of outrage from the company or from commentators. The company may be excused on the grounds that it was busy doing the right things to reassure consumers, shareholders, and regulators and didn't want to risk the chance of mixed messages. But someone should have been added to the mix with a voice of fury.

Have we become so immune to disgusting criminal behavior that we don't condemn it? Several people who "found" syringes and stuff are being prosecuted. But this happened well after the fact and received minimal publicity. Someone else needs to say, "It's unacceptable to lie, tamper, and defraud." Otherwise, the message to the public is that this kind of action gets you a ton of publicity, and you might, but probably won't, suffer any consequences. Business in general suffers when that happens.

Whether people stop to think specifically about this crisis or not, the real losers are the press and consumer groups. This was clearly copycat behavior. The press claim that they only report the facts, but the flaw in that argument appears when you see an incident like this. The reports become the incentive for the next incident. The press ignored its own role in expanding a crisis.

Consumer advocacy groups apparently only comment on consumer behavior when consumers are photographically wounded by large corporations, not the other way around. Either a group represents consumers or it doesn't, and they were conspicuous in their silence.

There is an old saying that you get good judgment from those times when you used bad judgment. Perhaps we need a new saying: We develop better judgment from experiences when we did a good job. The Pepsi tampering incident shows that a company that uses good judgment can survive a significant threat, and that you can learn to do things better by doing them well.

SANDOZ PHARMACEUTICALS — "SHAME ON YOU?"

"The reporter has already made up his mind," our clients complain, and frequently they're right. The question to consider is whether a company can get the "right" message to a desired audience *despite* a reporter with a hostile point of view.

An excellent case study is the experience of Sandoz Pharmaceuticals, makers of Triaminic, a popular children's cough and cold medicine.

The CBS *Morning News* has a regular report called "Shame on You," which skewers companies misleading consumers. Reporter Arnold Diaz went after Sandoz Pharmaceuticals, accusing them of ripping off consumers. Sandoz had changed the formulation of the product to make it "taste better," presumably so children would take it more easily. To do this, they recommended the dosage be doubled. The price of the bottle stayed the same. Diaz took the point of view that Sandoz had also doubled the price but was hiding the fact.

Sandoz agreed to an interview, which was the right decision. However, the interview didn't go well. Here's what happened and why:

The reporter started by holding the product toward the camera, saying, "The makers of Triaminic, a popular children's cold medicine, say it's new, improved, and tastes better." In other words, he repeated all the key words the company wanted the desired audience — parents with small children — to hear and reinforced the perception that the medication is already popular with parents. But then, the Sandoz spokeswoman said, "We improved the product so it gives more *value*." Words are the first and most important part of communication because they

36

Mark Cullum/Copley News Service

serve as the anchor of a message. People build what they remember around the words. By adding the word, "value," Sandoz invited another look at the product. The reporter pointed out that the reason the product tastes better is because it's a different dosage. You must take two teaspoons instead of one. The reporter pressed the Sandoz spokeswoman, skeptically asking if the consumer doesn't have to buy twice as much, or in other words, if Sandoz hasn't effectively doubled the price.

Viewers were privy to an unusual and revealing segment in which we heard the questions the reporter asked, as well as the answers given by the interviewee.

While it is true that in the editing process, the reporter's questions are usually dropped, that does not mean one should ignore the questions. It creates the perception that the interviewee is evading the topic. The Sandoz spokeswoman ignored every question. For example, the reporter asked, "You have to buy twice as much to take the same amount, don't you?" The spokeswoman replied, "One bottle lasts the duration of a cold." She may have believed she responded to the question, but the ear expected to hear "yes" or "no" in response to the question. When we didn't, we perceived that she ignored him. Politicians are usually the worst offenders.

All answers need to begin with what we call an "acknowledgment," a word or short phrase indicating that we heard the question. Sometimes

37

the acknowledgment is also the answer. The reporter asked, "You have to take twice as much, don't you?" The ear expected to hear "yes" or "no," and since we already knew the answer is "YES" from an earlier segment, there was no reason not to say "yes." The spokeswoman, still stonewalling, said, "There is still the same amount of active ingredient per dose."

The reporter asked, "Don't you use it up twice as fast?" The ear expected again to hear "yes" or "no," but there are some answers which are not a clear "yes" or "no." This was probably one of them, and the ear would have accepted "not necessarily" or "it depends" as an acceptable substitute. "It depends" was probably the *correct* answer/acknowledgment, which makes sense to parents with small children who know the strength of a two-year-old in the middle of the night.

I, as a parent, have pried the small jaws open, poured in the medicine, closed the mouth, and declared victory, only to remove my hands and have the determined miniature tyrant spit it all out. Adding insult, the medicine is red.

The reporter returned to the question, "Don't you use it up twice as fast?" She again reported the answer, with no acknowledgment phrase, "One bottle will last the duration of a cold." The reporter followed up with, "How long did a bottle of the old Triaminic last?" The spokeswoman was stumped. She looked down. She looked to the side. She was flustered, and finally she said, "Reask me that question." The reporter slammed her, "Finally, a question she had no double-talk answer for."

The Q&A should have gone like this:

Question: "Don't you use it up twice as fast?"

Answer: "Not necessarily. Children take it more easily because it now tastes better, and parents told us that was their top priority."

Question: "Don't you have to take twice as much?"

Answer: "Yes, but our customer surveys showed that when children are sick, the most important thing is getting them to take effective medicine, which Triaminic is, and the new dosage is easily swallowed by small children."

Question: "Are you telling me there's been no price increase?"

Answer: "For most people that's so. Now that the medicine is more popular with children, as well as their parents, we believe it will be more effective because there is less waste and fewer temper tantrums."

What should have been a triumph for Sandoz became a disaster. First, the spokeswoman added a word — "value" — to the messages "new, improved, tastes better." Second, the company is still following the advice, "Forget the question, it never gets on the air. Just say what you came to say." And third, the answers were gobbledygook and jargon. Do you go into the drugstore and ask, "May I have a bottle of medicine that will last the duration of a cold?" Most of us go in and say, "What works for a three-year-old?"

The episode was unfortunate. Triaminic *was* new, improved, and tasted better. And any parent knows it's important for young, sick children to be able to take medicine easily. If the spokeswoman had answered as suggested above, with a truthful acknowledgment but an immediate return to the real issue, that message would have come through to the parental audience. For most parents, price is not the most immediate concern, especially when a child is ill. Although the reporter was determined to ask about price, Sandoz could have responded to those questions and been equally determined to get its message across.

The worst-case scenario would have been if the reporter had phrased the question about price, "Won't some people in some cases end up spending more money?" An honest acknowledgment would have to be "yes" or at least "probably," but that should still be followed by, "But we respond to what our consumers want and they told us loud and clear to make the medicine taste better so children, particularly very young children, would take it more easily. And we listened to our consumers."

Part of the "shame on you" goes to CBS, not Sandoz. Just because a company spokesman doesn't sound like a professional TV person or do everything perfectly is no justification for savaging them. Even if a corporate spokesperson makes the mistake of sounding canned and staged, that's not a justification for ridiculing them.

While a healthy skepticism between press and corporate America is, well, healthy, pouncing on corporations whenever they make a mistake only creates a climate of distrust and dislike. Corporations need to focus on the fact that if they have a concise, targeted message with compelling illustrations, it can get through to the right audience, despite badgering questions of a reporter with an attitude.

THE CAR DEALERS LAUNCH AN ETHICS PROGRAM

Oxymoron. What a contradiction. Familiar jokes — military intelligence, business ethics. And car dealers, particularly used-car dealers have long been the butt of jokes about ethics. Every comedian has a routine about the stereotype of the high-pressure, gimmick-laden sales pitch designed to confuse.

The car dealers are ahead of us. They have publicly committed themselves to an ethics program of fair dealing. They have published a "Car Dealers Code of Conduct," which is to be prominently posted in participating dealerships. It has eight major points, including treating customers with courtesy and respect without discrimination; being knowledgeable about regulations governing vehicles; being honest; accurately representing the vehicle's condition and its ability to meet the customer's needs; providing the customer with clear explanations; acting professionally; and, finally, acting within the bounds of law and ethics. Quite a mouthful and quite a commitment.

The program is more than a poster for the wall; it includes a certification and training program run by the National Automobile Dealers Association. The certification seminar is followed by two tests. Those who participate and pass receive the right to post the Code of Conduct and to call themselves members of the Society of Automotive Sales Professionals.

Is this perfect? No. Is it a great idea? Yes, and it's a good example of a national organization taking a leadership role to move its members in a direction which will benefit the industry in the long-term.

The Code of Conduct is actually a sophisticated communication strategy aimed at the general public, regulators, and car dealers themselves. The public pronouncement of the Code holds up a standard. Any customer experiencing treatment inconsistent with the standard can now point to the

Code and say, "Look, you treated me wrong, and your own Code says so."

The Code drew predictable criticism from some quarters, particularly the pro-regulation consumer groups who have no faith in business and the consumer. They want government to prescribe even the tiniest details and punish transgression, yet they are oblivious to the costs of regulation. The critics' main argument is that the Code won't change anything overnight and has no enforcement mechanism.

They are wrong on both counts. The Code won't change anything immediately, but "overnight" is the wrong time frame. Government regulations don't change anything overnight. They just give the appearance of it. One points to the new regulation and claims success. Market behavior lags far behind and frequently never changes, or changes at great cost to the consumer. The Code sets a clear direction for adherence by car dealers. Eventually, all dealers who want to stay in business and who want their customers as ambassadors for other customers will follow it. Peer pressure and customer satisfaction are the most powerful enforcement mechanisms in our society.

Most municipal ordinances work this way. For example, no policeman materializes if a smoker is smoking in a no-smoking area. But irate citizens drive him away. In New York City, where "pooper scooper" signs about the law are on every block, the law is enforced by others on the sidewalk. Littering laws work the same way.

These regulations have the sanction of municipal regulation, but they have absolutely no enforcement teeth. On the rare occasion when a policeman sees you tossing a soft drink can in the street or out of your car, he'll stop and write a citation — if he's not too busy with muggers. (In a car, watch out. The cellular phone has given other drivers a powerful tool to report the litterbug who heaves trash out his window and thinks he's safe because no squad car is in sight.)

Hurray for the car dealers. Not only because the Code is a public commitment, a step forward, and a model for other industries to emulate, but because it's a good example of a trade association leading the way. Predictably, because the training and certification requires time (on top of a long work week) and costs several hundred dollars, many salespeople were unenthusiastic. They pay the short-term price. There was a lot of grumbling. Trade associations, which depend on their members' dues, too frequently defer to grumbling without focusing on the long-term interests of the industry. The Car Dealers Association has been the best kind of new model, a leadership one.

THE STRIKES AND STRIFE
AT CATERPILLAR

Nyah, nyah. Did too. Did not. It's the sound of children taunting each other, or the sound of labor relations at venerable Caterpillar, the maker of high-quality, heavy-duty equipment. These people don't need labor lawyers, they need a marriage counselor.

The specifics of the well-covered labor strike are as follows: The United Auto Workers (UAW) had clung to "pattern bargaining," insisting that all companies in an industry adhere to the same wage agreements. In a global economy, it's global insanity to ignore foreign competitors' cost advantage.

However, this isn't a fight about wages, or even layoffs, which is what union leaders contend. It's about power and control. Caterpillar is doing well; foreign competition is having its own problems. The company is expanding and the average UAW worker makes almost $50,000 when overtime is included.

Caterpillar is trying to control its future, and that means the ability to assign workers, remove antiquated job classifications, and so on. Other companies would tell you the future also means a leaner company, more empowered workers, and truly empowered teams. Teams require freedom, and freedom requires few rules and an erosion, if not abandonment, of the "we/they" concepts of labor versus management.

Other companies in the same or closely related industries seem to grasp this, as does the UAW. Barely two hours drive from Caterpillar, Deere & Co. union officials, members, and management look alike, talk together, and more important, listen to each other.

By contrast, Caterpillar and the UAW are sniping at each other. The company defeated the union in 1992 when a strike collapsed in the face of a threat to permanently replace striking workers. Both sides (notice the use of the concept "sides," implying a conflict where two "sides" are pitted against each other, thus there is a "winner" and a "loser") continued to look for control. UAW officials tried to get workers to slow down production by following rule-book procedures (which apparently workers disregarded). Meanwhile, company officials "disciplined and fired union members for mostly petty actions such as wearing T-shirts that disparage the company," according to *Business Week*.

Both sides are paying lip service to the concept of teamwork, but both sides are simultaneously clinging to minutely detailed work and labor rules to attack the other.

What's missing from this dispute is leadership, the Dutch uncle, someone to step in and say "This is ridiculous." The company is actually right: Pattern bargaining is a relic that should have been disposed of years ago, but in a real marriage or relationship, "being right" isn't the issue. "Being right on track is the issue," and at companies where management truly values and trusts the workers (think of Southwest Airlines, and Texas Industries), the CEO would know when to laugh at himself and would understand that workers' concerns, even unreasonable concerns, need to be addressed so the team can pull together. (If Herb Kelleher, CEO of Southwest Airlines, saw a T-shirt about him, he'd want one.)

The workers are the losers because they have plum jobs today. The company is also losing because it will require layers of management, not to mention providing lifetime work for its lawyers, to fiercely supervise workers and aggressively defend charges of violating labor laws. In these cases, management is distracted from the research and focus on the future.

This company needs a lot of honest internal communication. It needs to restore humor and goodwill to its workforce. Most of all, everyone needs to set aside the mentality of power and control. Neither "side" appears to be interested in change, so this story is mainly useful for other companies to figure out how to prevent getting cornered. The real "pattern" which has emerged here is the losing one of confrontation.

It reminds me of the marriage where one spouse lorded over the other for years, but when the immature partner finally grew up, the other one refused to be magnanimous and used the opportunity to get even.

Unions, even the UAW, are demonstrating some willingness to face reality. It's possible, some would argue mandatory, to look for those positive signs and individual leaders and move into the future. Where's a good marriage counselor when you need one?

"WE MESSED UP"

"I deeply apologize to our customers . . . " began Intuit Chairman Scott Cook on March 2, 1995. Cook was in the second day of press conferences and statements to deal with public outcry over the discovery that two popular programs, MacinTax and TurboTax, had program glitches which would cause occasional errors in calculation. (Not good for programs doing your taxes.)

Intuit came in for closer scrutiny than it normally might have because of Intel's debacle last fall with its Pentium chip. In that case, Intel stonewalled for months, finally confirming reluctantly there was a problem but defensively claiming almost nobody was affected. Intel refused for months to replace the chip, to recall it, or even to talk about it. Would Intuit behave the same way?

Intuit's popular software have almost 65 percent of the market for tax preparation programs, and about 80 percent of their buyers buy each version year after year. These programs are the fruitcakes of software. That is, customers trust them, and they buy them year after year without analyzing the purchase decision. It's an accepted part of the season. These program/products are an annuity for Intuit, both in revenue and in maintaining a customer base.

Intuit actually recognized the problem early and did acknowledge it to customers who called in. Intuit's technical assistance people are very close to the customers, and they quickly developed a way to help people work around the problem, and the "bug base" people (what they call the people who "de-bug" software) knew about it and fixed it immediately for the 1996 version. In fact, they fixed it so fast that information about the problem never made it into the company's internal quality control system.

The first lesson for other companies is about how information flows. Intuit didn't make an announcement, apparently because the people at the top didn't realize it was a problem. The people elsewhere thought, we fixed it. No problem. The customers experienced the problem, though. Intuit, of course, confirmed it to customers when they called, and computer users are an aggressive group. Letters quickly found their way into trade publications, others started asking questions, and finally Intuit had to respond to public challenges, "Is there a problem with MacinTax and TurboTax, and if so, why have you covered it up?"

Intuit took several weeks to figure out what was going on, and this made them seem to be following in Intel's path. The companies and their cultures are really quite different, but the general public just sees two computer companies.

Then Intuit acted. They issued a statement to confirm the problem, explain it, and put forth the remedy. The original release was complete and straightforward, and tried to set a positive tone. The first paragraph said they were making "available, free of charge, a revised version of [its] tax preparation software," and Cook was quoted explaining there were "calculation errors," but they were committed to make it "as easy as possible for any affected user." The first paragraph also reiterated a key promise of the company; they "guarantee" the accuracy of the software and will pay any IRS penalties caused by their software. They set up an 800 number to assist customers.

But the first statement generated a round of "why did it take so long?" questions. So the next day, March 2, 1995, Cook issued a "personal letter" which he also read at a press conference. While it must have been personally embarrassing to Cook to stand before the world, he handled it extremely well, and he had a lot at risk.

Intuit's two programs have four selling points. They are, and the public believes them to be, the easiest to use, the best in terms of tax advice, the most reliable, and the best selling. The glitch calls into question reliability, and the perceived delay attacks the concept that the company will help you make the programs easy to use. The company is really selling trust; the two products are simply the use of that trust for the consumer, and Cook pointed that out.

There are several elements of what Intuit did correctly, and what Intel did not do. The chairman himself was personally involved. He was the point man. He was personally at risk. He talked right to us. Next, he apologized, and he sounded as if he really meant it. Companies apologize too infrequently. He went right on to say they had fixed the problem and the process that had caused them to be unresponsive. No justifications, no wiggling around. He made a clear promise to consumers, backed up by the commitment to pay for problems the company caused.

He did not get hung up in haggling over the numbers about how many people might be affected or how many calculations might be affected. Intel went astray by insisting that a minuscule number of customers might have the problem, claiming that even if they had it, it wouldn't matter, that millions — or was it thousands? or tens of millions? — of calculations were required to experience the problem. To the listener, this sounds like caviling. We think *"It might be me!"* And most of us are not sophisticated enough to figure out how to analyze whether we are affected. In other words, by the time we know we have the disease, it's too late.

Intuit's discussion of how many were affected, "less than 1 percent," is significantly down in the body of the release.

The company didn't put restrictions on who could get new versions. In other words, no complicated differences between people who bought direct and paid full price versus people who bought from a retailer versus people who got it as a freebie.

Intuit maintained its crucial communication with its customers and target customers, using the press as a key vehicle, and restored and improved its credibility.

The press coverage of the issue was instructive. The *Wall Street Journal* coverage of the first day's announcement was a short blurb buried in the second section. "Intuit Moves to Correct Problems in Tax Software," said the headline. Intuit's local press in San Jose had a large headline screaming, "Intuit to Replace Error-laden Tax Software," which was more than a little overdone, even starting with a joke. "Q: What do you get when you calculate your Intuit tax return on a Pentium computer? A: Audited." Still, the article favorably compared Intuit to Intel, printed the 800 number prominently, carried a picture of the software box and repeated the pledge to pay IRS penalties. The AP story carried high in the body of the copy a comment by an industry analyst and expert explaining that errors aren't uncommon. But the AP story predictably carried comments from such individual users as sculptor Bruce Beasley, who complained the program missed $8,000 in income. (He also popped up in the *Business Week* version of the story.)

The press will always tell a story through, or at least including the view of an individual user, which is why problems, even if they are in reality tiny, become magnified because the reader or listener identifies with the individual quoted.

What if Cook had gone before the microphones several weeks ago, before they knew exactly what happened internally? His message would have been exactly the same, except he would say "we *will* fix it," instead of "we have fixed it." Many companies believe they have to have solved the problem before coming forward. The Intuit experience demonstrates that even a short wait can be damaging. The Intuit experience also shows that grace, honesty, and absolute commitment to the relationship with the consumer will pay off.

LOWERING (THE PERCEPTION OF) DOCTORS' SALARIES

Americans have always had a deep ambivalence about being rich, or at least about being perceived as being rich. Star athletes, CEOs, and doctors are always defending their high salaries and claiming they deserve them. Most Americans who are now "rich" — two-income couples making $75,000 a year or professionals of any sort — identify themselves as "middle class" in surveys.

As health care reform attracted the media spotlight, doctors' salaries received unwanted attention. Now, starting in 1995, the American Medical Association (AMA) has decided to bring down the "average" physician's salary. Their technique is to reformulate what numbers they include in figuring out "average" and to include for the first time the salaries of medical residents. Since residents make very low salaries as part of hospital staff, the $177,000 annual figure will drop.

The AMA's decision and announcement attracted media attention and criticism. *Business Week* called it "a public relations dodge." Was the AMA right in its decision to jiggle the statistics? Yes. Should they have announced it differently? Yes.

Perception affects reality. To most Americans, six-figure salaries appear "high." Most people without "high" salaries believe that those with "high" salaries can obviously afford to pay more taxes and deserve fewer breaks from the government.

The AMA was actually right; it was time to re-examine the formula used to produce the "average" salary. Residents are full-fledged physicians. They are continuing their education and developing their specialty at a hospital. The bargain is that the resident works for relatively low pay in order to see great volumes of patients and to work around doctors who have years, if not decades, of experience. A residency is not just a chance to practice on patients; it is a way to transform judgment and experience from the brains of older physicians to younger ones.

All the stakeholders — patients, hospitals, residents, older doctors and the community — win.

Years ago, residents made no money. My father made zero salary through medical school, internship, and residency — a 12-year total of negative net cash flow. Gradually, hospitals paid interns and residents a stipend, then a low salary, and finally a salary equivalent to a grocery store manager. The AMA is absolutely right to include them. They are "real" doctors.

The predictable criticism from the left-wingers is the analogy that you don't include graduate teaching assistants' meager dollars in assessing what history professors make. This is the classic debate technique of confusing the issue by raising irrelevant issues. We do include or recognize the difference in the salaries of nontenured professors, or guest lecturers, or any of the other ways universities try to deliver services (courses) while containing costs (salaries).

The greater question for business is how to communicate a significant decision that involves changing a basic formula, particularly in the context of anticipated criticism.

The general strategy should be: First, validate the decision by involving outside experts. Even if a company pays high-level people like a former Attorney General or FBI Director or someone with a recognized title like a Federal Reserve Board Economist, their expertise and integrity helps. Most people of that caliber (but, I recognize, not all) are not hired guns. They take on an assignment to assess or analyze something, and you get their honest opinion.

Second, citizens are bombarded with so much information that the best defense is an aggressive offense — design a plan and then triple it. A simple announcement with one press release and a few follow-up interviews is a guarantee of failure because the scenario will go like this: company announces; opposition bitterly criticizes announcement, putting negative messages into play. Negative messages are memorable. So the exchange is not an even one.

Third, local contact through local media and our individual physicians is crucial because that's how most Americans get information. It is time-consuming to organize a "local strategy," but it is the safest and most effective role.

A word about message is relevant; the announcement shouldn't have been defensive — "we deserve it" — nor should it have been filled with what salespeople call "features" or with facts — "doctors have 12 years of training." The average individual doesn't care, just as you don't ask your banker if he or she has an MBA or a degree from the London School of Economics. This is the moment for aggressive messages like "a long overdue truthful accounting," or "you deserve the best medical care in the world, and your doctor goes into training to provide it." Don't argue that an ophthalmologist who specializes in glaucoma deserves $185,000 a year because he trains for nine years and has to know phaceoemulsion, etc. The listener doesn't know what you're talking about and doesn't care. It's like bankers arguing that they need more fees because their margins are being squeezed. No one cares except the squeezee.

My prediction is that for the next few years the AMA's ritual of announcing average salaries will include a repetition of the charges that this is a public relations ploy, but that after three or four years the formula will be accepted, and the media will move on.

THEY PROTEST TOO MUCH

Kohlberg, Kravis, Roberts (KKR), the takeover and financing juggernaut, rolled through the 1980s racking up huge profits. They were so interesting that predictably, *New York Times* writer Sarah Bartlett wrote a book. It was like a TV drama — success, huge sums of money, ambition, greed, and betrayal. KKR certainly turned out to be a "Money Machine," the title of the book. Certainly, they are an American success story. *Fortune* magazine estimates KKR, through its holdings, is one of the largest American institutions. Bartlett, who covers banking and financial institutions for the *New York Times*, undertook to write their history, their short history, since they've only been around for a decade. Despite their well-publicized behavior in hotly pursuing companies, Henry Kravis and George Roberts, the "K" and "R" of KKR, didn't like seeing it in a book. Despite a public posture of "what book? we don't care . . . " they used all the muscle and leverage that Bartlett described to try to suppress coverage of the book. This kind of behavior never stays a secret, and it does more to confirm what Bartlett wrote about these guys than the book itself.

The book, *The Money Machine*, was *not* a trash job. It was harsh — Bartlett believes that KKR evolved from a firm that helped companies grow and expand while making money for investors into an outfit that started buying and burdening companies with crushing debt for the short-term benefits of the KKR owners. She is hardly alone in this belief. *Time* magazine noted, "KKR's concept of bootstrapping changed over time. Kohlberg's original notion was that he and his partners should invest their own money in deals and, most important, should glean profits only if and when owner-managers and other investors did." *Time* notes that by the mid-1980s, "KKR's interest and those of its investors began to diverge."

Another aspect of the book, shocking only to readers learning about the world of investment banking for the first time, is the level of fees the deal makers rake in. Again, *Time* points out in one deal in 1983 (the early days), KKR invested less than a million dollars of its own money and $50 million of its investors in a $442 million deal and charged $4.5 million. A few years later, KKR was investing $2.5 million of its own money in a $2.4 billion deal but charging $23 million. "No one ever stopped to question the logic of whether it really took 10 times the brainpower to orchestrate a $3 billion deal than it did a $300 million deal." But that's the point; these are money-making machines, and they benefit all who join. KKR built up a network of investment bankers, lawyers, and other "professionals" who got rich and collected exceptionally high fees. *The Economist* called the fees "enormous" but described the subsequent management fees as "solid." In one example, investment banks charged $20 million dollars for processing a minor refinancing.

But all this was written about before. The new material in the book was relatively minor. One of the original partners felt betrayed and left. People who made investment decisions for pension funds and other institutions were given a chance to "get rich quick" in a way, well, not available to the rest of us. (Psst. Want to buy some stock at $100 a share? Sound expensive? In a few months, you can sell it for $900 a share.) This is not good for the free market, public confidence, or the economy, but it's hardly an earth-shattering revelation.

The most interesting thing was Kravis's and Roberts's reaction. They not only want to be successful, they want to be loved! They're upset that the book does not portray them as Mother Theresa. It's true, they have given generously to the arts (a sure-fire way to redeem one's name) and other causes. Heavens. The first John Rockefeller paved the way.

What did they do about the book? Exactly what Bartlett might have predicted. They hired a fancy libel lawyer and threatened the publisher, Warner Books. They leaned on the press. The *New York Times* was apparently persuaded to move a story off the cover of the Sunday magazine and to cancel an already completed news story. Now, that's really muscle. Can you imagine if Exxon tried this?

Interestingly enough, despite widespread and generally good reviews on publication, the second wave of publicity about the pressure tactics appeared in the *Washington Post.* They actually got an editor at the *New York Times* to explain the decision to move Bartlett's excerpts from the cover of the *Times Sunday Magazine* by saying, "We didn't want to give the appearance that we were unduly promoting a book by one of our own writers. If there were a controversy, we would have covered it. It wasn't our job to create the controversy." This will come as news to countless other companies who have tried to convince the *Times* to see the virtue of their position.

Actually, Bartlett is far harder on her colleagues than the name subjects. The book implies that financial journalists traded access for objectivity. Bartlett calls this a process of "mutual seduction." The journalists got information, exclusivity, stroking, hot tips, and in return, they cast KKR in a favorable light. Actually, the institution coming off worst in Bartlett's book is the *Wall Street Journal*, which holds itself out as impervious to influence. In those famous words, "Say it ain't so Joe."

No, it shouldn't surprise anyone that Kravis and Roberts are behaving true to form. They exercise power, skillfully and successfully. They *are* a "money machine." The surprise is how much the press is helping them.

The lesson for others here is "don't make it worse." Or, even if it's broke, don't smash it. Perhaps the Shakespearean, "She protesteth too much" is appropriate. Bartlett wrote about the deeds. The KKR official's response was "the book does not merit comment," but their actions spoke louder.

"Good Source of Fiber"
"Toasted Whole Grain Oat Cereal"
"Low in Fat"
"No Artificial Colors or Flavors" — CHEERIOS BOX

"Why can't I have Cheerios every day?"
— MAVERICK LEZAR, AGE 3

NEW CHEERIOS?

They don't go snap, crackle, and pop, but Cheerios are a staple in most American households. Almost every house has a box in the cupboard. Cheerios made news when General Mills decided to bring us "NEW" Cheerios; however, the news was actually how they chose to tell consumers, or in this case, how they chose not to tell them.

Usually, a "new" formulation is big news. General Mills didn't announce it, however. The actual information was included in the annual report (not usually the vehicle for hard new announcements). It was picked up by someone who said, "Wait a minute." So, the news became not "new" Cheerios but whether General Mills was trying to slip something by. Yet, it's certainly the company's right to decide whether to reformulate and what to tell the public.

What should they have done? In hindsight, they created the perception that they were trying to downplay the reformulation. Reporters linked the "new" Cheerios with an investigation that found minute quantities of pesticides in a few boxes. The company said, "No link, no way."

Hindsight is the great advantage we all have; unfortunately, we can only put it to work for the future. What appears certain is that General Mills didn't have a mechanism for internal debate about communication structure and strategy. An internal communication team that cuts across divisions and functions is a useful resource utilized by few companies. For one thing, it serves as an internal sounding board and a way to spot minefields before stepping on them.

Teams are, of course, all the rage this decade, but few adopt the idea that communication is a state of mind to be driven through the company. For teams to work well, the following conditions must be present: The team must have access to top management or obvious support from the top. Otherwise, no one takes it seriously. Next, the inclusion of an outsider/insider is a vital element when the team considers strategic decisions. The outsider provides a safety valve, a "deniability" (in political jargon), a way of considering previously incorrect or difficult topics.

For example, McDonald's made news when an elderly woman sued the company after dumping a cup of scalding coffee in a take-out cup in her own lap. Most press coverage looked incre-dulously at the woman's claim that McDonald's was at fault, yet a jury awarded her millions of dollars in punitive damages, which was later knocked down by a judge. Yet, the *Wall Street Journal* later probed the issue and found that McDonald's had 700 other suits against it for the same charge!

Surely there was something to be learned from that volume of litigation. Either the coffee was too hot, the disclosures needed to be different, or the method of handling complaints needed re-examination. (The woman had originally asked for compensation for medical care, which couldn't have been more than a few hundred or thousand dollars. That's nothing compared to the cost of legal defense or losing the suit.)

Back to the "how to announce" dilemma — when you reformulate, do you make a big deal of it or not? The attempt to reformulate Coke is usually cited as the case study, and traditional wisdom holds this as a bad example. However, one of the largest bottlers of Coca-Cola told me, "It was pure genius." It created a national debate, energized Coke drinkers, and put passion back into drinking Coke. When was the last time you felt passionately about your soft drink?

Notice the basic philosophical difference. The Coca-Cola Company is traditionally customer-focused and includes customers in its debate. So an "open" announcement made sense. Our general rule of thumb is that when a key audience will find out anyway, it makes sense to be open from the start, capitalize on the positive aspects of news, endure the predictable hits or howlings and bad news, and look on it as an opportunity. The risk is that you can only have "new and improved" so many times and it stops being news, but a truly "new" Cheerios is legitimate news. Cheerios is an American classic (my kids eat handfuls of it as snack food).

Marketplace Communication

The question isn't whether General Mills did it right or wrong on this one, but rather is the process in place to examine the strategy and make it "new and improved" on the next go round?

THE TOWER OF BABEL

Remember the biblical story of the Tower of Babel? People spoke so many languages that their whole economy collapsed in chaos. In today's global economy, doing business means coping with similar conditions. There are nice success stories of companies successfully handling this communication challenge.

Many companies do business in many countries. Our image of professionals carrying briefcases, pouring over spreadsheets, and doing deals isn't the only way to do business abroad. Many companies do business in multiple languages, but their workers are not college educated and are at the low end of the wage scale.

We've just defined life for Sky Chefs International. Operating from 32 cities, they prepare 64 million meals a year for 35 different airlines. In order to deal with all this, their 8,000 employees speak 38 different languages ranging from Russian to Tagalog. Now, suppose you also want them to work autonomously and produce the highest quality goods and services *without* time-consuming and expensive supervision and inspection procedures? That's a challenge.

Sky Chefs tackled this by an aggressive program to explain their mission and goals to every single person in the company. They distilled their vision of what it would take to be successful in the future to 13 concepts, or elements, of excellence. How do you communicate this in 38 languages? They used an innovative nonverbal language. They clipped and pasted until they had compelling pictures of the 13 standards which comprise their corporate mission and strategy.

"The Customer as Number One" shows the traveler who is pleased, well fed, and refreshed. "Culinary Excellence" shows trays of wonderful-looking food. "Teamwork" shows the entire team with suppliers on one end and customers on the other.

"Communication" is also one of the elements, and that concept is depicted as people talking close-up and at a distance. Because the needs of their customers are constantly changing, they must constantly communicate.

Most air travelers don't think much about the people in blue work clothes loading food into the aircraft. We're too busy hauling on our allowed three items, jockeying for a position in the overhead rack, and grabbing magazines. We don't want to think about the support systems that produce the comfortable flight, the acceptable food, and the Diet Dr. Pepper or V-8 juice when we want it. We just want it when we want it. And Sky Chefs knows it has to deliver.

An axiom of business leaders is that you can learn something from every successful company. One of the noteworthy things about this company is that they stress respect and manners. They say that first, they treat their own employees and each other as they would treat their customers. Everyone must learn to say "please" and "thank you" in all the languages. Now that's something in itself, something two generations of American school children should learn. Most of us who've collected a million frequent flyer points can say *merci, danka,* and *gracias.* But what about *spasseba* (Russian), *shayshay* (Chinese), *rreggato* (Japanese), *kam'un* (Vietnamese), *ma'hlo* (Portuguese), *kob'koon* (Thai) . . . only 29 more to go.

MORE EXAMPLES

The power of example is one of the most powerful communication tools.

One thing about traveling widely and working with many companies, I see lots of examples of good and bad communication. It has made me a fervent believer in the power of example as a communication tool.

There's an example of a CEO who said, "Our employees are our most important asset." He put his money behind his words. Richard Branson's tiny Virgin Atlantic Airways won £600,000 in a lawsuit against British Airways. Branson divided the settlement among all the airline's employees to "thank them for persevering during a difficult time." Can you imagine the lengths those employees will go to for their employer?

Customer service anecdotes, or personal experiences, can be a powerful advertising tool for a company. For example, we recently spent a weekend in Washington, D.C. Our baby's doting godfather gave her a party at the Ritz, and when I found out that part of the festivities included a seafood buffet, I was dubious. This is a child who thinks Cheerios are exotic.

The Ritz staff professed to be delighted to see her. Not only did she get a high chair but also such toddler delectables as a banana, cranberry juice, and grapes. More important — she also got lots of attention and affection. I confess, though, that she and her godfather spent the better part of dinner tossing corks at his other guests. I have told this story over and over again. Free advertising for the Ritz.

People also repeat negative experiences, and these are particularly damaging when they confirm stereotypes. Women- and minority-owned companies are frequently hesitant to try to work with very large projects because we fear that we will be treated unfairly. Yet many companies proclaim they want to work with minority- and women-owned companies. Several years ago, the now-defunct Superconducting Supercollider, or SSC, wanted help explaining why Congress should spend $8 billion of your tax dollars on it. Our firm was solicited to present a proposal. It took about five man (in our case, woman) days, to create and submit a proposal. After it was submitted, we learned that a week *before* the deadline, Texas Governor Ann Richards had instructed the Foundation for Scientific Leadership, the sponsoring group, to kill the project. But the Foundation let all the firms they had solicited toil away anyway.

You don't have to be a rocket scientist to realize that it's precisely women- and minority-owned firms that can least afford this kind of charade. We don't mind competing, but we sure do mind spinning our wheels. And the insensitivity indicates that the SSC and its related agencies really don't have much interest in working with women and minorities. They're just checking boxes to meet regulations.

Everyone loves what's called "human interest" stories — the tragedies or near tragedies where neighbors or others pitch in to help. One family on a traditional summer vacation trip had a big problem. The action or reaction of several companies sent a very bad message. But one company's reaction communicated caring and commitment, the kind of reinforcement of a corporate message that money can't buy.

My parents used to say, "Actions speak louder than words," and it's true. A company can't say, "We want to help you" in its ads, and then when you walk in the door, their actions send exactly the opposite message. On the other hand, when a company's actions reinforce the corporate line, consumers get the message.

For example, one Indiana family driving around the country had a car accident near Galveston, Texas. The family had a 17-year-old son with muscular dystrophy, and their van had special equipment.

Hertz, Avis, and Budget *all* refused to rent the family a van for a *one-way* trip home, but American Airlines flew the family home — for free.

Northwestern National City Mutual was the insurance company for the driver of the *other* car. They provided a van with a wheelchair lift so the family could visit San Antonio and the Alamo while they were in Texas.

What happened? Hertz, Avis, Budget, and the other rental car companies are good companies. But some employee, some bureaucrat, looked at the book of rules and regulations, and it said, "No one-way trips." Period. No exceptions. No appeals. Forget it. I'll bet if the clerk had called corporate headquarters and said, "Look, here's the situation," they could have hustled up a van for a one-way trip.

But whoever answered the phone for American had the good judgment to say, "Let me see if we can help." That's good corporate communication. It says the company encourages its employees to use their heads, *and* that those advertising slogans about caring about the customer are really true. So Avis and the other car companies didn't try harder. As for American, it really is *something special in the air.*

Part II

THE CEO AS LEADER

> *"The goal is simple: Reach employees, investors, customers, and regulators; inform them honestly; and finally — here's the tough part — make it positive."* — MERRIE SPAETH

SUPERB HONESTY

The condition of the CEO's health has become a matter of public concern. What do you say, and how do you say it?

Most companies are still doing a mediocre job of delivering bad news, whether it's layoffs, mergers, plant closings, or the departure of the CEO. All these indicate change and thus potential threat. Even worse than change is uncertainty. What if the CEO isn't leaving? What if he's just sick? Maybe dying? And what if his condition involves something very scary — like brain cancer?

Obviously, from a communication point of view, the goal is simple: Reach employees, investors, customers, and regulators; inform them honestly; and finally — here's the tough part — make it positive. Use the occasion, however grim, to reinforce why you're taking certain actions; what the company's future is — whatever. There are always positives. The trick is to do this and be honest; that is, it can't sound saccharine or forced.

There's no tougher situation than telling the world that your CEO has brain cancer. The business community was presented with the interesting example of two parallel situations. The CEOs of Tenneco and TLC Beatrice International were both faced with brain cancer. They chose to handle the situation in totally different ways.

Beatrice did not even reveal the condition of CEO Reginald F. Lewis until he went into a terminal coma and died a few days later. Tenneco announced it from the start. In my view, Tenneco created a beacon of light for honest communication — and for communication as a strategic business tool that merits top corporate management's attention. Every American corporation should get a copy of Tenneco's press statement and the accompanying physician's letter as an example of strategic communication.

The press statement was issued in the unusual form of lengthy personal comments from Chairman and CEO Michael Walsh, whom every living human being called "Mike." It presents information honestly — this guy has brain cancer. "The average survival is five to six years; some do better, some do worse." And it is presented in an upbeat way. The doctor involved is a leader in researching new therapies.

This statement "sold" at the time because Mike Walsh's personal tone and intense personality leapt through the words. Here are some of the phrases you might expect: "I remain absolutely committed to continuing the critical work that our excellent team and I began months ago."

Here are some of the phrases you might not expect: "Our shareholders, our employees, and our many friends can be assured I intend to face this disease with the same commitment to meet it and beat it that I have brought to every other challenge in my life." I believed it.

The doctor's letter to the board likewise offered some expected comments ("Consult me any time.") but also some unusual sentences: "I have never seen an individual handle a matter like this any better than Mike has." I believed it.

Unfortunately for Mike and for Tenneco, it didn't turn out to be the case. Oh, at first it looked as if this might be one more adversary that Mike Walsh might defeat, just as he defeated bad guys as a U.S. Attorney. He made no secret of what was going on, going to staff meetings with the mechanism to dispense medication strapped on him, lying down in his office (briefly), or joking about his "haircut" (no hair from the treatment). His hair grew back, the spring in his step sprung back, but the cancer did, too.

Typically, Mike Walsh insisted on candor. He was honest, open, and refused to be grim or bitter. He died in 1994.

Beatrice's CEO never had a chance to allow us to see how he handled the disease because by the time the world knew about it, he was gone.

Death is the most personal of experiences. I prefer Woody Allen's great phrase, "I don't mind dying. I just don't want to be around when it happens." Who of us has the strength of will and stamina to allow ourselves to die publicly? It's too easy to say Mike Walsh did it the "right" way and Reginald Lewis did it the "wrong" way. It's not that simple. By all accounts, Lewis, the scrappy yet elegant founder of one of the world's largest African-American-owned companies was a private man. He, too, was conscious of being a role model. He may not have wanted to be publicly seen with no hair or an uncertain gait. That's his right. And his company was privately owned. So it was his right to run it.

From the company's point of view, however, Mike Walsh's example has many benefits. First, it allows the company to plan. Tenneco made a smooth transition to President Dana Mead. Beatrice International has had a rocky time, first with Lewis' half brother and now under his wife. Candor allows those who are part of the company to plan and adjust.

We demand a lot from today's CEO. Public dying is probably one thing we shouldn't demand — yet. Mike Walsh made it his life's work to be a role model. He can add death to his credentials of leadership.

CEOs AND SPEECHES

Reprinted with special permission of King Features Syndicate

Giving speeches is an accepted part of being a CEO today — even though polls continue to show that many top executives prefer death to public speaking. There are several books which should be on every executive's bookshelf.

Most books on how to give a speech or how to write a speech have very useful information, but executives, PR departments, everyone who writes speeches (or tries to), and anyone who does any public speaking ought to have these three books: Jack Valenti's *How to Write a Speech*, Lilyan Wilder's *Professionally Speaking*, and *Executive Speeches*, subtitled "51 CEOs Tell You How To Do Yours," by Brent Filson.

When I'm teaching communication, people always ask for recommendations on speech books. I usually remind them of the famous words of E.B. White and William Strunk in the classic, *The Elements of Style*. (If you've misplaced your copy, get another. It's in about the 117th printing.)

Remember, they say, "Omit unnecessary words."

The author of *Executive Speeches* and the CEOs he has interviewed demonstrate that speeches are more than delivered text. One interview with an executive at Republic Bank in Texas stands out in my mind.

(Remember them? They're extinct today, and this attitude explains why.) This executive thought he could stand up and regurgitate facts and numbers — and that was a speech. He'd tell me, "Don't put any jokes or quotes in it. That isn't me." Well, being an executive wasn't him for very long.

Executive Speeches is the first really modern book I've seen on the subject because the author recognizes that today's speaker needs props, gestures, stories, video — even a band in one case — to reach the audience. Executives who refuse to consider these speech enhancers, and who hang on to their pile of slides or overheads, are willfully refusing to recognize the competition for ideas and attention today.

Yeats said, "Speak in the language of the people." Some of us need help. Grab these books.

STUPID, STUPID, STUPID

"I'm afraid I'll do something stupid." "I don't want to look dumb." "I'm concerned I'll screw up." These are all reasons we frequently hear from people explaining why they don't want more of a public presence, why they don't want to be interviewed, and why they don't intend to try something new — usually in front of other people. It's not enough to counsel the CEO that he needs to be the standard-bearer in communication; we must assure him that he can manage the blooper, survive the pratfall, negotiate past the dumb comment — in short, he can survive a public display of his own stupidity.

To take risks is to ensure that at some point you will do something really, really dumb or embarrassing. The only way to ensure you don't is not to do anything. As the runner's girlfriend says in the movie *Chariots of Fire*, "You can't win if you don't run." To win you have to play.

Bloopers fall into different categories. First and most feared, there is public speaking. One CEO was addressing his top managers about the importance of diversity. He said, "We can't just look at whether someone is a man or woman." That didn't come out quite right, so he tried again. "What I mean is that we have employees who are both men and women." Still not quite right, perhaps even worse. The audience was beginning to titter. The CEO went on, "We have to be concerned about bisexual employees." The audience was now howling. The CEO put his head in his hands and laughed along with them. After he wiped away his own tears of laughter, he said, "This stuff isn't easy to talk about, and I guess I'm an example. But it is important, and I want to be an example of that, too." And he continued. He snatched victory from disaster.

My favorite example of keeping your cool was a speech given by Chief of Staff James Baker to President Reagan's political appointees in 1982. He charged right in, saying the Administration had done a lot, but, "There are two promises the President has not been able to keep. The first is the promise to put more Americans back to work, and the second . . . " He paused. Finally, he turned to Ed Meese and asked, "What is the second promise?" An audible whisper, "Balance the budget," and Baker was back on track. The audience was in stitches. Baker's facial expression was a big smile. Like the CEO, he laughed at himself.

Anyone who has cats is familiar with the strategy of pretending you meant to do something no matter how foolish it looked. Years ago my roommate had a cat. I watched it fall in the toilet, climb out, and perch on the side that seemed to announce, "I meant to do that."

Contrast Baker and the CEO with the cabinet secretary breakfasting with top business leaders. The secretary began with a 10-point plan. Unfortunately, after the fifth point, he lost track. For the remainder of his remarks he kept asking aides, "What was number eight?" or "Did I mention exports?" The executives left shaking their heads.

Public speaking ensures that something over which you have no control will go wrong, usually the equipment. Again, the proper stance is to dismiss it and keep going. During my first speech to a conference sponsored by the Federal Reserve Bank (yes, Alan Greenspan and me), the sound system stopped working. (And, yes, I had practiced in the room with the technician.) My microphone was useless, and the audio tapes I had planned to play from the podium were out of the question. I stepped to the front of the stage, recalled my projection lessons, and continued. About five minutes later, the sound came on with a loud "POP," making everyone jump, including me. For the rest of the conference, I was the lady who jumped.

One of my senior vice presidents spoke to a conference hosted by KPMG Peat Marwick for its clients. Although she, too, practiced in the room with the technician, in the middle of her speech she noticed smoke coming from the A/V room behind the stage. Nothing to do but step in to investigate and announce to the audience. "This is not a good sign," she said. The audience laughed.

Handling bloopers like these requires the patience and practice that comes with many appearances. Those who take the message "don't use equipment" or "have everything written down" got the wrong message. Things will always go wrong.

Of course, it takes a special amount of self-confidence to behave as President Reagan did during a visit by the famed Lipizzaner horses to the White House lawn. The Lipizzaners are stallions. Somewhere close to the White House was a receptive mare. The staff didn't know this, but the stallions did. Their anatomy changed accordingly. While we tried to ignore the change, President Reagan paused, gazed, and said, "This story is getting awfully long," and he drew out the word "long." The audience gasped with laughter.

President Reagan also managed to read an entire set of remarks with Victory, a baby miniature elephant, tugging at his ankle with her trunk. And when the press corps photographed him receiving an eight-week-old puppy from Mrs. Reagan, the puppy demonstrated that he wasn't housebroken, and the President was photographed receiving more than the puppy. Mr. Reagan wasn't fazed and asked, "Does anyone have a handkerchief? A big handkerchief."

Another category of blooper entirely is the stupid remark. It may be made in private or semipublic. One of my clients greeted a new employee who was very, very round in the middle and wearing a flowing dress. "When's the baby due?" he asked enthusiastically as a prelude to telling her that he, too, had a new baby. "I'm not pregnant," she said — very coldly. In this case, apologize and say it fast. "I'm so sorry. We have an eight-month-old baby, and I'm very interested in the topic. I apologize and hope you'll accept it." She nodded coldly.

Don't ignore the blooper. Don't overexplain or be overly apologetic. If it's a truly sensitive subject, such as race or divorce, it may be appropriate to handwrite a short, personal note later, saying, "Thanks for being so gracious. I look forward to working with you."

Notice, these are bloopers made by smart people. I'm not talking about what Molly Ivins, the Austin columnist, calls "the seriously dumb," mostly politicians. Former New York City Mayor Edward I. Koch explained to the *New York Times*, "The reasons that many politicians do dumb things is that many of them are just plain dumb. It shouldn't shock you."

It's not really a blooper, but it's a mistake, so I'll include it. It should be categorized as the "mean response." Several rotund welfare mothers were pounding on Nelson Rockefeller's desk. One of them shouted, "You don't know what hunger is." The Governor of New York replied, "Madam, how wonderful that neither you nor I know what hunger is." It seemed mean-spirited. By contrast, when a reporter asked President Reagan about reports that he couldn't hear at Cabinet briefings and dozed off, Mr. Reagan replied, "Eh? Could you repeat that? I must have dozed off."

In the aftermath of the Connie Chung interview, a reporter screamed at Speaker Gingrich, "Is your mother a liar?" (Chung had told Mrs.

Gingrich that a remark would be "between you and me," then aired a comment about Mrs. Clinton.) The Speaker looked very peeved and angry. He snapped, "I'm not going to respond to that." He got it partially right. The correct response is to look unfazed and say with an animated, pleasant expression, "I'm not going to reply to attacks on my mother."

Mercifully, perfection isn't the benchmark. For executives today who are sincere in trying to do a good job and who care about their colleagues and employees, their attitudes will shine and carry them through bloopers. Actions do speak louder than words, although the words can sometimes be awfully funny.

CEO SALARIES

Is a CEO worth a million dollars? Two million? Fifty million? Lee Iacocca's salary went up to $4.8 million at the same time Chrysler announced record losses. That caused a lot of talk at the time, but in retrospect it seems like small potatoes. In 1993, the CEO of Disney made more than $200 million at a time when the company had significant problems with its European Disney property. Mr. Goizueta of Coca-Cola pulled down $86 million one year. Some critics are recommending a system that links a company's financial performance with the CEO's salary. Salaries, or the compensation system, tell us a lot about the CEO and his priorities.

The question is not "how much" but "how to explain it" and to whom. When it comes to salaries and compensation, American business is curiously focused only on one group of key players. Other key players receive messages which are quite different from what the company intends to convey.

There has been a lot of attention to the huge salaries paid to CEOs of public companies. Top managers defend large salaries as fair compensation for the stress and complexity of "managing" billion-dollar enterprises. Others point out that many of those companies have experienced layoffs, stagnant stock prices, and shrinking markets. Economists say they are at a loss to explain the disparity between a company's performance and what a CEO is paid. Executives communicate what they think is important, or who, in many ways. Some executives, like Harold Hook at American General, will show you who should be important by drawing a circle around the CEO. They put shareholders, employees, customers, the public, even vendors and creditors on the circle. Each of these "stakeholders" have some claim on the company. Thus, the CEO's compensation should depend in part on how good a job the CEO did for these constituencies, recognizing that the long-term survival and prosperity of the company make possible the rewards for all.

What some CEOs are telling us with very high salaries is who is important (besides themselves of course) and who isn't. When a CEO's salary soars despite a lackluster stock price, a decline in market position, or some other indication of long-term problems, the CEO is saying that stockholders aren't important, and neither are employees, the public, customers, or creditors. When the CEO's salary soars, the CEO is trying to impress one small group — *other* CEOs. These astronomical salaries tell us the CEO's top priority isn't leading the company but competing for recognition with other CEOs. They're lusting after those "top 100" lists.

How should a CEO be evaluated? Formulas that measure shareholder value can help. ITT's stockholders complained for years that the CEO and top executives were overcompensated while the stock stagnated. In 1991, the company's board changed the compensation formula. It was very effective. ITT's stock rose almost 50 percent in two years and is cited by corporate reformers as an example.

I remain concerned that simple formulas like this are misguided in the long-term. Articles that praise ITT's stock performance note that the company has many problems. Its overall revenues have declined. While I don't believe in mindless worshipping at the alter of growth, other important indicators are also lagging. Several ratios which measure how well a company is deploying its assets or reaping a return are also low, and research and development has been cut.

Clearly, other companies are trying the same thing. General Dynamics has a scheme to give large bonuses to executives if they can push up the price of the stock. (Remember, GD announced layoffs of a third of their work force). We all know companies manipulate earnings, and therefore stock prices. ITT has sold many assets and bought back its own stock. These create temporary "improvements," but not the long-term strength needed for the goal — again, survival and prosperity.

Long-term progress does depend on stockholders, and systems which link stock performance, compensation, and time send a message to stockholders that they are important. For example, Citicorp gives executives the right to purchase stock in the future at the year's closing price but only if the stock reaches target prices significantly higher in the future. Institutional Shareholder Services in Bethesda, Maryland, approves, writing in its annual review, "The goals are difficult enough that executives won't benefit unless shareholders get a good return."

But shareholders aren't the only key group. The employees, customers, public, and perhaps vendors are important for long-term performance. Bilateral formulas linking compensation only with stock price ignore their importance. The argument is that investors' willingness to risk their funds makes jobs and other contributions possible. That is true, but the employees' willingness to work also means something. The problem in designing a formula to measure that reduces this equation of trust to a formula that is fraught with problems if not doomed to failure. However, that doesn't mean it should be ignored.

The board can at least enunciate what it thinks the CEO should be trying to do. The individual or audience can then judge whether the company is living up to its words. For example, if a board believes it's important that everyone prosper together, it won't do what CompUSA did. They fired 40 workers to "cut costs" but also announced in the same news article million-dollar golden parachutes for top officers. Cutting costs for this company was undoubtedly important. The chain was experiencing significant losses, but apparently cutting costs still allows millions of dollars to be paid if another company takes over the company. The excuses were predictable — "they need to keep top talent." But the clear message this sends to employees is that there's enough money for cushy departure packages for top managers. Risk is not equally divided here. If the company is worth managing, saving, and growing, the executives should be rewarded — but with stock in a package like Citicorp's, not with cold cash and certainly not in the midst of "cost cutting."

Companies need to make a much greater effort to explain to their various "stakeholders" what the CEO and top management do or I predict there will be increasing attempts to regulate salaries (as with the ill-advised and impractical attempt to limit what a company can deduct in the salaries category to $1 million). American business concentrates almost exclusively on trying to explain compensation to analysts.

It's not a popular sentiment, but Steve Ashton, CEO of a small but thriving photography company in Oregon, expressed how most people feel when he said in *INC* magazine, "When things go bad, cut pay at the top first. When things go well, reward at the bottom first." If the board of directors really wants to ensure long-term prosperity, they'll pay attention to Mr. Ashton's advice. If they do, they can be sure the CEO will pay attention.

SHOULD A COMPANY PRESIDENT DO HIS OWN ADS?

Frank Purdue became famous by appearing in his own advertisements. Somehow the "tough man" was perfect to promote the "tender chicken." The top man can be a good choice for the job of promoting the company or its products.

We are seeing more company CEOs appear in their own ads. Sometimes it works great. Lee Iacocca got across his personal pledge for quality.

"First, we took a good, hard look at our own company. If we found something that slowed things down, or didn't add value or improve quality, we dumped it."

The message made sense, and Iacocca's personal delivery skills were superb. Both those things need to come together in the ad or else the CEO's presence is a hinderance, not a help.

When the CEO or president has a message that implies personal commitment it enhances his presence as an advertising spokesman. For example, Victor Kiam's, "I liked the razor so much I bought the company." This works for someone who can say, "I built this business myself," or "My family has worked in this industry for two generations." In Dallas, the three Minyard cousins who run the Minyard grocery chain can say "from our family to yours," because it is their family.

What about delivery skills? The CEO does not need to sound like James Earl Jones. In fact, like Kiam, his voice can be gravelly and he can look like one of Santa's elves, but he needs a certain command of language.

"The Remington Micro Screen — quick, comfortable, and shaves as close as a blade, or your money back." The copy must sound as if he wrote it. That is, it really has to sound like the guy talking.

"At Chrysler, we believe that standing still is a great way to get run over. In this business, you lead, follow, or get out of the way." Sounds like him.

Not everyone can be Lee Iacocca. In one low-budget local radio ad, the proprietor says, "I'm Pasquale Trizola of Trizola Resources. My company will produce an affordable, professional newsletter exclusively for your employees or customers."

He had perfectly decent delivery skills, and we know his name and reputation are on the line. This adds weight to his message.

Tip-offs that your executive shouldn't be pushed in front of the microphone? First, an inability to understand how to reproduce the spoken word. "Come in and buy *a* re-frig-er-ator from us to-day."

However, this isn't an absolute disqualifier. The Men's Warehouse, a national chain of men's stores, has CEO George Zimmer on radio and television saying you'll get top quality from his stores at a better price, and he says, "I guarantee it." The pronunciation is theoretically all wrong; each accent in "guar-an-tee" is hit with a sledge hammer, but he speaks with conviction. He sounds as if he believes it. (Occasionally, these ads include real taped messages of voice mail that customers have left for him personally — a great technique that adds credibility to his claim.)

In his case, the message and the deliverer match as well as being consistent with the audience. The Men's Warehouse wants the average guy to know he is welcome. The fake British accent adopted by so many announcers would send the wrong message. And if the message and the deliverer don't match, watch out. There was the proprietor of the fashion store who looked like the absentminded professor, and the expert on airline services who looked like a grease monkey.

Finally, there's the hard-to-define quality of charisma. If you have to stop and ponder whether your guy has it — he probably doesn't. The best way to describe charisma is Former Supreme Court Justice Potter Stewart's wonderful line about pornography: "It's hard to define, but you know it when you see it." How else can you categorize something Henry Kissinger, Tom Peters, and Dr. Ruth all have? Charisma is credibility, as mentioned above. The listener or viewer needs to believe that the speaker believes what he's saying. It's excitement, and usually (but not always — witness Dr. Kissinger) it's enjoyment. The speaker makes us want to learn more, experience more, and be part of the topic.

Reasons for CEOs to be in their own ads? It's fun (CEOs deserve some fun), it saves money, and it shows that you'll do anything for the company. But not every CEO should do it.

THE EMBARRASSMENT IN YOUR INDUSTRY

"The bank doesn't go out of its way to court black customers. If we did, we'd go broke. Our history record with them is horrible," said the chairman of one bank, in print, in the *Houston Chronicle*. Hardly a quote taken out of context, the chairman also told the reporter that "Arabs have a poor record of repaying loans." He did feel that "Chinamen . . . were thrifty and work hard."

Predictably, in this day of both heightened sensitivity coupled with political correctness, reaction was strong and swift. A community activist used the comments to castigate all of banking. "These types of comments are evidence that much of the banking system has changed very little," said a local redevelopment community director.

The occasion of the remarks was a "need to improve" rating from Community Reinvestment Act (CRA) regulators received by the bank in question, an issue of interest and concern to every banker today. The CRA government police wield significant power, enough to force a Maryland bank with no history of discrimination, no specific charges against it, and an excellent record of community service to open brick-and-mortar branches in black neighborhoods far from its normal area of service. The CRA is only partially about increasing credit and funds to areas and individuals previously limited in access. It's equally about the government's ability to direct previously private funds to accomplish social goals.

What this individual banker needs to improve first are his own communication skills and ability to deal with the media. What should other bankers do? "I didn't say it," one told me. "I just want to ignore it." Not the right strategy. Why? What should they do?

The risk is that, unchallenged, the bank chairman's quotes appear to represent the industry when in fact they are grossly at odds with both the attitude and actual practice of American banking today. The question is how to get that across, and the answer is to analyze audiences and target the right ones.

One school of thought, of course, is "don't respond because that just highlights the charges and repeats them." There is truth in that analysis and risk in an alternate path. But life is analyzing and accepting risks. An alternate approach would be to ask bankers who feel differently from the quoted bank chairman to identify the key audiences — regulators, community leaders in minority areas — and reach them by letter and telephone, stating their bank's philosophy, commitment, and track record. This semipublic commitment to progress serves to isolate the chairman's quote and position him as a renegade in the industry.

In this case in particular, that approach should prevail because the quotes of the regulators and activists indicate understanding that the industry has made progress. The activist goes on to say, "We have a long way to go," with which most bankers would agree. Silence from other bankers can be taken to indicate approval or acquiescence.

Consider a wildly different issue — the debate over abortion. A tiny group of self-styled radicals on the fringe of the pro-life or antiabortion movement has advocated the righteousness of violence. The "pro-choice" movement insisted that more mainstream but still antiabortion groups denounce the talk of violence. Finally, several acts of real violence took place, including the murder of a physician in Florida. Pro-choice groups loudly castigated the established pro-life groups, charging that their failure to condemn violent talk ultimately contributed to the killing. The media and apparently most Americans concurred. Finally, the pro-life groups followed the urging of William Price, leader of a Dallas-based conservative pro-life group, which had criticized the radical element of the pro-life movement for several years, and called on other groups to speak out.

This is a chance for an industry to learn a much less expensive lesson. Industry members and other bank chairmen should activate the phone lines to their voluble colleague and tell him to wise up, not just button his lip, and learn what modern communication skills are required to run a company today. And they should use other avenues of communication to get their message across to key groups. But they shouldn't ignore the remarks and hope no one notices.

WHAT DOES THE BOARD KNOW?

Should a board of directors know or care what the company's employees think? Do they get an adequate picture from the CEO himself and top management? Is just "looking at the numbers" — the financial performance of a company — a proxy for how well the company is really doing, and how it is going to do in the future? Boards should have more, not less, information. What they find out may surprise them and may save a lot of headaches.

The Sunbeam Corporation made headlines when they dismissed the CEO, Paul Kazarian. Some analysts were surprised because Sunbeam's financial performance had not been suffering. But Kazarian ranted and raved and apparently had horrible communication skills. He displayed the classic "Dr. Jekyll and Mr. Hyde" personalities, and the directors were in the dark until it was almost too late. Only when a group of top managers said, "It's him or us," did the board learn the extent of potential damage.

A board of directors should pay attention to the communication skills of top management, particularly the CEO. Communication should be open enough that action is taken before there's a near catastrophe. And here, as in other areas, the liability directors face is becoming greater. In the January 1994 issue of *Bank Board Letter*, a publication for directors of bank boards, the issue of director liability is addressed. The editor lists eight issues that he advises directors to pay attention to including — you guessed it — employee attitudes.

A board should have an up-to-date view of employee attitudes. Employee attitudes tell a board a lot about management's effectiveness. For example, one of the country's largest banks was unpleasantly

81

surprised when an employee survey revealed that 67 percent of employees did not trust management to tell them the truth. Why is this important? Well, take cost cutting. Employees will not take cost-cutting initiatives seriously unless they believe they are necessary and that everyone, including top management, is involved and committed.

Employee surveys are the first tool to determine what employees really think, what they are planning to do, how much they are willing to commit to a company, and what they really know and think about the company's products and services. The caveat is that such surveys should be done by a team comprised of insiders and outside experts and must be impeccably honest. It's too easy to create questions and surveys designed to give you the answer that you want as opposed to the correct information. Today the target audience of any survey is very sophisticated and will try to scope out what is the "right" answer for the survey taker. Surveys must be ongoing, that is, one survey taken one time only gives you a benchmark. It's a snapshot, not an album. For example, the bank mentioned above found double-digit positive gains over a two-year period in response to questions about whether the bank was committed to making the work environment more friendly to family issues and more diverse.

Another caveat is that perfection is not the goal. Surveys give a sense of the environment. It's disturbing to some CEOs and board members to discover something like the fact that only 80 percent of employees feel that a certain product is truly the market leader when that's what all the marketing material calls the product, or that only 75 percent of employees feel that the company has a vision for the future. It's important to focus on the fact that this majority feeling creates a very positive environment or dynamic. Trying for 100 percent is self-defeating. So understanding how to interpret the findings and apply them is yet one more skill required of top management and the board.

(One finding that has come out of every survey we've seen or done is that management will learn whether employees feel that their ideas for improving the business, cutting costs, or starting something new are really welcome and whether they feel rewarded for contributions. Again, there's usually a big gap between what management thinks employees think and what they really think.)

Today, the board needs to make sure that the CEO has excellent personal communication skills and an understanding that communication is a key strategic business tool; it fosters the sense of mission for the corporation — and dollars are at stake.

The CEO is not only the main messenger for the corporation, he defines its style.

Marketing guru, Stanley Marcus, says that companies only get 25 percent of what a customer is prepared to spend. One key reason is that customer service is poor, and one reason it's poor is that communication throughout the organization is mediocre.

Look at companies where the CEO is an effective communicator, again both in personal skills and in understanding how to use communication as a business tool. Tenneco and Southwest Airlines, for example, have extraordinary leaders who take communication seriously and are very good at it.

So, members of corporate boards — pay attention. If you do, your company can perform better. If you don't, you're handicapping the potential of the company, and, in the worst cases, you increase your own liability.

"Vision, smision, it's 1% inspiration and 99% perspiration." — A FORTUNE *500 CEO*

VISION

Does a company need a vision? America's large companies make news just because they're large, even more when they're troubled. The CEO's words are reported and scrutinized. When Lou Gerstner took over IBM in 1993, he made headlines saying they didn't need a "vision," they needed more basic business skills. Many people took umbrage at his comments, but one other *Fortune* 500 CEO said, "Vision, smision, it's 1 percent inspiration and 99 percent perspiration."

"Vision" has become an overused word, like "quality" and "caring," but that doesn't mean its usefulness is at an end. "Vision" means "to see," with the additional implication of seeing clearly; it means having a view of what the future is going to be and where we fit in it. People who have a "vision" have the ability to use their minds the way most of us don't. A vision is special; it is exciting, and it is tantalizing.

Most people don't have a vision and don't understand the leadership role in defining and articulating it. Hence, former President Bush's toppling into the ungraceful phrase "the vision thing." Defining and articulating a vision is the hardest work a CEO can do. It draws on skills they didn't learn in business school.

Presidential press secretaries are never supposed to say, "what he really meant was . . ." But in this case, what Gerstner probably meant was that the company didn't need to get all tied up in long-term exercises, that it had good products and services, that attention to costs was paramount, and that it requires basic rethinking of business process — things that don't lend themselves to *traditional* vision statements. (However, note that Southwest Airlines' vision is that air travel competes with automobile travel, and that to pull people out of their cars, they have to be the low-cost provider. And they've done it.)

What was particularly interesting was the public reaction to the Gerstner comments. One letter writer commented, "It is important to note that Lou Gerstner is not the only player in this transformation; tens of thousands of IBM employees have to row the Big Blue boat forward, too. Hence, a unifying vision is critical, even if it means restating elements of success for IBM for decades." The writer suggested, "IBM will build on its strengths in technology, creativity, global presence, and customer relationships to be the premier advanced-technology company in creating and delivering computing and information-processing solutions to individuals, businesses, nonprofit organizations, and governments worldwide."

Despite the overly long sentence, this writer is grappling with stating what IBM is and to whom. Another letter writer forced the discussion into the sentences, "Who are my customers? What do you want me to sell? How will I be paid?" He says if your managers and line employees can't answer the question, you have a real problem.

Another former IBM employee distilled the vision as "something that can be articulated to everyone, both inside and outside IBM" and suggested, "Our mission is to be the most successful information-technology company in the world."

I think sophisticated, hip, roll-up-your-sleeves CEOs like Gerstner become impatient with missions because *they* have heard the words so many times that they've lost their impact. They appear to have lost connection with the bottom line or with people. They forget the impact those words have on others.

If a company can't articulate what it's in business to do and what it claims makes it different from others, it can hardly expect its employees or customers to articulate the message and pass it on.

Mission statements are difficult to write. Arthur Andersen, one of the Big Six accounting and consulting firms, struggled for a long time before it finally came up with "Our mission is to help clients succeed in the global marketplace by exceeding their expectations and delivering value in everything we do." In between came slogans such as, "All accounting firms are not alike," which had the unhappy effect of stressing the similarity between firms instead of differentiating Arthur Andersen's special qualities.

Famous mission phrases that have produced generations of leaders include the Marine Corps' "Semper Fidelis" and West Point's "Duty, Country, Honor."

Marketplace Communication

Perhaps Gerstner and others misunderstand the simple purpose of vision. For those mired in the trenches, we want to know that someone is up there on the hilltop, that he can see his way clear to the next valley, and has scoped out a way for us to follow him there.

> *"The employees don't understand that unless we move forward and keep up with the world situation, they will lose by default."* — JIM CUMMINGS, PLANT MANAGER OF THE NESTLE PLANT, CHESTERVILLE, ONTARIO, COMMENTING ON THE WORKERS STRIKING AND DENOUNCING NAFTA

WHAT WE LEARNED FROM NAFTA

In Chesterville, Ontario, they weren't too happy about the North American Free Trade Agreement (NAFTA). "I've got my sombrero already," snapped one worker to the *Washington Post.*

As the world has become a global economy, the reaction of the Chesterville workers should be of concern to employers. The question is not why the employees are unhappy. We are all discomfited by change, and when change means moving our factory and way of life out of town, we are upset. The question for the future is why don't the employees understand what Mr. Cummings, quoted above, is saying.

Coverage of the NAFTA debate was a window on the deep division between how management and workers view the world. Management should not neglect to address that division.

This is not the place to address the historic tension between Big Labor and Big Business. This is about more basic, straightforward communication. If workers knew very little about NAFTA, it was because their companies spent very little or no time discussing issues like free trade, the Mexican economy as a new frontier, how capital flows instantly around the world, and so on. Companies did not communicate with their workers until the passage of NAFTA was upon them, and then that communication was tainted by being part of the political debate. (That is, workers viewed the companies' posture as being part of their political lobbying, not an effort genuinely designed to inform them.)

Companies have sharply reduced internal communication and when it does exist, it usually deals with day-to-day things like compensation, new plans, new plants, new products, new personnel, new challenges

Danby/Bangor Daily News

like process improvement and so on. It should not have been a surprise that employees didn't realize the U.S. has 70 percent — the lion's share — of the Mexican market. This is a key fact in analyzing why Americans should support NAFTA, which will mean more exports and more export-related jobs for U.S. workers. Most workers thought Salinas was a small coastal town in California. Failure to keep your employees informed can prove costly.

When companies finally got around to briefing their own employees about NAFTA, they discovered to their dismay that their workers didn't believe them. This shouldn't have been surprising. A number of surveys revealed that employees do not believe management is straight with them. Multiplex, a St. Louis-based manufacturer that prides itself on articulating important issues, found 72 percent of employees felt they were "given little or no information by management."

Some companies do a good job informing their workers about overall trends, economic conditions, and general public policy issues. For example, Mary Kay Cosmetics has a public affairs series where guests come in and talk about everything from tort reform to health care to water conservation. Employees can attend and ask any question they want. Texaco used to circulate daily clips. Federal Express routinely uses its global internal television capability to address such issues as the economies of Asian markets.

Today's complex issues mandate that companies do this with their employees on a regular, proactive basis. The time to discuss issues is before you debate them, with the debaters representing different points of view. During the NAFTA debate, people weren't really discussing, they were articulating hardened positions — positions created by fear (employees) and desire (employers). This was tailor-made for political posturing. Although much ink was poured on the subject, little true communicating occurred.

If business doesn't play a role in informing and educating its employees about the issues that affect their daily lives, albeit on a very broad level, they relinquish that role to the press. The press is driven by daily news, groups with an ax to grind, and politicians. None are good sources of true information, and none are versed in the challenges of growing and running a business today. They aren't really even interested in business.

Legal reform, health care, educational trends, conservation, wellness, and other issues will have an important, bottom-line impact on each company. It behooves us to enlist our employees early.

The final reason to communicate frequently and honestly with employees on these and other issues is because it sends an important message to them — that we view them as reasonable, important people; that we respect them as informed citizens; that we think they're worth the time and capable of understanding what affects their world.

This also prepares people for the impact on their pocketbooks. When Future HealthCare, a small pharmaceuticals research company, decided it needed to get dental and health insurance costs under control, they were briefed on the state of employee benefits nationwide, using the U.S. Chamber of Commerce's material. That set the stage for investigating Future's own benefits, performing a cost-benefit analysis on them, and having the employees rank for themselves what they valued and what they didn't.

If business takes the time to do this, whether it's free trade or the next issue down the pike, employees are much more likely to support the company's needs and positions. During the teeth of the debate, we won't have the inflammatory, divisive pictures, as we did in NAFTA, of sign-carrying employees shouting, "We don't HAFTA."

Part III

COMMUNICATION AS PART OF OTHER THINGS

JUST WHAT IS "SEXUAL HARASSMENT"?

Ever since the confirmation hearings for Supreme Court Justice Clarence Thomas, sexual harassment has been a big topic for employers and employees. But just what is sexual harassment? It is dangerous to have a major problem so ill-defined.

Because sexual harassment is illegal, many companies are trying to communicate with their employees to prevent complaints and litigation and to create a better workplace. They are publishing handbooks and running seminars on the topic. But a survey around the country shows that there is a lot of disagreement about what qualifies as harassment. When such an explosive topic is poorly defined, lack of understanding about what is and isn't okay creates confusion and actually may encourage complaints and litigation. Clearly, demanding sex in return for keeping a job or getting a promotion is harassment (not to mention disgusting).

But here's the problem, as described in the *Wall Street Journal* by the woman who is the president of Ryka Athletic Footwear: "Every woman has her own gauge of sexual harassment. For some women, it might be just a comment. For others, it could be someone coming up and touching her."

There are big differences between those things. If a glance, a stupid crack, a leer, a dirty joke, a fondle, and extortion are all equal, the result will be to make men very uncomfortable around their women colleagues. And women are discovering that their male employees will use the law against them. Jenny Craig, the diet and health company whose customers are overwhelmingly women, found themselves the target of charges of sexual harassment from male employees who objected to all the "girl talk" — discussion of menstrual cycles, boyfriend trouble, and so on. The women protested that this was how women talk among themselves, but that is, of course, precisely the argument men made about the pinups, leers, bad jokes, discussion of sexual conquests, and so on.

The press covered the discussion about this part of the issue in a one-sided manner. Many women dismiss such talk, the juvenile pictures, and so on. We just brush it off. But we weren't quoted. Any woman who said such things was described as a "tool of the right wing," according to Betsey Wright, President Clinton's former chief-of-staff.

The current state of affairs (no pun intended, of course) has reduced the ability of workers to laugh at themselves. At one bank, a male teller objected and "felt sexually harassed" when coworkers posted pinups from *Playgirl* magazine. The women posted the pinups as a joke and to make a point about how women feel. But because one male teller "felt harassed" — another male teller presumably has a better sense of self and knew not to let this upset him — the women were reprimanded, demoted, and transferred.

Have we lost our minds? Can't anyone see the difference between this situation and the construction job where male workers posted *Playboy* "Playmate" pinups and made leering, threatening remarks about women whom they supervised, or with whom they had to work as team members?

John Uhlmann, president of the Uhlmann Company in Kansas City, had the most sensible thing to say about the issue. He said, "There needs to be a distinction between what is bad manners and what is illegal." And he added, "We need to come up with a better definition."

Arguably, the bank women aren't even guilty of bad manners. They were trying to be funny, although apparently they failed according to one person. Sensible rules involve the need for communication, for awareness about status or rank, and for a third-party appeals process or intervenor. There needs to be responsibility on both sides, and the harassed person, historically female, needs to shed the victim's mentality. For example, if a person believes that certain overtures or actions are unwelcome or constitute harassment, it's that person's responsibility to tell the other person.

I am aware of the stories of women who say they tried to tell the boss "No" only to find a poor performance review or other retaliation. In theory, that's what the Equal Employment Opportunity Commission

(EEOC) regulations handle. Mucking up the process by legitimizing instances like the male teller's objection to the onetime *Playgirl* pinups or by accepting a definition that says harassment is in the eye (or other part of the anatomy) of the victim only results in trivializing the issue and denying justice to people who have truly suffered sexual harassment.

The only way to create an environment that overcomes the potential for harassment is to stress values and good manners. Treat other people the way you want to be treated.

Otherwise, the only people who will not end up being harassed are the lawyers . . . as usual.

NEW, CASUAL CLOTHES

We've all heard the saying, Clothes make the man. Some companies are discovering new meanings to that old saying.

Our workplace used to be strictly segregated — by clothes. Executives wore suits, ties, dark socks; women, stockings and heels. Oh sure, maybe people in advertising and movies wore wild shirts and ties, and academics could wear knitted ties, but the expected costume has been rigid. After work and on weekends, we relax and dress down.

Companies are discovering that by loosening the dress rules, they loosen what people think they can do. Let people dress casually, and communication between groups improves. Let them wear anything they want, and they come up with new ideas. The rapidity with which "casual Friday" has spread shows how quickly corporate culture can change. *USA Today* said that more than 70 percent of major U.S. companies have a weekly "casual" day. Chrysler has two a week!

The marketing department at Citicorp designates some days for casual dress and calls them "marketing out of the box." They have found that it encourages people to approach problems in a new way. Southwest Airlines is a pioneer in this field, and in the summer months all their employees wear shorts and blue knit shirts. The flight attendants love it — I've always wondered what it must be like working in those straight skirts and heels many airlines still require — and it reinforces their image as the airline you hop on for a fun weekend in Santa Fe or Corpus Christi.

Even big companies like Alcoa have experimented with casual wear. First, it was a reward for employees who contributed to United Way, but dressing down proved so popular that it's now an everyday option. Alcoa also determined that employees speak out more frequently. And loosening the dress code can build morale, as the Zale Corporation discovered. Zale, the nation's largest retail jeweler, went through a major restructuring and Chapter 11 proceedings. Andreas Ludwig, then executive vice president and CFO, said that everyone was working six and seven days a week, so the company made Friday a casual day to reward and encourage team spirit.

When companies allow individuality in dressing or casual days, they are sending a clear message to employees that they want to try new things, that it's all right to challenge previously held beliefs, that there is more equality among employees, and that innovation is important.

Companies that institute "casual days" are finding it necessary to issue some new definitions. Federal Express wrote to all employees that "Casual is not grunge." It's up to the company to decide whether "casual" means "anything goes," or just that it's okay to ditch the ties, jackets, pantyhose, and heels.

Generally, top management sets the tone, but once a company says "Change is okay and you're empowered to set new rules," watch out because employees will do just that. That's good. Torn jeans and T-shirts with slogans like "Compost Happens" are probably not.

The CEO, however, should set the tone, issue general guidelines (like Federal Express), and leave it to individual departments to handle things. Casual day becomes less casual if there's a lengthy list of dos and don'ts.

One problem companies are still grappling with is how to handle vendors or professional consultants (the lawyers and accountants) who arrive appropriately attired for noncasual day. Some companies try to make outsiders conform to casual day, and that's a mistake. The caller may have other clients to deal with who don't have casual day.

Another area of sensitivity is that minorities and women, so recently arrived as accepted players in the corporate power game, can be diminished by appearing in casual clothes. One African-American executive once told me he never wears anything except a formal three-piece suit because people always thought he was a janitor. I witnessed a similar situation myself. At one of our seminars for a bank, one African-American executive arrived casually dressed in a nice T-shirt and slacks, and one of the senior executives who opened the course obviously thought he was the coffee delivery service.

Still, change never comes without glitches and problems, and in an era when a level organization and empowered employees are goals for many corporations, casual day reinforces the messages that we're all in this effort together; we're more equal than less equal, and that work is not totally separate from real life and what we do for fun — all good things for American business as it strives for competitiveness in a global economy, a set of "new clothes" as it were.

SHOULD A COMPANY PUBLICIZE GOOD DEEDS?

One company sends a press release announcing a donation of a few hundred dollars to a local charity. Another does not announce a $100,000 grant to a women's shelter. Which is the correct approach?

The first question to ask is not "What's right," but "Which audiences are important?" Employees, shareholders of a public company or investors of any sort, vendors, creditors or financial backers, customers, regulators, competitors, and the general public are normally targets, but they can vary in priority. It is crucial for business, particularly American business, to educate the public about its commitment to the community, the industry, and the general well-being and economic welfare of our nation. We live in a time of appalling ignorance about the market system and distrust or lessening trust about business. (Indeed, to read cartoons or to watch television is to see that business people are *routinely* portrayed as greedy, unconcerned, abusive, rich, and exploitive.)

Although there is broad debate about how much business should contribute in charitable contributions or services, most Americans would probably be as wildly off base in their estimates as they are in what profit they think business makes.

Once the strategic question is answered, the issue becomes audience, vehicle, appropriate tone, and how to manage communication.

There is nothing self-serving in letting key audiences know about your support. The law firm that gave $100,000 to the women's shelter didn't want to be perceived as promoting itself. That's the wrong view. (Not "overly conservative," just wrong.) It deprives the public of learning that the law firm is a leader in the community and that the women's shelter is important enough to warrant significant support from a main-stream firm. It deprives special audiences, such as other law firms and lawyers, of knowing that a women's shelter was considered a legitimate recipient by a peer firm, and that the benchmark for grants from law firms was going up. (Forget the $5,000 table to the local charity ball as your contribution. More is expected of law firms today.)

Nonprofit groups are frequently understaffed and lack sophistication. So an additional option arises if the donor organization handles the an-nouncement for the recipient. That means using its personnel to put out the letters and the press release and to disseminate other information.

Charitable contributions or goodwill activities are particularly effec-tive when they underscore the company's business strategy. For exam-ple, the *Wall Street Journal* was sufficiently impressed to write about the ability of Chase Manhattan Bank to find a way to provide bank accounts for the homeless. After other major money-center banks turned down a homeless service organization, Chase Manhattan analyzed the prob-lem — homeless people have no home address to send statements — and looked for reasons to solve it rather than barriers to explain why the problem was unsolvable.

One Chase Manhattan officer, John Imperiale, solved the problem by arranging post office boxes for the recipients. He also discovered a new, if unorthodox, customer base. "Homeless" is not, as it turns out, synonymous with "no money." Virtually all of the "homeless" received monthly government checks of one sort or another. The homeless pop-ulation has a hard time guarding the cash for reasons mostly due to personal habits. Some homeless people actually got significant checks from legal settlements.

This effort produced top-notch publicity and visibility for Chase Manhattan and reinforced their reputation as a bank that thinks cre-atively, is customer focused, and can truly analyze costs.

There are also ways to publicize good deeds beyond press releases sent to the local press. Some companies and organizations produce a regular report, annually or quarterly. This approach allows them to go beyond cash grants or donations of products to include the efforts of their employees as volunteers in the community. Baptist Memorial Health Care System in Memphis is a good example of this. Other com-panies like ITT use their employees' volunteer activities in their ads, which reach not only customers but employees, the public at large, reg-ulators, shareholders, and vendors.

Frequently executives say "But we'll be criticized," and they worry that donations will not seem very large when contrasted with the big-dollar numbers of revenues, CEO salaries, acquisitions, etc. That is a legitimate worry, but to give in to "what might happen" paralyzes a company and eliminates a very important communication to a company's publics — namely, that the company does consider it important to contribute to public causes (however defined) and is making an effort to do that.

Another comment is "We want to keep a low profile." Again, that's a reasonable approach, and I, too, grew up with the admonition that true charity does not seek recognition, and the anonymous gift is more charitable than anything else. However, in today's volatile and litigious times, the low-profile approach also means the company has forfeited its list of good deeds, which should be put into the public domain *before a crisis* to condition how both the media and the public filter bad news.

The Schwan company is just finding this out. The decades-old maker of ice cream was accused of selling ice cream that caused salmonella poisoning. Suddenly, a low-profile company had no choice about being high profile as 15,000 calls a day flooded in from customers along with 100 calls from media. This solid corporate customer became known to the public not for its Pink Divinity (a rocky-road type holiday special with almond flavoring and bits of almonds), but for its ice cream's "side affects such as vomiting, nausea, dizziness, and death."

Finally, companies should not forget alternative methods of communication — newsletters; letters to clients; customers or vendors; video clips; even an occasional advertisement — may also be appropriate. These have become increasingly important as the large urban media (both print and electronic) have become attentive to disaster, disruption, and disgusting material. Without question, to be positive is to be viewed as wimpy. Thus, a company has to find other ways to get out good news and not forget about bad news.

Companies need to change their mind-set to actively, if not aggressively, let their communities know they are pitching in.

"Manners are simply the oil which smooth out social and business interaction. They are essential, common sense and neglected." — Ken Marvel, Chairman and CEO, Fitz & Floyd

WHAT MANNERS TELL US

The senior partner was lunching with the promising recruit. Discussion went well. The potential employee had good grades and high recommendations. The senior partner passed him the butter plate. The recruit took it, buttered his roll, then licked the butter knife and replaced it on the butter plate.

The young banker was doing well with her new customer until she took her napkin and carefully wiped off the lipstick on the water glass.

The sales manager was about to close the deal when he took his napkin and blew his nose. Then he carefully refolded the napkin and left it next to his plate.

These all happened. Look around and see how many baby boomers in their 20s and 30s hold their utensils. Not since the 1500s have we seen such clutching of a spear, as if the filet were about to get away.

Good table manners communicate that one was well educated outside the computer lab, that one had the breadth of understanding to seek out a good role model, and that one expects to be treated with respect.

I am not talking about today's informality of manners, such as the elbows on the table. Nor are we discussing how manners fit into equality of the sexes — should women always precede men or should men hold the door? Letitia Baldridge has thoroughly researched the issue in her books, and if one doesn't have them handy, simple rules apply. Treat the person the way you'd like to be treated. Be courteous.

We are not discussing elegant dining, like knowing which wine goes with brook trout or even that you hold the glass by the stem, rather than clutching the bowl of the glass.

If Letitia Baldridge is too daunting, try *Tiffany's Table Manners for Teenagers*. It's short, illustrated, witty, easy-to-follow, and not just for teenagers anymore.

Apparently the decline in teaching manners is related to the movement of women back into the work force. Ken Marvel, chairman and CEO of Fitz and Floyd, makers of fine china and giftware, says that Mom neither has time to teach manners anymore nor does she have time to monitor them.

Admittedly, there are whole new challenges in manners. What is the proper way to hold a Big Mac? How do you eat a taco while driving? Every culture evolves, but the general philosophy of manners should endure. Manners are to convey respect and further social intercourse.

A number of schools and courses in remedial etiquette have sprung up. The Emerging Leaders program at the University of Denver includes ethics, integrity, interpersonal skills, and etiquette. They view manners as part of fulfilling the mandate from businessman Bill Daniels, whose financial contribution stimulated the university's examination and formulation of an innovative leadership curriculum. The memo of understanding says participants should be "honest, principled, fair, humane, courteous, respectful, reliable, punctual, accountable, loyal, enthusiastic, mannerly in both business and social settings (ie: table manners, social graces, etc.), committed to excellence, community-minded, socially aware, and socially responsive."

Businesses should support such programs, and a good place to begin is a simple in-house seminar on etiquette. Why? Because it is a first point of entry into the Daniels' list of what we should, as a culture, expect from businessmen and women. One can debate for a long time what is "fair." Is it "fair" to downsize a business, knowing longtime employees will lose their jobs? It may be unfair to the employees who are dismissed but fair to those who will stay and benefit from a more cost-effective organization. It will be fair to shareholders if it increases the company's ability to compete and creates shareholder value. Those are tough questions. How you hold your knife is easy. Yet commitment to good table manners is a first step to commitment toward good business manners in general.

(Digressing slightly, please send Mr. Daniels a letter encouraging him to fund a grant to a good law school to get them to develop a curriculum and protocol for what developing lawyers should and shouldn't do as they are taught to abuse the legal system.)

Businesses are reluctant to underwrite etiquette courses. Several have told me that they feel this sends the message that they are intruding into their employees' lives. To the contrary, it says that the business is concerned about their success to the point that the business will support personal improvement and learning.

Businesses that ignore bad manners are endorsing them. Underlying the now highly volatile subject of sexual harassment is the undeniable issue of bad manners. If companies had stepped in and said, "It's just plain bad manners to have nude pictures in your work area, to make suggestive remarks, and to have wet T-shirt contests, and it's downright revolting to pinch or grab," we might have much less regulation and many fewer lawsuits. Before these actions were illegal (which brings a whole other dynamic), they were just . . . bad manners. Good manners. Good business.

CREATING A CULTURE OF GOOD MANNERS

Changing your corporate culture is a hot topic right now, and one important aspect of "culture" is often overlooked. It's the power of good manners.

Manners are viewed as an antique topic. Bad manners are like the weather. Most people complain about them, but it doesn't do much good. But unlike the weather, there's a lot you can do to create a culture of good manners in your company.

Good manners are important, of course, because they express concern about the other person and recognize his importance. And good manners mean a successful company. Look inside a business that functions well and you'll find good manners. Look behind customer satisfaction — they're there as well.

Good manners can spring up anywhere in an organization, but they are most powerful when they flow from the top down. That is, the CEO's behavior will be emulated by most other members of the organization. If the CEO screams and rants and raves, or if the CEO overlooks it when someone steals another person's credit, that sends a powerful message that manners aren't important.

One of the most visible manifestations of good manners is the thank-you note. When we consult with companies going through a crisis, if the CEO doesn't have personal note cards, we get some. A one-line message — "You're doing great" or "I appreciate your team spirit" — goes farther than you would imagine. Some visionaries, like Jim Adams of Southwestern Bell Telephone, actually carry note paper around with them to do this. J. Edgar Hoover sent notes of recognition — now, before you say "Whoa," remember, he created an organization intensely loyal to him and passionately devoted to his mission. That's quite an accomplishment.

We have our own small example of how employees imitate behavior. Our little company is 9 years old and has grown to 14 people. For the past several years, we've had an annual office retreat. We search for beaches, from the beach at Mustang Island, Texas, to Cancun, Mexico. This idea was born several years ago after six stressful months working on a large client's bankruptcy. We were either going to get away or kill each other. So we got away. The opportunity to visit and relax — with spouses, children, and significant others — proved so valuable that we've repeated it each year.

I received thank-you notes from everyone in our group and — this is really amazing — from husbands, significant others, even the children. My first reaction was astonishment, but our office manager, herself a writer of thank-you notes, pointed out that I am an active note writer.

Our team sees me writing notes to friends, clients, colleagues, and others saying "Thank you," or "That was a great article" or "We really appreciated your help." So they believe it's the right thing to do. They see the value.

Some companies, particularly (but not exclusively) in the retail area, are experimenting with allowing employees to write thank-you notes to customers. This is an excellent way to foster the sense of relationship between customer and sales associate (and, therefore, with the retail establishment). However, the effort is undercut by pre-printed thank-you notes. These usually say something like "Thank you for shopping with us. We appreciate your business and look forward to serving you in the future." I cannot believe that a sales associate who knows the difference between Albert Nippon and Chanel cannot jot the same sentiment by hand. Here's what the pre-printed version communicates to me: "We would like you to believe that you have a relationship with us, but we aren't ready to differentiate you from hundreds of other recipients of this card."

I admit that others may feel differently. Some of my office associates like the cards, and point out that we rarely make our own cards for occasions such as birthdays, graduation, or sickness. We buy them from makers like Hallmark and congratulate ourselves on our choice.

This is certainly true, but the clearly individualized note still stands apart. After many years of doubt and soul searching, I was baptized last fall. A number of people in our church took the time to write me a short note. One physician wrote, "This will change your life and you had a lot of courage to stand up in front of us all."

Perhaps note writers are intimidated by some imagined need to say something fresh and new in each note. Actually, many will repeat the same words over and over again. I have a piece of plain paper framed in my office. It says, "Merrie, you did a great job. Thanks. Ronald Reagan." Of course, if you can be creative, more power to you. After a particularly difficult and problem-filled event at the FBI, Director William Webster scribbled a little note to me saying, "You were grace under pressure." Since I felt like Grace Being Served for Dinner Under Glass, it was very welcome.

Some of the most powerful notes simply say, "Thanks for sticking with us," or "I appreciate your hard work." These small but resonant notes of personal attention show that our associates, supervisor, or CEO cares and notices. They are literally worth gold.

Some people imagine that their handwriting should look like John Hancock's on the Constitution; that is, flowing or at least closer to what penmanship teachers tried to instill with cursive writing. They should look at many of the other signers of the document. The cramped, crabby letters of some signatures would make any doctor proud.

You don't need to fill up the whole piece of stationery (it's usually a small folded piece of parchment) or the whole card. I'll admit that I like cards — similar to post cards that fit inside an envelope — with inset border lines so there is less space to fill.

Can these notes be typed? Yes, if employees know that you're a note writer and do your own. Can they come through e-mail? This is an emerging area of manners, but again, yes, particularly for companies where there is a culture of executives reading and responding *personally*, not filtering or dictating through a secretary.

You can create a culture of good manners, too, but in this case "Do as I say, but not as I do" won't cut it. No memo creates good manners. Only the real thing works. The good news is that when you practice good manners — like writing thank-you notes — you'll see them replicated, and you won't even have to ask.

USE HUMOR

Reprinted with special permission of King Feature Syndicate

Have you ever seen a group or meeting of business executives and noticed they usually have grim expressions on their faces? Ever wonder why? Did they all lose at tennis? Why do business people look so sour? Smart companies have decided to do something about it.

In some companies, you're not *supposed* to smile. Those companies have created an unofficial but rigid code of behavior that frowns on smiling and humor; in short, enjoying yourself. It starts when someone, somehow, in some situation, says, "You're not being serious. This is serious business." Well, no one wants to be frivolous, so we all turn our lips into a frown and "get serious."

The trouble is that this creates a distinction between "work" and "real life." And being "serious" makes it hard to develop the deep motivation or passion about one's work that is found in the best companies. Companies such as Southwest Airlines or Microsoft, have a definite culture of having fun. And it is fun to be involved in something meaningful, something that makes a contribution to our lives.

The Telephone Operations Division of GTE is involved in the country's largest reengineering project. They took a hard look at themselves, their environment, the demands of their customers a decade from now

107

and decided that they needed to totally rework how they are organized and approach the marketplace. This is no small undertaking.

It turns out that one important way to accomplish this is to allow people to have fun again. Just how does a mammoth organization order its people to have fun? Well, for one thing, you can't order anyone to be funny. The CEO can't send out a memo: "To: All Employees / Subj: Fun & Humor / Please be advised that the company has adopted a policy of humor."

You have to lead by example. Executives who themselves smile and use humor in their presentations, who appear to be enjoying themselves, will change the corporate norm for presentations over time. At GTE, one executive vice president giving a speech decided to illustrate a point by breaking into a lusty — although spoken — chorus from the country-and-western tearjerker, *Come from the Heart*. Another vice president showed up at the national headquarters on Halloween dressed in prison stripes and lugging a ball and chain!

GTE stresses that having fun is one element of empowerment, that empowered employees try to put themselves in the position of another employee. That makes listening and keeping people up-to-date on projects they worked on more important. For example, don't write a memo to someone with instructions. Walk down the hall and discuss it with the guy.

Now, all this may not seem funny to you but empowerment requires humor and enjoyment. In our normal lives we look for things that make us smile and laugh. We crack jokes to brighten up someone's life, break the tension, or just get everyone on board.

Southwest Airlines is a company that has made having fun part of its corporate culture from the beginning. CEO Herb Kelleher's original attitude was that people hop on Southwest for a fun weekend, so the flight attendants needed to reinforce this image and experience. It's hard to do that if you're bored or hostile. Southwest employees are empowered to interpret the rules and be humorous. For example, men regularly propose to their intended ladies on Southwest flights over the intercom system. (The lady always says yes, which the flight attendant reports to the loud applause of passengers.) One flight attendant recites the standard, "To fasten your seat belt insert the buckle," but pauses half way to say, "And if you don't do it, we open the door at 20,000 feet and toss you out." Another pause while the passengers absorb this and guffaw.

Camille Keith, vice president/special marketing of Southwest, reports that while conducting job interviews costumed as a queen for a parade not a single applicant asked her about her attire or cracked a smile. "They wouldn't fit in," she said. "We didn't make a single offer."

Instead of suing another airline using Southwest's ad slogan, Kelleher challenged the other CEO to an arm-wrestling match. Weeks of publicity attended the "preparation" for the event, for which Kelleher worked out publicly by using bottles of bourbon as weights. Over 1,200 Southwest employees turned out on their own time, waving banners and wearing buttons, to egg on their champion. (He lost immediately to the other CEO.) The companies decided both could use the slogan.

There is actually a burgeoning humor industry providing seminars and opportunities to laugh for corporate America. Comedy groups like Second City of Chicago appear at Arthur Andersen meetings impersonating senior partners. The actors behave in an increasingly bizarre fashion until people catch on that it's a put-on.

The managing partner of Arthur Andersen's Business Systems Consulting group decided that they would introduce a major project with a self-produced skit poking fun at the firm's tendency to bury clients with data and reports. The videotaped skit looked like a schmaltzy soap opera, with clouds and music in the opening and "thought" balloons throughout (those small round balloons over the heads of cartoon characters that let you know what the character is thinking). The last thought of the recognizable senior partner is, "Where did I go wrong?"

One banker at Texas Commerce Bank illustrated a presentation on capital markets' capabilities with a popular, purple stuffed animal made by one of her clients. Another used a golf club cover in the shape of a shark to characterize the competitors to their discount brokerage operation.

The workplace is changing, and anything that helps humanize it and promote flexibility is positive. Humor seminars send a message, if nothing else, that more is acceptable than in the past.

There's no surefire way to learn to be "funny," but real humor is not yuks and jokes. It's poking fun at yourself, being serious about work without taking yourself too seriously, and learning new ways to defuse stresses and crises.

GTE must be an interesting place to work these days. And it must be a whole lot easier tackling a mammoth project like reinventing yourselves when everyone is on the same team having a good time.

EMPOWERMENT

Customer service is something every company says it needs and values. But those of us who are customers have seen an awful lot of customer nonservice. What management communicates to employees about their role in the company ultimately comes through in the kind of "service" customers see.

Problems will happen. How do you train your people to deal with a problem? Well, you empower them to fix it, fast, even if it's not supposed to be that employee's job or the customer is unreasonable. Here's an example from the telephone company. It demonstrates employee empowerment.

We had a major thunderstorm, and trees all over Dallas attacked the telephone lines. Working from home because of a new baby, I was effectively out of business. I reported the problem — to a machine. Two days later I had still not talked to a person, but I had pushed a lot of buttons. Finally, I dialed "0" for operator and complained — and, suddenly, there was a person's voice at the other end. Unfortunately, the person I was talking to processed new orders and had nothing to do with repairs, but miracle of miracles, she said, "I'm sorry you've had trouble. I'll help you." And she did. The repair man arrived later in the day and fixed the line. How did that happen? Southwestern Bell Telephone says they have pushed the responsibility and the decision making in customer service down to the employees who actually deal with the customer. This sounds like common sense, but for years if you processed new orders you didn't help people who needed repairs.

It's a good example of internal communication: The employees communicated their capabilities up to management. Management made a significant effort to solicit input from employees and to let them know their ideas were wanted, and would make a difference. The message comes from the top.

110

I was once in an elevator with Southwestern Bell President Jim Adams when members of a cleaning crew got on. They saw him, yet got on anyway. Then they greeted each other by name. In most companies, the cleaning crew would have been afraid to share an elevator with top management, much less chat.

To turn an annoyed customer into a satisfied one, simply reach out to your employees and listen to them.

FALSE AND DECEPTIVE

Celebrities are not content to just be celebrities. Today, they want to be regarded as authors, too. Publishing companies are giving in to this vanity. The healthy desire to make money is causing them to shortchange a more important commodity — trust. When you see a book "by" Dr. Ruth Westheimer, you probably think she wrote it. Most of us do.

Book publishers are violating the relationship between business and customer with their growing tendency to sell books written by stars. But the stars don't write a word. In Ivana Trump's case, the real writer just followed her around. In some cases, ghostwriters rely on clips and anecdotes. In the old days, you got some hint of this when the book cover said "by Zsa Zsa Gabor as told to . . . " or "by Charles Lindberg with . . . " In Dr. Ruth's case, her book on the history of erotic art was written "with" (as opposed to "by") an art historian. However, the cowriter is anonymous, so in these books the real writer has disappeared.

This is wrong. It does a disservice to all the real writers around. It misleads the consumer. It's insulting to everyone. This practice says to writers, "Writing is so unimportant that it's sort of like a burger at McDonald's. No one cares whether it came from Alabama or Argentina." And to the customer it says, "You're too dumb to know or care anyway."

Book publishers defend themselves on precisely those grounds; that is, the consumer neither knows nor cares. One literary agent says book publishing is just like the movie business. Stars' names help sales. That may be true, but the last time I looked, the names of the director, producer, assistants, and everyone else involved in making a movie were scrupulously listed in the credits. Another publisher claims they are just giving the public what they want. This is the oldest ploy in the — pardon me — books. It's used to justify all the porn and violence in today's books, movies, and television news. It's the justification for fast food and empty calories. And there's a lot of truth to it. The public does apparently want those things. But government and industry still must try to ensure that the consumer has the facts. You want burgers? You get to know the grams of fat. You want to see *Terminator II*? You can find out its rating. Book publishers claim a special privilege to disregard the truth, in that the printed word and the concepts of freedom of expression are sacrosanct in our society. However, the publishers' arguments move the concept of "book" away from the category of freedom of expression and squarely into the category of "product." As such, someone is going to ask how the existing laws on claims or advertising apply to them. The Federal Trade Commission has rules that demand truth in advertising and claims. For example, ads that say "Recommended by most doctors" should be backed up by a survey proving that most doctors do recommend the product. Or warranties that say "Free replacement for six months" need to live up to that. The idea is that a truthful marketplace allows the fair exchange of products and services, and a corrupted marketplace stacks the deck against it.

There are already some examples in other industries. We are outraged to discover that a rock singer had someone else's voice on his records, but the consensus on what's acceptable is that a singing star can apparently lip-synch in a live performance. That is, the voice we hear is actually his or her own voice, but we hear it on a recording. Unlike many Broadway actor-singers, apparently these stars cannot handle the strenuous performance aspect of, well, a performance that requires one to sing and dance at the same time. (Actually, it would be more truthfully described as "sing and strut," "sing and grind," "sing and shake," "sing and slither," and so on.)

The equivalent of this in publishing should be that it's okay for Ivana Trump to verbally transmit her thoughts to a writer who edits and expands them, but the division of creativity and responsibility should be acknowledged. (Notice, I'm not arguing for absolute truth: "Ivana had some snappy one-liners, but the writer had to organize them, build up background material to make them sound useful, and do every bit of the actual writing.")

The diminishment of writing is of grave concern to me and every real writer. (One need not be a great writer to be a real writer and to respect the act of writing.) Few corporate chieftains write their own speeches. On the other hand, they are rarely paid for their speeches, while Ivana Trump was being paid for her name. Even fewer politicians write their own material. Jesse Jackson and Speaker of the House Newt Gingrich are among the very few politicians who apparently write most or all of their own speeches. It was upsetting to hear the news that Speaker Gingrich, a respected and employable professor, is looking for a ghost-writer for his controversial book.

Where's an overzealous regulator when you really need one? Isn't there some agency that can bring a deceptive trade practices suit against these celebrity books? Throw the rule book at them — out of respect to writers and writing, and also as a signal that truth in representation is a crucial principle of a truly free market.

*"Communication techniques and vehicles can help companies
in the 'next wave' of exporters."* — BILL McNUTT, PRESIDENT,
INTERNATIONAL DIRECT MARKETING CONSULTANTS

DIRECT MARKETING

Will the fax machine go down in history along with the inventions of barbed wire and the repeating rifle?

Exporting is one of the hot trends of the 1990s. Not just companies, but other groups — Congress, business, the public — want to increase exports. The conventional wisdom is that American companies have great opportunities if they reach out. According to Bill McNutt, president of International Direct Marketing Consultants (IDMC), "Communication techniques and vehicles can help companies in the 'next wave' of exporters." Interestingly, the first difference is the mind-set, the state of mind, and the decision by the individual company about exactly who is a target customer.

Amazingly, 85 percent of *all* exports are done by fewer than 300 companies. Big companies dominated exports historically because they could afford to hire or move *people* overseas. Today, with advanced communication, so-called "cross-border" communication techniques are available for small and midsize companies. IDMC, a business that guides American companies to increased exports, says that technology today offers small and medium-sized companies the chance to communicate via direct marketing. It's not just L.L. Bean that can sell abroad. Today, drug and medical supplies, office products, high-tech, and hundreds of other things made mostly by small companies could and should be marketed directly overseas. But the first step is this state of mind; the company needs to think that it *has* international customers, or has the possibility for them. Then, all that's needed is a fax machine, an international toll-free 800 number, a computer modem, and an electronic bulletin board. One small computer firm in California reaches customers around the world solely with its bulletin board. An international courier service then delivers the product. (Incidentally, technology allows the international courier service companies to communicate internally with their personnel, track your deliveries, make sure they go to Rwanda or wherever they're going, and do it for you at a low enough cost so you, their customer, can afford it.)

Tapping the potential in exports illustrates the importance of knowing which type of communication is the most powerful or persuasive. Traditionally, we have believed that verbal communication, preferably in person, is the most powerful. This is an exception. English has indeed become the international business language, but it's almost always a *second* language for a foreign customer. He is usually *more* comfortable communicating with you in writing via the fax or computer. International toll-free calls, however, allow foreign customers instant, free communication. The American company can deal with their orders or service requests fast, but doesn't necessarily have to answer the phone in a minute.

Expanding exports illustrates the difference between the proverbial "steak" and its "sizzle." People like to shop "in" the United States. Selection and price are frequently cited reasons, but there is an undeniable cachet or implication about American goods. Of course, technology only provides the tools. One still needs a business plan of what to sell to whom. But technology has opened the door to communicate with more customers in more places than we ever dreamed possible.

Let's turn to the parallel of the fax machine as the modern equivalent of barbed wire and the repeating rifle. These two inventions allowed settlers to move en masse to the American West. Before barbed wire, animals roamed freely. Wooden fences were time consuming and expensive to erect. Plain old wire, strung for miles, was easily circumvented by animals and by humans who would help the animals be free. Taking up residence in the wild was hazardous. Anyone who has seen old movies depicting wars or fighting in the 19th century recalls the image of load, shoot, clean, refill, ready, shoot again. By the time you get to "shoot again," the hostile forces had slit your throat or bitten your leg. (An alternate image for history buffs was presented in the movie *Zulu*, where the British form a block of tiers of soldiers, each group fires, then drops to their knees for the reloading exercise. Alas, without an accompanying regiment, American settlers were out of luck in desolate spots like Texas.)

The government was committed to a policy of encouraging settlers in order to bolster territory claims and satisfy the desire for land and freedom. By happy coincidence, these justified military support and intervention. Barbed wire allowed the relatively cheap, convenient, and effective division of a lot of land. The repeating rifle let you get the evil forces before they got close enough to get you.

According to McNutt, the fax may be seen as the modern equivalent because it allows the exporter a technological way to enter and hold new territory. It allows the exporter to divide territories and "hold" them because of instantaneous communication. Export ho!

GENERAL MOTORS

General Motors is always in the news — work stoppages in facilities manufacturing parts for other factories, competition, global worries. When John Smith, the former manager of GM's European market, replaced Robert Stempel, who was forced out after a little more than two years as CEO, he predicted that he had his work cut out for him. Most of the analysis focused on GM's restructuring challenges, but the auto giant actually had a huge communication challenge.

General Motors' problems over the last decades certainly include communication, bad communication. The company didn't listen to the messages from the market and didn't communicate the implications of those messages to key constituencies, such as the unionized work force.

Decades ago, the market — that's us, the buyers — began telling GM that we wanted higher quality, better styling, and better service. GM didn't listen. Years after the Japanese began to steal market share, Detroit finally got the message and made big strides. But two groups didn't hear the raindrops on the roof. GM's management, in particular, refused to concede that it was too large, too cumbersome, and too well paid. Similarly, GM's unions refused to believe that their work force was too large (at least for market demand), too cumbersome (in terms of work rules), and too well paid.

Now CEO John Smith has a major challenge; aggressive communication can help. He needs to pound home to the unions that changing market conditions means they need to change — or die. Obviously, changes such as those at the Saturn plant are what's in order: more teamwork and less confrontation; more flexibility and less rigidity; less "We always did it this way" and more "How can we do it better?"

Mr. Smith might go around handing out copies of the *New York Herald Tribune*. That's right. The *New York Herald Tribune*. Back in 1963 New York City had eleven daily newspapers. They employed four times as many workers as today. One by one they went out of business — done in by a changing market, by obsolete work practices, and by out-of-sight costs. The union leaders insisted on protecting their cherished work rules, and the entire industry suffered.

But there's another side to this equation. It will be impossible to get the unions to believe this is serious unless management changes are equally drastic. This means cutting management jobs, compensations, and perks. *Business Week* put it this way: "GM's troubles run so deep that it must recreate itself or tear its management apart in the effort."

Analyst Doron Levin listed 10 things GM needs to do, such as "End class distinctions among the employees to convey the message that everyone is in the same boat. In turn, executives must erase distinctions that have historically divided GM workers."

One company president who had to downsize made his first action closing the executive dining room. He announced, "If we can work together, we can eat together."

Mr. Smith could make that same statement. In fact, he could go a step further and say, "We'll all eat together — or we won't eat at all."

"It's a little late in the history of civilization to remind people that reporters are not cheerleaders." — DAVID BRINKLEY

DOES BUSINESS WANT GOOD NEWS?

Most of us in the media hear a common complaint that the press never reports good news. However, sometimes, those of us in the media wonder if American business wants us to cover good news.

The critics are right; positive stories don't get enough attention. The reasons? First, a lot of "good news" isn't news — it's not new or timely; that is, it doesn't have to be dealt with that day.

Second, there is indeed a predilection for bad news. It is perceived as sexier. Sometimes it's more interesting. Readers and viewers like it. And sometimes reporters are just lazy. They look for predictable stories: earnings up, earnings down; new product introduced, new product pulled off shelves; management shakeup. Fraud, failure, embezzlement, and conflict are a sure sell.

At an all-news radio station where I worked in Dallas, we set out to have a regular report on something positive. We called it a Profile of Business Success. Predictably, some were companies that succeeded, such as the retail clothing County Seat stores. The company involved their customers in redesigning and repositioning their stores.

Other success stories are about small businesses that just survive, such as a car insurance company in a low-income neighborhood in South Dallas, or spot a brand-new niche, like Millie Whitmore whose company writes family histories. Her services are so hot she is doubling in size every six months and has produced a "do-it-yourself" kit.

Still other successes look at how a company overcame a specific problem. Collmer Semiconductor conducted a single-handed campaign to change custom laws, then recovered hundreds of thousands of dollars in overpayment. We paid special attention to minority businesses, like MBE Enterprises, which bonds construction projects. We can tell you first hand there are good minority business-men and women out there. Finally, we looked for cases where doing the right thing is also good business, like the Container Store, which has a special "shop for the blind" service and has created a whole new category of fiercely devoted customers.

Enough positive examples. What about the problem? When we con-tacted a company about a Success Profile, the executives sometimes reacted as if Dan Rather and his camera crew had walked in the door. "Where did you hear that?" snapped one executive when I called to inquire about their superior safety record. "I don't think I'm allowed to talk to you about that." Sometimes companies just aren't helpful. Calls aren't returned. Information doesn't get to us. Finally, companies try to turn positive stories into hype. One company's PR department tried to rewrite the profile, expanding it by a third and adding gushy lan-guage that would never appear in a news report.

Sky Chefs figures in this book as a good example. One of the compa-ny's own premier tenets states that it's important to learn to say "thank you" in every language. However, they reluctantly responded to our inquiries, refusing to help us with the pronunciation of "thank you" in some of the languages their employees use around the world. Then Sky Chefs criticized the report that went on the air.

One CEO said to me, "Why should a company have to cooperate just because you want to cover them?" That is a reasonable question. First, in general, a company should cooperate when the story will be written whether they cooperate or not. A company can't have input if they don't cooperate. I suspect the greater reason companies don't cooperate is a deep skepticism about the press and the feeling that the media can't be up to any good no matter what they say they want to cover.

This creates a negative circularity. Business expects that the media will never willingly cover good news, so they are reluctant to present it. The media, not seeing the positive stories, continues its focus on the problems, layoffs, product failures, union disputes, shareholder gripes, and other negative stories. At the 1964 Republican convention, David Brinkley said, "It's a little late in the history of civilization to remind people that reporters are not cheerleaders." While that's true, report-ers can report good news occasionally. We'd do it more often if business gave us a hand.

THE RE-ENGINEERING RHYTHM

Re-engineering made Michael Hammer and James Champy a fortune. Is it a way of totally restructuring your corporation to equip you to compete in the future? Or is it just another fad, a code word for downsizing and layoffs?

Re-engineering usually, but not always, *does* mean fewer people, but it's a by-product of rethinking how a business works. If re-engineering is simply a way to dress up a head-count reduction in the mind of top management, employees will figure it out quickly and the whole process will become suspect.

What if you do want to rethink, redo, and restart your company and the processes that run it? But you're afraid that your employees have seen article after article on layoffs, and the minute you mention "re-engineering," your employees will panic.

First, are you *really* committed to true re-engineering? If so, as the CEO or Division Head, you need to be personally involved, supportive, and allocate your own time. Otherwise, you will repeat the experience of many quality projects which started with a bang, then foundered.

The CEO is the key source to articulate the reasons for re-engineering. It's important that employees "hear" the messages and that the information is easy to understand. A company re-engineers to get ahead of the curve, to ensure survival, to gain a competitive edge, to increase customer satisfaction, to increase profits, and to increase market share. These are good and vital things for a company to do. So company officers must articulate those messages in speeches, informal conversations, letters, and company publications. The messages must come from internal sources, such as executive and company publications, and from external sources, particularly the press.

But articulation of these crucial messages is only the initial step. When employees tell me, "I'm so sick of hearing corporate platitudes," it means the key messages *have* been articulated but they have not been supported or made relevant to the target audience.

People remember something that affects them. Change is inherently disruptive and usually scary. To compensate for this disruption and fear, it's important to validate the concept that the process is worthwhile for the company and for the individual. According to Charles Ketteman, Worldwide Director of Business Consulting for Arthur Andersen, "Many of our clients are realizing that effective implementation of quality management concepts is not enough. Global competition is demanding radical change — 50 percent improvement in cost or quality over a short period of time — to win the marketplace."

All the articles on re-engineering can now work to your advantage as props and speakers' material. Pull out quotes and examples showing that a telecommunications company did indeed take 42 percent permanently out of the costs of their financial systems, or that Blue Cross/Blue Shield of Metropolitan Washington cut the abandonment rate on their telephone calls from double digits to zero. This shows that other companies accomplished the "significant" or "dramatic" goals you've set. (What you're doing, of course, is using the validation of the media to replace the scare and horror stories of layoffs and failed projects.)

Verbal and written material must also include anecdotes that illustrate individual experiences — successful ones, obviously. For example, it's true that the head count in one department of a large urban hospital declined, but one person found a job as the administrative head of the Security Division, which was increasing its staff. She didn't have a background in security but had worked in the division on other hospital projects. She understood the culture of ex-police officers and law enforcement officials and the challenges they faced in a radically new environment where it wasn't possible to wrestle a suspected perpetrator to the ground and pat him down for weapons.

Anecdotes like these take work to compile, and they must be specific enough so they seem real to the listener. They are invaluable because they make credible the message "It will make things better." Without them the listener hears the message and thinks, "Yeah, right, better for you at the top, but I'm going to have more work with fewer resources and that's only if I keep my job." If top management says, "We'll listen to you," it needs to be supported by an anecdote such as the one from Blue Cross/Blue Shield of Metropolitan Washington. The people handling claims and complaints pointed out that they did not have telephones on their desks to take incoming calls. So if someone called them back, that person had to leave a message at a message center. By the time the employee got it, the customer was frequently unavailable. By giving employees their own phones, customer satisfaction increased and the time to process a claim was reduced.

Anecdotes from other companies also broaden your employees' idea of what actually can be re-engineered. Most employees will arrive at the process thinking it means either reducing people or reducing costs, when actually it means rethinking processes — all processes.

For example, the *Miami Herald* decided to re-engineer their sales approach. They found that 85 percent of sales came from 15 percent of customers, but those customers — home builders, car dealers, and so on — frequently didn't have sophisticated advertising departments of their own. The *Herald* made its ad representatives responsible for the 15 percent of customers, allowing them to spend much more time helping them get a customized approach. The advertisers were happier, the salesmen and women had more interesting jobs, and the paper made more money.

(Lest this story be misleading, one result was some reduction in the size of the sales department. The fact that rethinking change will mean disruption for some people shouldn't be ignored; it just shouldn't be allowed to overshadow the whole process.)

Other wonderful anecdotes from re-engineering involve Pittsburgh Plate Glass reducing their working capital needs by 80 percent in two phases of re-engineering. Another large company re-engineered its sales tax function and saved $10 million dollars while improving the employees' jobs. Technology turned out to be the missing element. The employees said to management, "We're so busy just filing forms, tracking things down, and paying the taxes that we don't have a chance to use our expertise to figure out how to manage the process." Automating the processing freed up the employees who could then ferret out uncollected refunds. In this case, the department didn't decrease by one job.

Why, with such great material, is re-engineering so frightening to employees and so frequently misunderstood? Why does it often miss the mark in achieving the kinds of savings and improvements in the examples above?

The first most common mistake is a lack of real understanding and commitment at the top. Again, too many CEOs think this is a nice way to package layoffs or head-count reductions. Second, there is too little involvement or buy-in from the top. They think it's a great idea in the beginning, then they wait for someone else to do the work and the report. The CEO is perhaps the only contemporary person who is drawn and quartered, at least in terms of time. But he must be involved, minimally to the extent of regular reports from all involved, and as the spokesman for announcements; thus, he has to know enough to be credible with what he's announcing. Third, there is not enough communication going to enough people frequently enough. As Phyllis Smith-hisler, formerly of Blue Cross/Blue Shield says, "Err on the side of more communication rather than less. It's hard to have too much communication." But this communication has to be multilevel, multimedia, and vivid enough to grab the hearts and guts of the target audience.

Maybe it shouldn't be called "re-engineering." Few of us have engineering degrees or experience. The communication aspect should be called common sense.

SOMEBODY'S LISTENING

Companies have traditionally made a distinction between internal and external communication. That old dividing line is long gone.

Material a CEO thought was designed for people inside the corporation is increasingly likely to be heard by important groups outside — and they may react very differently than the inside group.

Here are some examples: Hurricane Andrew hit not only Florida, but the insurance companies as well. American International realized that the disaster would focus public attention on insurance companies and be a good time to make a case for increased prices. This is actually good sense and a great strategy. Insurance companies have been hard hit by a string of disasters, which bring skyrocketing claims. Regulators in many states, particularly where they're elected, can be hostile, uneducated, and happy to go for the quick, nasty headline rather than creating an environment where people can find affordable insurance.

However, the insurance company circulated an internal memo that contained such phrases as, "This is an opportunity to get price increases now." They made two big mistakes.

First, they forgot that internal documents are frequently seen by others — the press, consumer groups, regulators, lawyers — and the phrase "Opportunity to get price increases now," particularly when lifted out of its overall context, is juicy. It seems like they're using other people's hardships for selfish advantage.

Their second mistake was losing control of the story. When another group released the memo to the press, it did so with its own spin; the company lost the opportunity to control the context of the debate. The press reports contained phrases like "The company instructed people to start *softening up* brokers." Those words weren't in the memo; they were the spin.

Another example is the battle over breast implants. The implant makers have seen lawyers take decade-old documents and release selective phrases, which made it look as though the companies knew about the risks and were covering them up. The memos are actually reporting on research. They are the researchers' notes on risks and benefits. Scientific debate encourages "On the one hand this, but on the other hand, here's something else." When the "something else" is selectively released, particularly with the anecdotal illustration of a person with a terrible problem, it creates the impression that the company knew about a potential problem and ignored or covered it up.

TU Electric of Texas filed for a rate increase. Reporters were steered by consumer groups to documents that revealed that the company belonged to 114 country clubs, spending more than $300,000 in fees. TU protested that it used the country clubs all over North Texas to entertain and visit with business customers. TU is a multi-billion dollar company, so the amount was minimal. However, it didn't change the impression that TU was spending lots of money on frivolous matters while it was asking customers for more money.

The solution is two-fold: First, communication training will help spot and prevent potential problems, as well as giving employees a new tool to do their jobs better. It means analyzing expression based on how various audiences will *hear* a message and what they will *believe* and *remember.* The examples above could almost be guaranteed to cause problems. No one inside the company monitored how other groups might interpret the message.

Most companies try to defend themselves in the wrong way — by protesting and explaining. For example, TU Electric responded, "The money comes from our profits, not revenues." As my great-aunt used to say, "Come again?" This fine distinction makes no sense, particularly to a mass audience. Then TU tried to say, "It would only be a penny a month even if the customer were paying, but he's not." This approach is misguided because it tries to explain and rationalize. It assumes the listener will know or want to know as much about the company as the executives and spokespeople. We don't. It also assumes we will interpret numbers and words as they do. We won't.

Someone should have seen the TU problem coming and recommended that the country club memberships and expenses be paid in different ways. Perhaps a few clubs would have arranged reciprocal memberships or individuals could have paid and been reimbursed. (Houston-based Texas Commerce Bank no longer pays for any country club memberships. Many companies no longer pay because of the appearance of funding pricey activities, which are hard to explain to stockholders and customers.) The spokesman should have remembered who is important — ratepayers or customers — and what we need to hear from our utility. "Everything we do is to provide our customers with dependable electricity and service."

Next, management needs a new attitude in order to understand that messages or information must be presented in several ways at once. They should have gone to the public via the press when they raised the issue with their own people.

You'll see more examples like TU's case — unfortunately.

> *"Companies cannot forget that their audiences are listening to them — even when companies hope they're not."*
> — MERRIE SPAETH

THE CASE OF
THE BLEEDING MESSAGES

Have you ever shared something that was good news for you, only to discover that it meant bad news for someone else?

Many companies have made an announcement that they must "cut costs." DuPont was just one such company in recent years. It announced it was going to cut costs by $1 billion over two years, including slashing 5,000 people from its payroll. Wall Street praised the announcement as good news. It had a positive effect on the stock price. But employees saw it as threatening — to their jobs, their future, and their opportunities. This scenario has been repeated many times in recent American business history. Same piece of news — very different reaction. Who's right?

Of course, both the stockholders AND the employees are right, assuming this is true "cost cutting" where one rethinks the actual processes of costs and finds creative ways to reduce them, usually making work more interesting and productive. The blunt head-count reduction or across-the-board flat cut of everyone's department, personnel, and expenses has a distressingly unsuccessful track record, frequently raising costs.

Cost-cutting initiatives fall into the category of efforts that cause change and disruption for some audiences, although carrying an immediate, positive message to one key constituency: the stockholder. A company needs to pay attention to "bleeding messages," where a message for one constituency is also heard with a very different reaction by another. The danger? In this case, employees see instability, and some are likely to leave. The company wants that; however, there are some people they want to keep. The employees may see their future constrained and jump ship. One of the worst examples was the old Texas-based bank holding company, Republic Bank, which announced a combination of cost cutting, hiring freeze, and head-count reduction of "attrition," implying that any program or person that could find a home elsewhere, should. The unsurprising result was that anyone who could find a job elsewhere did, leaving all those who could not. It should not be a surprise that this hurts productivity instead of helping it. Potential recruits wonder about the future of this company and go elsewhere. Customers don't like cutbacks. They worry about the level of service and relationships with trusted suppliers.

When a company wants to send a message to one constituency today, it's mandatory to think through the impact on EACH other group, and develop and implement a plan to explain it persuasively. In this example, DuPont is trimming costs and streamlining operations so that it can bring pure research to the market faster. They hope this will bring more stability, more opportunity to employees, and better service and products to customers. These kinds of secondary messages need to be delivered in a number of ways. The single obligatory letter from a department head — "Oh, by the way, we're doing this because the company needed it" — won't do. Company executives have to make the time to meet with groups of employees. Despite the advantages of modern technology, e-mail, and that sort of thing, the face-to-face encounter is crucial. It allows the employees to see the face and hear the vocal tone of the person delivering the message. And these venues usually allow for questions, creating two-way communication. This encourages participation by the employees even if it doesn't produce terribly satisfactory answers. You can't have an empowered workforce or a team if all you do is talk at them.

The media needs to be solicited. Most companies neglect the media as a tool to reach their own employees. This is because they want to control the information received by employees, but that measure of control affects the message actually received. The media needs to be part of distributing messages and information before employees "hear" it through the press as well. (This, of course, requires training and skills, as well as a comfort level with techniques that most American businessmen and women are just developing.)

One final thought. It's not possible to talk about cutbacks, efficiencies, and trimming costs with employees if senior executives receive pay raises and luxurious perks. The second message — of wealth — causes employees to discount the first, and, in this case, no amount of insisting "We earned it," or "Our job is so hard," or "It's not very much money in a multibillion-dollar company" carries weight. Companies cannot forget that their audiences are listening to them — even when companies hope they're not.

BUSINESS MESSAGES

Businesses communicate with key groups in many ways. Sometimes, a business sends a message that's quite different from what it wants to send.

I make my living advising companies on communication problems. Sometimes I wonder if I shouldn't be teaching values instead. It is a truism to say that it's important to do the "right thing," but usually it turns out that the right thing is not only the right thing, but good business.

Here are some examples of good — and bad — communication that show a company's real values. First, a good example. A few years ago, a Luby's Cafeteria was the scene of the country's worst mass murder. Media from around the country covered the dead bodies and dazed survivors of the tragedy. Luby's executives made an on-the-spot decision to keep all the employees of the restaurant on the payroll, even though the company wasn't sure if they would ever re-open that location. Their actions backed up their family oriented message.

Now bad examples from the Sam Walton enterprises. First, a Hypermart employee was keeping a vigil at her son's death bed. The little boy had been shot in a tragic accident. It took him five days to die, so his mom missed work. Hypermart fired her for her absenteeism. After the media wrote a story about this callous act, the company rehired her. Second, there was a philanthropic organization called Hot Diggity Dog that hired elderly, disabled workers to sell hot dogs outside Sam's Club. (Used to sell hot dogs, I should say.) Hot Diggity Dog was so successful that Sam's decided to kick out the old folks and sell the hot dogs themselves. Third, Wal-Mart informed distributors all over the country that it will only deal directly with manufacturers (LARGE manufacturers).

Now, how would you interpret this? The clear message from Walton enterprises is that they are willing to renege on commitments and bully little guys. As a customer, is this a place you trust?

There is constant debate about which "constituency" or target audience is the most important. It's a pointless debate because all the stakeholders are important for a business to survive and prosper in the longrun. The business needs good employees at several levels — management and/or specialty needs and the "troops"; a business needs customers (preferably good customers); it needs vendors; and finally, it needs money from some source. Other groups, such as regulators and the public, are separate groups that overlap with all the other groups. Regulators' importance has risen over the years as government has made them the custodians of the public trust in some way. Shareholders or investors are bolstered by the SEC and other agencies, employees at the Department of Labor, and the myriad of alphabet soup commissions that are supposed to ensure fairness.

One thing all these stakeholders have in common is an interest in what's going on in the company. One luxury business, particularly American business, doesn't have is deciding when it will allow that interest and when it won't. Americans have gotten used to having information, and have it they will. That means that they are constantly receiving information whether the company thinks it's sending it or not.

I predict that one of the largest battles of the second half of the 1990s and the first years beyond will involve salaries of top management, particularly the CEO. Is it "fair" or "right" — to investors or employees — for the CEO to make 150 times what a plant worker makes? What if the company loses money or has a fiasco such as EuroDisney, as Disney has experienced? This is not a financial analysis, and attempts to solve it with financial rhetoric will fail. It's a debate about values and it echoes the concern with values currently finding voice in many areas of our society today. It can only be engaged with a values perspective.

I am not arguing that there is a right or wrong answer to the question about the highly paid CEO whose company lost money. I am saying that it's a new way of grappling with the issues that American and global businesses need to prepare for now.

Companies need to learn that we listen to them — all the time. Even when they think they're not talking to us.

BEING INCLUDED

One of my favorite clients, someone with whom we have had a long-standing relationship, said the women in his organization were "so prickly." He couldn't figure out what they wanted. He said I wasn't "at all like that." Is that a compliment? I pondered the comment.

An ad in the *Wall Street Journal* caught my eye. It was one of those plain vanilla, boring boxed announcements. Kidder Peabody was announcing the new managing directors. My eye idly scanned the list; I turned a few pages, then turned back. Of the 36 names on the list, only two (Cheryl and Eileen) were obviously women. I called Kidder Peabody to get some facts and ran into a stonewall. Are Masakazu and Loren men or women? "We can't tell you." What's a managing director? A secretary told me it was "sort of like a vice president." A big deal? "Yes." How many managing directors are there? "Can't tell you." How many are women? "Don't know. Talk to the HR people." I called them. They said, "Talk to the PR people." I called them back, they said, of course, "Talk to the HR people."

Being a paranoid member of the media, I assume the answers are all bad; that is, they reflect poorly on the company. In the mid 1990s, when about half of all business school students are female, and between a quarter to a half of new hires are women (and it's been this way for a decade), shouldn't more than two of 36 promotions be women?

Of course, there are many reasons why women take different career paths, but male management fails to understand the need to be included. What women want is not exact similarity, not "equality" — whatever that means — but being included as a person worthy of equal attention and opportunity. A white male would never have noticed the Kidder Peabody ad. It would have seemed perfectly normal to him. Women and minorities see the world differently because we notice instantly when we *aren't* there.

Pictures of top management and boards of directors are my favorite visual. The lack of women (and minorities) or the lone "woman's" slot is so apparent. At the level of board of directors, the defense is always that there are few women who are CEOs. This is only partly true. There are few women who are CEOs of public, *Fortune* 500, or *Business Week* 1000 companies. The reason is that their boards are overwhelmingly male and perpetuate the image of what a CEO should look like without ever being aware of the automatic limitations on the parameters of their thinking. There are many women CEOs of middle management and small businesses. There are many women lawyers and academics.

What a board wants is a woman that some other company has validated by inviting her on the board first. This leads to such situations as Martha Seeger, former governor of the Federal Reserve and an admitted heavyweight, serving on the board of a dozen large companies. Paula Hill, director of the Business Leadership Center at the Cox School of Business at Southern Methodist University, heads an innovative effort which has been praised by *US News & World Report*, she sits on no corporate boards.

The affirmative action debate now raging in Congress is a public policy debate about how to look at the world. Conservatives and women who regard government as ineffective, counterproductive, and expensive see the world differently from men. The fundamental reason is that although there are growing numbers of women in business everywhere, women are not included as men are.

When we look at a picture of leadership in corporations, universities, or Congress, the picture is still overwhelmingly white and male. Women and minorities have special, higher hurdles to face.

"The objective of diversity training programs is to better the relationships among people who work together. Despite the best intentions, however, some diversity training produces the opposite effect." — H.B. KARP, IN TRAINING MAGAZINE

DIVERSITY TRAINING

Diversity is the hot word in workplace discussions these days, and it's no surprise that training in diversity is the newest fad. Companies should be careful what they do, or they'll send an unintended message about diversity.

When most of us think of training, we think of learning something that will help us and our companies to be more effective. But so-called "diversity training," which is supposed to encourage employees to think that a diverse work force is a good one, is so poorly thought out and executed that some companies have found it causes more problems than it cures.

At Baxter Health Care in Deerfield, Illinois, the diversity manager asked people to tell how they feel about abortion or gay rights, and then pitted people with opposing positions against each other.

Another company asks people to express stereotypes they've heard, such as "blacks are lazy" or "women crack under pressure." Women and minorities are then encouraged to express their rage over these comments.

Too frequently, diversity "training" sessions become an opportunity for women and minorities to say publicly things that have built up for years. An administrator for an Ohio sheriff's office was one of five white males in a group of 30. The administrator lived in an integrated neighborhood. In the training session, he said he found himself blamed for causing everything from slavery to limitations on women's opportunities.

These techniques, and other confrontational and divisive sessions, violate one important rule of training: They forget to take into account how we remember things. The pro-life person in accounting will remember the argument with the pro-choice person in marketing, which does nothing to foster a diverse work force. Verbalizing stereotypes only makes them more memorable, and having individuals boil over with rage will ensure that everyone remembers the divisiveness, not the diversity lessons the trainer intended.

One cardinal communication rule is to ask yourself what you want your target audience to remember after you are long gone. Don't allow more controversial or quotable messages to compete with it.

Another important tactic is to define up-front what "diversity" means and what you hope to accomplish. Diversity doesn't just apply to race and ethnic background. Bill Boyd of Sunbelt Motivation & Travel recognized regional differences in his travel agents. Southerners like to visit with customers during discussions about reservations, asking personal questions, and doing what the Northern or Eastern agents considered gossiping. The Southerners viewed it as good manners and friendliness. The Northerners and Easterners viewed it as wasting time.

One technique that I personally do not believe is very productive is to hammer people with statistics. Reeling off numbers about how the world is changing is really not "training," yet it is a common place for diversity trainers to begin. That is, the trainer or facilitator gets up and says:

"From 1983 to 1993, the percentage of white, male professionals and managers in the work force dropped from 55 percent to 47 percent, while the same group of white women jumped from 37 percent to 42 percent. African-Americans will rise from 10 percent to 12 percent of the work force by the year 2005, while Hispanics will rise from 6 percent to 11 percent. At companies like Amoco, women and minorities are 40 percent of the work force, and one of every six employees is not a U.S. citizen."

The trainer smugly thinks he or she has made the case that, change is necessary, but the white males in the audience hear it and think, "I'm toast." African-Americans hear it and think, "Hispanics are doing better than we are."

Two important aspects of successful diversity training appear to be to organize and position it as the "right thing to do," and as an ongoing effort. No one-day, one-shot seminar will suddenly make everything perfect. A good one-day seminar can raise important issues, change how people react initially, and create a benchmark for behavior. But without successive reinforcement, the original day of "awareness training" soon fades. "Awareness" can be a very important step to changing behavior, but one can create awareness and end up without changed behavior. We believe the best training creates a structure, incentive, and team spirit for people to monitor their own values and behavior, and change or moderate them to fit within a fairly flexible group norm.

Positioning diversity efforts as a "moral imperative," as Taylor Cox, Jr. of the University of Michigan calls it, underscores the issue of fairness. This is actually a significant philosophical difference from courses that position diversity training as pragmatic or worse, as something driven by regulatory pressures. A survey by the Conference Board found that top management said they view diversity as part of good management and a competitiveness issue. This places it roughly on a par with cash management. By contrast, Anthony Carnevale and Susan Stone, writing in *Training and Development,* urge CEOs to consider it a leadership issue.

That's another problem with diversity training. People in management often think that it's something they don't need. A survey by Towers Perrin said the number-one factor in successful workforce-related programs (including diversity) was greater awareness and commitment from senior management. Too many senior executives believe this is something they can farm out to consultants, have those at a lower level handle it, and perhaps never change their own behavior. This is a recipe for failure. All the diversity training in the world won't wipe away the picture of a CEO whose advisors and close counselors are all white males. Or how about the one who uses his leisure time to go off to the Masters in Augusta for a white male CEO round of golf.

Finally, leadership does not mean unthinking tolerance of everything. For example, being a single mother is not bad, but it is still far better for children to grow up in two-parent households.

If top management is committed to instilling a respect for diversity at their company, they'll get top training for their employees, and their involvement won't stop at the classroom door. They'll keep tabs on workforce behavior after the training is over. Unless all that is done, the corporation is sending a message that diversity training is not serious. White males will think it's poorly thought out and delivered and resent the waste. Women and minorities will recognize that nothing has changed. All the good intentions in the world won't make up for that.

SCHOOL DAYS

Most of us remember school as the 3Rs. The foreign language was French (unless you count Latin). Technology wasn't even a subject, and only a few strange kids carried slide rules around with them.

Today, technology is emphasized at good schools, and foreign languages include a selection ranging from German to Arabic. St. Mark's School of Texas in Dallas begins Japanese in third grade.

At the nation's top business schools, the curricula is undergoing a similar revolution. When I went to Columbia Business School in the late 1970s, we took finance, marketing, operations research, statistics, organizational behavior, and some other courses. Columbia considered itself advanced because we had a semester on corporate ethics and governance and a specific focus on "entrepreneurship." There was no mention of communication.

As "quality" was regarded decades ago, communication was thought to be a "soft" skill and certainly not part of the real academic focus. Communication was something added later, only when it was important in a crisis. These exact comments were written by the quality guru, the late W. Edwards Deming.

Things are changing. At the Cox School of Business at Southern Methodist University, we teach graduate business students "Strategic Communication," "How to Manage the Media," "Communication as a Strategic Tool for Business," and several levels of Presentation Skills, including a focus on negotiation, sales, and motivation. As the ad says, "This isn't your father's Oldsmobile!"

At the Stanford Graduate Business School, students take courses in public presentations and analyze how different groups express themselves differently. At the Stern School at New York University, Fred Helio Garcia examines the role of media in helping a business accomplish its goals or hindering it, particularly in times of crisis.

The new emphasis on communication, even if it is only starting, is a welcome change from past practices. It will lead, however, to some generational misunderstandings as media savvy graduate students flow into corporations and climb the corporate ladder. They will run into several generations schooled in the thought that the press is, at best, an unwarranted intrusion and, at worst, a damaging, hostile force. Those students who have also honed their presentation and negotiating skills will be criticized as "too smooth" and "too sharp" since we always attack what's new and different, particularly if we don't have those aptitudes ourselves. The old forces always take the kernel of truth and build the attack around it.

Like "quality," it will take some time for "communication" to become a way of life. I predict that it will because at levels below graduate business study, in the leading elementary and secondary schools like Germantown Friends School (GFS) in Philadelphia, come newsletters with headlines like the one above and articles about how first and second graders are getting up on their feet to make presentations to their classmates. Far from grandstanding or schooling a generation of new politicians, this technique forces students to organize and express their thoughts in a cogent manner and to defend them in subsequent question and answer sessions.

At the Hockaday School in Dallas, a K-12 school for girls, and Cistercian Academy for boys, students write poetry and read it aloud. These opportunities to speak aloud benefit not just the speaker but the group, because the rest of the children learn the importance of listening. They get lots of practice.

At GFS, lower-school students take communication lessons as part of philosophy courses that examine values, ideas, and moral questions. In upper school, debate has returned as part of the curriculum, taught by veteran teacher Pat Reifsnyder. Mrs. Reifsnyder taught me American History years ago, and I still remember how she structured the year by having us collect the campaign slogans and platforms of the *losing* Presidential candidates throughout our nation's history.

In the newsletter that came my way, the article about communication teaching at the school ends with the paragraph: "But what sets GFS apart from other schools is a deeply felt attitude that communicating clearly can help solve problems and contribute to a more complete understanding of one another. And that is knowledge for life." I agree, and I can imagine how well equipped these youngsters will be for business school at SMU or Columbia when they arrive. Business needs to be ready for them.

CUSTOMER SATISFACTION

The hot new business buzzwords are "customer satisfaction" — knowing your customer, then making sure your customer is happy. Customer satisfaction is supposed to keep customers loyal and differentiate one company from another, bringing business profits. But how docs a company analyze the elements of customer satisfaction and communicate that to its own employees?

Companies are discovering that the most effective, long-term way to achieve customer satisfaction is to create a culture of client satisfaction, and that actions speak louder than words. This isn't something that can be ordered from Office Depot.

Stanley Marcus, the retail genius and guru behind the Neiman Marcus department store chain says that customer satisfaction means always doing more than the customer expects. He has written several books on the subject. The day before Christmas, a customer in rural Texas called the store in tears. She had ordered a dozen small gifts to be used as party favors for a dinner that night and asked that they be gift wrapped.

They arrived — without the gift wrapping. It was too late to find suitable wrapping. Marcus didn't hesitate. He sent two wrappers by plane. They finished wrapping just as the dinner guests arrived.

My husband and I were out with another couple celebrating a birthday at Sam's, a chic Dallas restaurant. We arrived and were seated. And sat. And sat. And sat. Half an hour later, I grabbed a waiter and said, "Hey, no water, no menus, no drinks, no rolls . . . *not* happy!" He disappeared. The manager appeared. She brought us our drinks, apologized and said, "This is on me." We thought she meant the drinks. After a nice dinner, we asked for the bill. No bill. Manager Dian Bradley explained, "This should be a special night. We want you to remember it like that." Thanks to her gesture, we do.

This was a great example of customer satisfaction. Here's how to achieve it. First, spot the problem and act fast. Second, act as if you personally care. Put yourself in the customer's place. Third, go beyond the customer's expectation. An apology is nice, but doing something to prove your sorry is even better.

Put yourself in the customer's place: I just ordered some children's pajamas and heavy pewter stocking holders from Lands' End. How heavy? Would they really hold a loaded stocking? The person on the phone said, "Gee, in the catalog, the stocking doesn't look all that heavy. Hold on and let me check because if it doesn't hold everything you want, it would be a real nuisance to send it back." She came back with the verdict that the holders would almost certainly be strong enough for the fattest Christmas stocking but if they weren't, they would come back and pick them up — at Lands' Ends expense. Now that's really thinking like the customer.

How does a corporation get this across? The best way is to publicize examples like Ms. Bradley or the person from Lands' End who helped me. A number of companies are putting their own people in their ads. One banker for Houston- based Texas Commerce Bank describes helping a customer who was taking out a home improvement loan. He was self-employed and traveled long hours, so the loan officer met him at his office at 5 a.m. so he could sign the papers. When a banker meets you at your office at 5 a.m., it signals a revolution in how banks look at customer service. It also sends a powerful message about how far bankers are expected to go to accommodate the customer.

A car dealership ad described a salesman getting a call from a customer's wife late on a Friday afternoon. She had a flat tire and needed help. He went and changed her tire. What was remarkable about this was that he had not sold her the car. He had sold her husband his car.

Customer service is a culture, and you see that in microcosm in the United States Post Office, one of the most ridiculed and inefficient organizations. Yet some postal stations offer superior service and are customer focused *despite* the bureaucracy. We put in a new driveway and fence. It took months. Since we live on a busy street, our mailbox was moved first to our next-door neighbors, then back, and then someplace else. Finally, the fence was completed but the box with the code allowing access was, of course, on the wrong side of the entry for the right-hand-drive postal vehicles. During the months of construction, I had called the post office many times with the latest instructions and updates. My carrier, "Roy," had become a real person although we had never met. When the gate was finally finished, he asked, "Would you trust me enough to have one of the appliances that opens the gate?"

I learned a number of other houses on our route have the same problem, and the carrier has a large bag of remote gate openers. Today, my mail is still delivered right to my doorstep.

The postal service needs more employees like Roy to compete with express carriers like Federal Express whose employees seem to compete for good customer service. Federal Express employees have become famous for delivering packages by bicycle, canoe, snowshoe, and sled when weather threatened to interfere with their guarantee of overnight service.

Customers don't necessarily need perfect service or trouble-free experiences to be satisfied. The attitude of the employees can make the difference. The Peabody Hotel in Memphis is a landmark structure, "where the South begins," according to some people. Famous for its ducks who live in the fountain in the central lobby, the Peabody suffered the decline experienced by many old hotels. The structure looked as though nobody cared, and the staff reflected the attitude. Room service forgot you? Tough, you don't look like you're starving. New ownership tore through the grand hotel, renovating and retraining but keeping the employee base of central Memphis. Today, the arriving guest is virtually overwhelmed by greetings and enthusiasm. "It's not the White House, it's the right house," says one doorman. The genuine sense of commitment differentiates the Peabody in an age when the business traveler has a hard time remembering whether he's staying in Atlanta or Albuquerque. There are still rough edges in the Peabody's service and physical plant, but the staff's attitude of ambassadors of goodwill keeps many customers coming back.

Incidents of satisfied customers need to be publicized internally. Too often only the problems get high-level attention. La Quinta Inns could be said to have "written the book" on customer satisfaction, sponsoring author Scott Gross' *Positively Outrageous (Customer) Service* book to hammer home the commitment to its managers and employees. Their examples of customer service are on display for everyone to read. Asked to arrange transportation for a guest's wife, hotel staff met her at the airport with flowers and song. She was overwhelmed. They stress, "Do the unexpected," as an element of great customer service.

Many companies have internal awards similar to Baylor Health Care

System's "Five Star Spirit," an employee recognition program in which patients, physicians, and coworkers can express their appreciation for excellent customer service. Video can be a great internal communication tool to enhance customer service. It allows you to display emotion, facial expression, and so on. Employees who watch someone doing things right will not only repeat most of the words they see used, they will duplicate the gestures and animation of the person they see on the screen.

There is no magic prescription to achieve customer satisfaction, but common sense, commitment at the top, good internal communication, and relentless repetition of the message about what customer service means can produce a lot of happy, loyal customers.

> *"A ritual of the business pages today during the acquisition process involves the prospective new management saying how valuable the company's personnel are, and 'how things will stay the same.' Nonsense. Everybody knows things will be different. A lot different."* —MERRIE SPAETH

ACQUISITION

One company buying another has become commonplace. It is hardly a topic for discussion any more. There is more attention to takeovers when one company doesn't want to be bought; for example, AT&T's pursuit of NCR and the Blockbuster/Viacom dance. Behind the headlines are acquisitions and "de-acquisitions" of whole companies. Sort of the way we buy a new sweater. "Oh, this fits," or "This is fashionable" and you buy a new one. Very little attention is given to what happens after the checks change hands. An old value applied during the acquisition process will pay dividends in human terms and help make the combined companies function.

A ritual of the business pages today during the acquisition process involves the prospective new management saying how valuable the company's personnel are, and how things will "stay the same." Nonsense. Everybody knows things will be different. A lot different.

Acquiring companies should be very careful not to say things automatically that they really don't mean and don't intend to carry out. Those comments have long-term effects, especially where people are concerned.

Two examples came to my attention. Kitty Litter, founded by entrepreneurial great Ed Lowe, was bought by two Chicago businessmen. Through the negotiations the buyers talked about tapping the founder's insight, judgment, and so on. After the sale, they unceremoniously bounced him.

The Union Life Company, one of the nation's most farsighted insurance companies, sold a subsidiary to Pioneer Life. Again, through the

DILBERT reprinted by permssion of United Feature Syndicate, Inc.

discussions, the buyer mouthed words of respect for the management. Nine o'clock in the morning, they buy the company. Five after nine, they tell the president to clean out his desk.

Again, everyone knows there is potential conflict between the new owner and old executives. And it is the new owners' right to hire and fire. The behavior of "once in, slash and burn," the philosophy that you say anything during the negotiations because once you own the company the poor saps who were there are history, has repercussions. Employees, vendors, and frequently customers or lenders will remember the contrast between "before" and "after." And they will question your veracity for a long time.

The role of the outside media in affecting internal opinion is extremely important. Employees of the target company hang on every word the acquiring firm says about the industry, the company, and the plans for the future. For example, one real estate broker blabbed to a local business weekly that he had been hired by a certain *Fortune* 500 company to look at buildings with a lower price per square foot than the current home office. "They haven't given me any geographic parameters," he told the press confidentially. Everyone in the home office spent the day of publication wondering where they were moving. It turned out that the acquiring firm was just looking for ammunition to negotiate a reduction in the lease from its landlord.

The potential new owner must say something about his intentions to key constituencies of the new company: employees, vendors, concerned citizens, customers. For employees, a good policy is what Jody Powell, former press secretary to President Carter, called — and took a bum rap for — "honesty in moderation." Don't overdo the accolades and protestations out of respect for people. You can acknowledge that there will be changes at the same time you say there will be continuing opportunity for employees who have made a contribution, if it's true. If it's not — well, better complete the acquisition quickly and quietly. The main message is don't think you can say one thing beforehand and something different later.

Part IV

COMMUNICATION TOPICS EVERYONE UNDERSTANDS

COMMUNICATION AND STRATEGY

When should a company think about communication? Too many companies still think it's something which is added *after* a company has done its "real" strategic thinking.

Newspapers offer daily proof that communication is still in its infancy as a key business tool. Companies don't include their communication talent in strategic decisions, although they frequently turn to them to clean up the mess.

In fact, one paper itself provided an example of a company that undertook actions without much attention to analyzing the message to key audiences. Proving that the media can be just as lacking in media savvy as other industries, the *Pittsburgh Press* went through a bitter labor dispute. It didn't publish for six months, and prospects looked dim. A situation like this hurts everyone. The paper's owners got hurt. The citizens of Pittsburgh suffered. The community was without news, and cultural and social institutions cannot communicate with key constituencies without papers. People can't look for apartments to rent, for lost pets, for movie times, or for church services. The paper's employees faced the loss of their jobs if the paper folded permanently.

How did this impasse come to pass? The *Pittsburgh Press* is a union paper in a union city — and union costs are indeed high. The paper used to have good labor relations, but they tried to save money by firing 4,300 young paperboys and phasing out a number of truck drivers' jobs at the same time. Any competent communication counsel could have told them that this was strategic suicide. It married the truck drivers — the Teamsters, known for crime, bully-boy tactics, and high costs — with the intensely sympathetic paperboys.

Why did this happen? Undoubtedly, when the paper planned these moves they thought communication with the paperboys and the citizens of Pittsburgh would be too cumbersome, too time consuming, and "not worth it." So they either didn't bother or they didn't do it effectively. The lawyers probably played a key role telling management that it was their right to fire the paperboys and that their argument would stand up in court. And what did the owners of the *Pittsburgh Press* get? They got big trouble because their argument didn't stand up in the court of public opinion.

This is an obvious example of the impact of not listening to good communication advice. More often, the negative effect is harder to measure. For example, one company trying to cut costs did not tackle the internally sensitive issue of the company's executive cars. So all the regular employees — on whom the company depended to watch costs — had to walk through an executive parking lot full of Lexuses and Mercedes to get to their cars. Guess what? The employees have been less than enthusiastic about participating in cost reductions.

Strategic communication means thinking through the communication aspects or implications *before, during,* and *after* a process or series of events. Here's a multilevel example involving one of the country's largest and most prestigious pathology labs which handles, among other tests, Pap tests. Physicians send the Pap smears taken in their offices to the lab. Four years ago, a technician doing the initial screening mislabeled as "normal" a slide of a patient suffering from cervical cancer. Subsequently, the patient sued the lab. An internal investigation determined that her smear probably merited, but did not receive, a review by a physician where it might have been labeled "positive" for the presence of cancerous or precancerous cells.

The explanation is couched with "mights," but in today's litigious environment, juries expect health care to be perfect. Mistakes are never forgiven, never understood, and always characterized as evidence of malpractice. (In a similar case, a lab in the Midwest, was convicted of criminal behavior.) The lab agreed to a multi-million-dollar settlement with the woman.

The patient refused to sign a confidentiality agreement common in settlements of this sort. That should have been a red flag to the lab owners, but because the litigation was over, they thought that the situation was finished.

Months passed. The woman, now dying, focused her anger on the lab and found a sympathetic TV reporter who produced an emotional series of "investigative" stories called "Fatal Mistakes." When the reporter called the lab, one physician talked to her over the phone explaining the situation, but refused to be interviewed. Weeks passed. Only when the TV station began to run promo spots about "Fatal Mistakes" did the lab decide to participate in the story and seek media counsel.

The lab physicians went through a crash course on dealing with the media under hostile circumstances. The reporter had written a "good guy/bad guy" story, with the lab as the bad guy.

Could this situation have been different? First, recognizing that dying patients go through predictable stages of anger, grief, depression, and acceptance, the lab should have reached out to her family, minister, and friends to explain the situation and express their sorrow. This patient was in anger when she placed that first phone call to the reporter.

Can this tragedy be explained? Although many women think Pap smears "tell" whether you have cancer, they are actually only a diagnostic tool. These tests are not perfect, and they are performed and examined by people who are not perfect.

Labs and OBGYNs explain little or none of this to women. In trying to motivate women to get regular Pap smears, the American Cancer Society and women's groups send the message that "the Pap test can save your life." This decades-long education effort, while important, effective, and still necessary has conditioned women to have unrealistic expectations. Yet, it is in this environment that physicians and labs must operate. To refuse to understand it is to invite problems.

The lab made no attempt to explain this to those around the dying woman, and perhaps that is understandable. But they could have communicated it to the reporter, or to the reporter's editor. Failure to do so resulted in a two-part TV story charging that labs kill women.

The lab should have considered their audiences: customers, physicians, and health-care organizations. Without giving it much thought, the lab sent only a short "Dear Doctor" form letter alerting physicians that the report was upcoming. They failed to think through what should have been in that letter, namely a reminder of the lab's recognized status as a high-quality health-care provider. The lab didn't even really have a good list of its customers, other than billing records, so that they could contact the person in charge.

The few days before and after the story were a mad rush to avoid total disaster and regain some control of the situation. Lab personnel consented to be interviewed, so the television station's story included a lab physician's comment pointing out the lab's high standards. The day after the story, the lab messengered a letter to each customer explaining their high standards and cost effectiveness, expressing their sorrow at the woman's death, and asking for their customer's help in educating the public.

Most of their customers are experienced physicians and large hospitals who understood the complexity and problems involved and stuck with the lab. Few called with comments like the hospital that said, "That was a terrible report. It was so unfair. We're canceling our account."

This is an example of a predictable situation with obvious signs of trouble that were ignored out of arrogance, fear, or ignorance. A farsighted organization should have recognized the environment, analyzed the risks, and prepared for the potential exposure: when the woman refused to sign a confidentiality agreement, when the TV reporter called . . .

Strategic communication asks, "Who are our audiences? How and when do we reach them? What do we need to prepare for? Are we ready to react quickly? What are the costs of doing something and of doing nothing?"

Today, the cost of doing nothing is very, very large indeed.

The message to the CEO is to include the communication counselor in your strategic thinking. This means that you must also know enough to assess whether you have creative, sophisticated help or not. Don't necessarily believe the lawyers when they tell you they've got it covered. And pin a copy of the *Pittsburgh Press* to your wall to remind yourself of the cost of being out of business for six months. Ask if you can invest a little effort to save yourself a lot of trouble.

WHERE TO PLACE THE COMMUNICATION PERSON

Most companies today have a person or department responsible for public information, communication, public relations and other similar functions. Not all companies do. There are still a few like Schwans, a well-known, privately held company that makes ice-cream products for schools and other institutional customers. When Schwans was accused of selling ice cream contaminated with salmonella, the company had to depend on the person in charge of communication, who was also government liaison and in charge of insurance, community relations, and a few other things. The company didn't even have up-to-date media lists.

Assuming most companies today are more progressive than Schwans, where should the communication department be located in an organization?

You can tell a lot about a CEO's priorities by who reports directly to him or her. Unfortunately, most communication functions and the people doing them are still buried in the organization. They *should* report directly to the top.

Communication should be a tool used by all divisions for all efforts. It's not something that you reach for *after* the work is done. But that's the typical attitude. Get the product ready or review the problem, and after everything is done, call in the PR people and have them do a news release. Wrong. They should be in there with you.

I have seen many situations where problems were created because communication wasn't valued. For example, a company reduced its workforce significantly. The lawyers treated it as a legal matter, focusing on potential problems from wrongful discharge suits. The shock waves from the layoffs drove customers away, scared employees, and antagonized shareholders. A good communication strategy would have anticipated those reactions, prepared for them, and mitigated or eliminated them.

A major jewelry chain lost a customer's diamond ring while it was in for repair. Unfortunately, the ring had belonged to the customer's grandmother who had survived the Holocaust, but could not apparently survive the practices of this company. The company tried to ignore the lost ring for months. Finally, the customer, who was pregnant, demanded to have the ring returned, and the company was forced to admit what had happened. The customer went into labor when she learned her ring was gone. The company's lawyers' attitude was "It was insured for $5,000. Give her the $5,000." Wrong. The woman went to the local consumer reporter with her story of woe. He went on the air. All of Denver knew that this company lost her merchandise.

Imagine you have a piece of jewelry that needs repair. Would you take it to this store? No, of course not, and that's the danger of treating customer problems as a legal matter. Even if this customer had not gone to the press, she was sure to tell every single friend about it. This is the kind of message that "travels"; that is, one person tells another who tells another.

This story has a happier ending. I was personally involved in it, but, alas, only after the consumer reporter made it a cause célèbre. Here's what happened next:

We called the reporter and apologized for not being responsive. The store called and wrote the woman an apology. The local store manager told her, "I'm so sorry. I've worked here 17 years, and this has never happened. Please let us try to create a new heritage and memory for your grandchild." You can buy quite a rock at wholesale for $5,000, and the store told the woman she could pick out any 2-carat solitaire, and if she didn't see one she liked, they'd find more. She managed to find one that looked fabulous. Her grandmother's rose-cut diamond had a lot of sentimental value but not much sparkle next to the new diamond. The store manager practiced her apology so she would feel comfortable on the radio show the next day. She went through her apology and her description of what the store would do, and the woman described her new ring. The consumer reporter thought for a moment and said, "That's more than fair. What a great store."

The woman will probably become an ambassador for the store and show everyone her fabulous new diamond ring. Of course, the entire problem could have been avoided if a communication approach had been part of the jewelry chain's initial response rather than a reaction to negative press.

Communication should offer an additional perspective, even on things that don't seem like marketing or PR. For example, a company in Chapter 11 was preparing for a hearing on a proposed refinancing. The first batch of funding, however, returned a third of the money to the financial advisors as fees, rather than going to pay creditors, reduce debts, or increase working capital. The communication person said, "I think the judge is going to have a problem with that, and I know the creditors will come unglued." The lawyers said, "Nonsense, this is a legal matter, we've all agreed on it." What happened? The judge had a problem with it, and the creditors came unglued. The company should have used the communication people for insight and advice on how others would perceive their recommendations.

Good communication can help leverage positive messages and information. Texas Commerce Bank had a great new group of derivative products. Their communication person was plugged in from the start. First, she made sure the presentations the bankers were putting on about these new products were as sensational as the products themselves. (Remember, you cannot have a staid, boring presentation with lots of overheads about products that are innovative market leaders, or you have a bad case of mixed messages. The presenter is saying, "It's new and exciting," but the message is destroyed by how he is saying it.) Then she galvanized the lines of internal communication so people in other departments knew about these products and knew how they could help customers of the other departments. At Texas Commerce, communication is part of marketing.

In today's increasingly competitive, volatile global environment, doesn't it make sense to avoid problems and leverage your strengths? Put that communication person at the CEO's right hand — and you'll take a big step in that direction.

> *"Business executives don't have to be perfect to be effective.*
> *They just need to take performing on camera seriously."*
> — MERRIE SPAETH

CORPORATE VIDEO

We're supposed to live in a television age, although we at *Marketplace* prefer to characterize it as the electronic age. But many corporations are turning to video newsletters and annual reports or internal television to communicate with employees and investors. Even Harvard Business School has started distributing lectures and advice on video. Apparently there are companies who will pay $1,900 for videotapes to learn how to meet productivity and performance goals.

Video is indeed a persuasive tool, but too frequently people forget they're doing television in the television age.

Big companies like American Airlines started video newsletters years ago. The J.C. Penney Company has junked paper communication between buyers at headquarters and stores in the field. The stores order merchandise on a live, private TV network. In 1979 the Emhart Company in Connecticut became one of the first outfits to do an annual report on video. Now many companies distribute annual reports on videotape. McDonald's sent out 300,000 tapes in 1994.

The benefits of all this are obvious. Alas, we don't read much, so video or TV become more convenient ways to disseminate information. It's more effective, too, because television is such a powerful medium. Video communicates with more than words — it has picture, motion, immediacy, and it's cheaper than a couple hundred thousand printed reports or newsletters. Let those trees live in peace. But video is not quite television. It's a controlled medium, like a company's brochures or ads. And television is actually a personal communication vehicle. The person on the screen is talking one-on-one to the viewer.

Companies make several predictable mistakes when they use video.

First and foremost, when conveying information, they are far too easy on themselves. In TV news, the reporter represents us. Either in person, via voice-over or simply in how the material is edited. The reporter asks the questions on our minds in the tone of voice we would use. In corporate video, the person reporting or interviewing the CEO is often afraid to be skeptical, to interrupt, or follow up. In television, if it looks like a setup, the credibility of the information is diminished. This is most obvious when a company faces bad news like layoffs or plant closings. But it's also true even if the information is positive.

I have seen far too many corporate videos done in talk-show format where the "host" formulates the question in a fawning manner. "Tell us the good news about the Midwest market, Mr. Smith." A real reporter would ask, "Is there still bad news from the Midwest or are things turning around at last?" Even positive questions are phrased so they appear objective: "The Midwest has had seven straight years of good news. Isn't this a tough record to maintain?"

(The trained executive knows how to handle questions like that. Acknowledge the question with one word. "No." Put on a headline. "The Midwest anticipated the competition and prepared for it." Prove it with a fact. "They merged two routes and brought two key vendors on-site to reduce cycle time and costs by 14 percent." Bring it alive with an anecdote. "As a result, the Payton account moved to us from our key competitor.")

Second, internal TV needs to be produced well enough so that it looks like television news, but it should not be so slick that it looks like an advertisement. Many corporations have a big status gap between the executives and the production people. In real TV, the production people, the director, and the producer are in charge because they know how to make the piece good and how to hold the attention of the viewer. Too many corporations disregard this. Programs are too long, not animated enough, and use too few enhancements. One of my clients was producing boring video communication despite state-of-the-art studios. I visited with the production people who described how one executive had responded to their attempts to coach him. "What am I? An actor?" he snarled. They stopped trying to give advice. Their attitude was that if he wanted to look boring, fine. They had tried to enforce time limits on another division, only to be overruled many times.

Finally, electronic communication demands more out of executives. That is, they **must** tackle the special requirements of good delivery over the airwaves. This means working between cameras, taking direction, and learning how to read a TelePrompTer. It means learning how to write for the mouth and ear, not the eye. That is, in "real" verbal intercourse, the speaker speaks in phrases, repeats something, inserts half sentences, and so on. Most corporate writers and executives write scripts that look and sound like memos. They are written and edited visually rather than read aloud.

The executive who wants to communicate on video needs to be comfortable. Television can spot someone who doesn't really want to be there and turn discomfort into destroyed credibility quicker than you can blink an electronic eye. Business executives don't have to be perfect to be effective. They just need to take performing on camera seriously. An executive shouldn't *look* slick or rehearsed (but he should be rehearsed).

After two generations of the television age, it's critical for executives today to be both Wall Street and *Sesame Street* wise.

DO WOMEN COMMUNICATE DIFFERENTLY FROM MEN?

One hot topic in communication and training is "do women communicate differently than men?" This is a ridiculous question because the answer is both "yes" and "no." What's happened, of course, is that every time someone observes something that confirms traditional female behavior (subservience, hesitance, circularity of expression, and so on), it confirms to the observer that women are different.

There are many other ways to examine these differences. Younger managers communicate differently than older ones; people who have experienced success tend to have different patterns of style than others; people who own companies, even small ones, who have been through the wars of company building, present themselves differently than corporate executives. In my own experience and observation, the biggest determinant of how people communicate is whether they adopted a "learning posture" early in their careers or lives. This kind of posture can be fostered by corporate culture, by unusual personal orientation, by personally modeling behavior on an individual, or by individual life experiences.

The importance of corporate culture should not be overlooked. For example, one popular "difference" is the claim that women "soften" their management comments, saying "that's a good idea" and then pointing out the problems. At the J.C. Penney Company, where corporate culture includes good manners and being positive, the idea is for all employees to find something positive and build on it.

Deborah Tannen in *How Women's and Men's Conversational Styles Affect Who Gets Heard, Who Gets Credit and What Gets Done at Work*, offers the

161

example of the male manager who gives his subordinates no feedback while they are working on a project. They feel ignored and left out. The male manager thought he was showing confidence in them by giving them freedom. He equated no interference with no problem. These differences, according to Tannen, are gender related.

They are equally likely to be personal manifestations or related to corporate culture.

One quote I've seen several times is the woman who ostensibly says, "This is a silly question, but . . . " Insecure women and men get weeded out of executive ranks early.

Most women, even those with insecurities, figure out how to work effectively, which requires communication with colleagues, vendors, bankers, and others. One can make an argument that women are positionally situated to learn differently. Sally Helgeson in *The Female Advantage* makes the point that successful women must learn not to compartmentalize their lives. You have to juggle being a parent, wife, partner, executive, and community leader; you learn something from all those roles and from making them work together. But the key is the word "successful," because many women don't do this particularly successfully (as many men don't).

The question is whether women communicate differently than men in ways that cut through all these other "differences." There is absolutely no decent scholarship to support either position, other than advice from personal experience. Here's mine:

➤ Women do need to watch that they don't confirm expectations of "female" behavior (crying, hesitancy, etc.), but this varies enormously from company to company. It's equally important to look at individual women role models in the company (if any) or individual models of success.

➤ Women have more flexibility of style and should use those options. A woman can attend a seminar on how to use humor, then talk about what she learned and how to incorporate it in the workplace. No one thinks she's weak or silly.

➤ More is expected of women. Gloria Steinem's comment still holds: "We'll have true equality when a woman schlemiel can succeed equally with a male schlemiel."

➤ Women should never try to act male. Obscenities, tough behavior, or physical behavior do not create the perception of equality but rather of someone who is trying too hard.

➤ Exceptional communication and presentation skills are required from top executives in all industries and professions today. However, a lack of talent or improvement in this area is more likely to hurt women because they are less likely to have corporate sponsors and more likely to have more responsibilities in the home that limit their ability to put in the traditional 150 percent necessary to rise. (Message: Start concentrating on these entirely learnable skills early in a career.)

Like many discussions today, probably far too much time is spent hashing over whether women are different than men. They are. They aren't. There's a lot of overlap. There are advantages and disadvantages to both genders. Some of it isn't fair. President Jimmy Carter reminded us that life isn't fair, and the press trashed him. But he was right.

E-MAIL

E-mail is mainstream. It is everywhere. It's generating controversy and calling for a new protocol specifically for this new communication medium. It's fundamentally changing companies that use it.

It's growing so fast, there are no real estimates of growth. One expert estimates that 900 million messages are sent per month. The United States Postal Service has lost as much as 33 percent of the correspondence between businesses, which the *Washington Post* reports is about 10 million letters a year, to electronic genies such as fax machines.

Companies usually begin using E-mail as a cost-saving measure. It cuts down the use of secretaries or other message takers. At the same time, it's also more efficient and much speedier. What used to take weeks, days, or hours shrinks to hours or seconds. A company using E-mail quickly discovers a lot about communication and about its own culture.

E-mail works best in companies where there are no or few barriers of status between layers of management, for E-mail is fundamentally an empowering technology. The lowliest clerk can communicate directly with the CEO (unless the CEO's secretary has access to his mail and intercepts it).

Messages become more frequent. Executives who used to dictate messages to secretaries are now in charge of their own communication and leave shorter messages since they now have to do them themselves.

A consensus, formal or informal, develops about what's acceptable and what's not. Be brief; be concise; don't be profane; don't assume things are confidential; don't insult; and don't include gossip. Michael Crichton's book, *Disclosure*, is probably closer to the mark than any of us care to think. (In his book, people read each other's E-mail and mystery hackers from outside the company send messages and clues via CompuServe.)

E-mail has become a force for change just because it fosters access. In companies successfully using communication as a tool for change the CEO checks and answers his own messages. The CEO of MCI, Burt Roberts, reports getting 100 messages a day. He uses it as a true research tool — sending a message to a dozen executives for a response. He needs E-mail to be accessible. MCI has 29,000 employees in 55 countries. They "talk" to him 24 hours a day. Jim D'Agostino, CEO and president of American General Life and Accident Insurance Company, gets a few dozen messages a day — most from top executives, a few from management around the company, and at least one from an agent or person in the field he has never met. In the first eight months of his presidency, President Clinton got 80,000 messages. We assume he farmed out the work of reading them.

Fame can overwhelm and invalidate E-mail. Bill Gates, chairman of Microsoft, apparently handled his own E-mail until someone published his identification code and, because of his fame, his system was overwhelmed like President Clinton's.

How do you know if the company president really wants to hear from you? I ask first if people call the president by his first name. Do they call him "Herb" (Herb Kelleher at Southwest Airlines) or "Mr. Kelleher?" A CEO who is called by his first name is more likely to be truly accessible. This is not an infallible rule because Fred Smith, founder and chairman of Federal Express, is called Mr. Smith by most executives below senior rank, yet he checks his own E-mail and responds. Most companies create a communication culture where the message is spread informally but unmistakably about whether the CEO really is accessible or whether his mailbox on the system is to create the false impression of openness.

E-mail can be a crucial tool in re-engineering because it helps rethink the traditional, sequential nature of many tasks and analysis. Arthur Andersen's Business Consulting practice re-engineered the hiring practices for a company that employed many low-skilled, minimum-wage employees. The process to gain approval to hire a new employee took two weeks because the packet of employment material went from one person's desk for sign off, to another's, to another's.

Arthur Andersen threw the information "packet" into the E-mail system with notification to the approving group, and the time required was reduced from two weeks to two hours.

Marketplace Communication

Companies are putting their newsletters, United Way appeals, flash bulletins, and information about their 401(k) plans into E-mail. The employee who doesn't understand page three, paragraph 10 can now ask just about that and get a reply without listening to more than he wants to hear.

Technology, as in all things, accelerates the pace of change. Originally, there was an E-mail network, and you had to go through laborious steps to access it. Today's software allows most users to continue with whatever application they are using, but send a message at any time. Many programs let you know when you have an E-mail message with an icon or message in a screen corner. Urgent messages can be accompanied by flashing icons, beeps, bells, or whistles. Read me now!

Finally, E-mail always brings with it — sometimes unexpectedly — a crashing down of the distinctions between "inside" and "outside" the corporation. It's just too easy to listen to, talk to, ask questions, and tap into all the other folks talking electronically. So E-mail will, we predict, speed research, accelerate trends to outsourcing, and speed the velocity of change (which was going pretty fast anyway).

E-mail, joined with the mushrooming Internet, has become a sales force, a library of magazines, a research tool, and a list of other potential uses we are just beginning to imagine and exploit. The *New York Times* reported how businessmen use E-mail to trade Mercedes, elevators, wheat, and chicken parts. We have seen the first E-mail used as a fund-raising device asking readers to contribute to a sick child. E-mail was literally lifesaving for one Newark, New Jersey, computer analyst, stricken with chest pains. He sent an E-mail message that he needed help to everyone in his department (the same key one would press to circulate the 401(k) plan or information about the company picnic); people came running, performed CPR, and called assistance.

E-mail: not just technology, but changing the way we think and how we do business.

NEWSLETTERS I: OLD HAT

There are fads and trends in all things, and the trick is to be ahead of the curve, be better than the rest, find a niche, and, as always, clearly know your audience and what you hope to accomplish. That's why most newsletters directed to external audiences fail miserably. They are derivative. They are published only because other companies, law firms, utilities, doctors' offices, and so on have a newsletter, so someone says, "Why don't we have one, too?"

I used to be a big fan of newsletters for external audiences. They could look like media, but be controlled. (In our analytical model, there are three routes to the audience: controlled material usually described as advertising, marketing, or other collateral; the press; and finally, personal contact, either in groups or one-on-one. Newsletters allowed a company the "look" of news but without depending on the vagaries of whether the press would actually quote your expert or carry your feature, opinion piece or letter.)

Newsletters allow companies or other organizations to pass their name by you monthly or quarterly. They carried "news" — by definition that included announcements and other real news — as well as analysis. Professional firms in particular used newsletters to promote themselves with clients and potential clients because this "analysis" always displayed their expertise.

Several problems, or rather changes in the external environment, have limited the effectiveness of newsletters. It's stunning that companies or consultants earning a good living helping clients understand how external environments have changed and require radical re-engineering of how they do business, fail to recognize this applies to other "processes" as well. ("Process improvement," a variation on re-engineering, means you look at every process. A newsletter is just one route, or process, for transmitting information, frequently coupled with motivation.)

First, the field is overcrowded. Every law firm, every company, and every doctors' group seems to have a newsletter. Enough!

When a vehicle is no longer differentiated, it loses its usefulness. Some argue that newsletters are still a way to pass a name in front of a client, but it's an expensive, time-consuming way to do it.

Next, there has been a radical redesign in how people, particularly Americans, receive information. It was started by *USA Today* (criticized initially, but now a global news force) and blasted into high gear by cable TV, MTV, and other forces. Even the venerable *New Yorker* was redesigned by a former editor of *Vanity Fair*. The design requirements for a newsletter are rigorous. It has to be attractive, easy to read, using all sorts of pictures, drawings, charts, quotes, cartoons — in other words, whatever works. Many newsletters fail this test miserably.

And even if the graphic design is exciting, the writing can't take second place. Newsletters are frequently written for people who already know the information. Wrong approach. Newsletters should be written with the same philosophy that governs every big-city paper — that the reader is very busy, needs to be hooked or interested in the first paragraph, cannot be patronized, must be addressed simply and clearly, and above all, cannot be bored. A basic, rigorous journalism course would help. (The worst offenders seem to be law and accounting firms, which fall prey to the mistaken idea that a newsletter must have "substance," so they look down on short, bite-size, simply written, graphically illustrated newsletters. And they absolutely veto the use of humor or snappy sentences — key tools in keeping your reader interested.)

Newsletters, even professional firms' newsletters, can be well written. An example is the Cleveland-based, worldwide law firm of Jones, Day, Reavis & Pogue. Their *Quarterly* is clearly written, interesting, and timely. It's worth noting that although the writing and subject matter are the main attractions, the graphic design is first-rate — the lines and columns are not bunched up, the artwork is modern but tied to the text. The writers resist the temptation to jam as much on a page as fits.

A good newsletter can still be a helpful way of reaching customers, clients, contributors, or potential audiences. Follow the comments above. The first key step is an analytical one. Who are we trying to reach? Why? What do we hope to accomplish? What or who is our competition? What other choices do we have to communicate? Is there any way to monitor or test whether we are meeting our goal?

A few ending thoughts. Technology has increased our options here as in all things — electronically delivered newsletters via Internet, fax, or modem offer new, cost-effective avenues to reach key audiences.

Audience interaction increases interest and awareness, just as it does in presentations. Fax-back polls are not yet overdone, and have been used effectively by magazines like *Working Woman* and *Inc.* They're certainly one useful tool. Others include cartoons where readers write the captions or summaries of other publications.

Organizationally, every newsletter needs a true managing editor with real power and a keen eye. If that's you, toughen your skin. The editor's job guarantees conflict. No conflict guarantees a boring publication. Complaints tell you that you're doing a good job. They tell you that you're successfully republishing what was old hat.

NEWSLETTERS II:
BOTH OLD HAT AND A VITAL TOOL

Is it worthwhile having a newsletter for your own people? There are loud arguments for and against. The intent of an internal newsletter is to provide a communication vehicle for the company's own employees. Newsletters can be extremely important if they don't fall into predictable topics.

Newsletters need to take a cue from *USA Today*. They need to be catchy, well illustrated, graphically designed to catch the eye, and use a variety of devices to illustrate material. But that's only the beginning of a good internal newsletter.

The word "news" in the title is frequently ignored in corporate settings, and material is old and out-of-date or viewed by the reader as corporate puffery. Newsletters, particularly monthly ones, face the challenge of being truly interesting. It can certainly be done. (Established monthly magazines like *National Geographic* are growing steadily, and single-interest monthlies, such as computer magazines, are exploding.) Good examples of monthly internal publications are Dallas-based Baylor Health Care System's *Progress* and Ameritech's *Vision*. For companies or organizations with large home office populations, weekly publications or even daily sheets are useful. An example of a good weekly is Memphis-based Baptist Memorial Hospital's *Greensheet,* a free weekly tabloid which "sells out" as it is put on the hospital's internal newsstands. "The *Greensheet* is more popular than breakfast around here," says Michael Calhoun, director of communication for Baptist Memorial Health Care System.

To gain respect and credibility, an internal newsletter must carry bad news as well as good news. It cannot cover up. For example, when a

170

member of top management is fired or asked to leave, the news release frequently says, "He resigned to seek other opportunities." The newspaper story inevitably notes, "He was unavailable for comment" or "could not be reached," leaving the impression that everyone is ducking the real story. Internal company publications frequently ignore the firing or resignation entirely, but carry glowing news about the replacement. This invites skepticism. The internal publication can be both credible news but true to its mission of corporate team player. It doesn't have to be *Forbes* and report, "the executive had been feuding with the CEO for months," but it can and should frankly say, "Management felt this division needed another manager," or "After discussions with management, he decided it was time to look for opportunity elsewhere." Both statements will be true, if incomplete. The "quotes" in the story will be something like, "He told our publication that the company has a top team of people," and "He feels he will leave many friends here" — also usually true. This is also incomplete but it at least avoids the appearance of totally ducking questions.

Many good newsletters also carry news or comments about industry conditions. I think this is particularly important. For example, in the fall of 1993, many companies were horrified to find their employees were against the North American Free Trade Agreement (NAFTA). The reasons were clear: Most managements had never discussed trade issues with employees and the press covered the treaty debate by depicting CEOs as for NAFTA and legions of employees against it. The employees identified with other employees, not CEOs.

Like a good publication, there has to be a place for real reader comment, input, and criticism, whether it's a letters column or a comment line.

An internal newsletter must be customer-focused. One study by the International Association of Business Communicators (IABC) found employees wanted to know about six major topics: the organization's plans for current and future operations, personnel policies, topics relating to "doing the job better," topics related to jobs, opportunities for advancement, and the affect of external events. The voluminous research done by the American newspapers for their own use suggests that readers also want human interest stories, "how-to" stories that will improve their individual lives, cartoons or humor, and sports.

The internal publication must serve the corporate mission, so it needs to have a clear point of view, usually articulated by the chairman. The key to this section is consistency of tone and honesty of message illustrated by anecdotes or quotes. Even if someone else drafts the chairman's words, it needs to sound like him. One large PR firm drafted letters for a chairman of a *Fortune* 500 company to send employees during a hostile takeover. The letters were warm, fuzzy, and caring. The employees all said, "Our chairman doesn't sound like that. He's never said those things in his life." And the letters did more harm than good.

The electronic delivery of information is changing how companies think of newsletters. The Cost Management Practice at Arthur Andersen has a monthly "newsletter" delivered by fax and by Lotus Notes. Dozens of companies are experimenting with "newsletters" or news flashes delivered via E-mail. This is clearly the wave of the future and will dictate that internal news "publications" be more timely, shorter, and breezier.

One reason not to have a newsletter? Because you've always had one.

QUARTERLY REPORTS

Quarterly reports are a good example of communication (in this case, to shareholders) that needs to be dramatically rethought. And some companies are doing just that. In the rapidly changing environment, some companies have created a new service helping business rethink the quarterly report.

I plan to do a survey to ascertain how many shareholders truly read the quarterly reports, and for those that do, whether they understand or retain the information.

Quarterly reports, like annual reports, have long been criticized as too dense, too packed with numbers, giving too much information that is hard to absorb and not enough real information about what's going on; being controlled by management and therefore being susceptible to manipulation for a positive spin.

Enter technology. The 800 telephone number, which we are so used to with catalog ordering, steps in to radically change the quarterly report, and just in time.

Quarterly reports can come to you free via telephone. We believe this is a positive trend, saving companies significant amounts of money (some of those quarterly reports cost hundreds of thousands of dollars), being more environmentally sound (by saving trees and even recycled paper, particularly the slick, glossy kind favored in reports), and actually giving the shareholder more, better, faster information.

"I hate the touch-tone phone menu system," says our anchor at *Marketplace*. What she means is that she hates systems poorly designed so you, the consumer and listener, flail away with the phone buttons, spelling things out while peering at tiny print, wondering what's coming in the menu, and having no way to repeat an item or reach a real person.

Dial 1-800-237-4273. You reach AETNA's line. You find the items — return on investment and earnings — easily accessible. You also find you can listen to comments from the chairman, get press releases faxed to you, and have access to other material much better written than the scrunched up traditional quarterly report. Plus you get the material *you* want, not what someone else thinks everyone should have.

Change promotes entrepreneurs, so we look with favor on new services such as Shareholder Direct, a Massachusetts firm that sets up these systems for companies such as IBM, Olin, and Conrail. They emphasize that interactive systems allow greatly expanded opportunities for a business to communicate with its investors. For example, a petroleum company used the system to communicate the details of a financial offering. A Florida bank used it to support the announcement of a direct stock purchase program.

This is akin to the changes in the banking systems, which have given us fewer tellers and branches (except in instances where the typically behind-the-curve Federal regulators step in, thinking they understand and can dictate the workings of the market when, of course, they do neither), but that means you can pay your bills at midnight and buy stocks at 6 a.m.

A caution: I said above a "well-designed system." I am particularly concerned about the need to be able to repeat items in the menu because verbal communication (which is what this mostly is, and it's verbal communication without props or a human being eyeballing you) is very poor at communicating facts, especially numbers. Repetition is key. Even matched with the dynamic that many listeners will be writing down the numbers and the faxed component, listeners need not only to be able to pick and choose but to hear it again.

As always, the ability to opt out of the system and talk to a human or at least leave a message that a human will return is the crucial element.

Quarterly reports — not just quarterly, not just reports anymore — provide a creative, innovative, cost-efficient way to communicate.

RESUME WRITING TO SELL

Most resumes should never be written. In those cases where you most think you need a resume, you probably don't. You need a different strategy.

Every editor has a seasonal article about college graduates or job hunters who can and cannot find jobs. The article varies from year to year depending on the media's view of the economy, but there are always obligatory quotes from job seekers who send out hundreds of resumes and get no nibbles. Most people say they need a resume when searching for a job.

I recently received a resume in the mail from someone who had apparently run a computer search of all firms with the word "communications" in the firm name, apparently thinking that this indicated companies that make telephones or install systems. His resume and cover letter told me that he was a defense department contractor, oversaw large contracts, and met quality training goals in aircraft manufacturing. Hard to see the relevance to a firm specializing in communication training and strategic consulting.

The inaccurate match indicates the job seeker isn't sophisticated enough to understand the difference between us and AT&T, or that he's too lazy to find out. It communicates that he is desperate. It tells me he hasn't developed job hunting skills, so I wonder how many other skills he hasn't developed.

It's no wonder that job seekers who send out hundreds of resumes are disappointed. It is hard to customize a resume for a company unless you are simply publicizing hard-to-find skills or achievement. "Headed team that developed Lotus Notes and wrote main programs" is a unique achievement. The person with that on his resume can develop one version, send it out, and wait to see what comes back. "Top proficiency with all word processing, spreadsheet, and legal research" is a combination of skills.

There are hundreds of books on how to write a resume and find a job. The job seeker should peruse them with skepticism. There are wide differences; one says, "put in personal references." Another says, "don't put in personal references, say they're available." But there are areas of common sense where there is wide agreement. Target companies in your field, and define the match between your skills and your prospective employer. Communicate the correct information in a resume that is clear, simple, easy to absorb at a glance, and shows your credentials in work and education.

This may be common sense, but it's ignored in at least half the resumes we see. Soft claims have risen to the stature of facts. Academic resumes are worst, with pages of titles of obscure articles published in highly technical journals.

Honors and civic work are appropriate as one rises in the corporation because it says that you're tapped for leadership projects and have developed a sense of how to position yourself and the corporation in the industry or community.

Personal information is not appropriate. One resume informed me the writer was 5′10″ tall, weighed 160 pounds, was a Weight Watcher graduate, and newly divorced. Shudder. Sex habits clearly follow.

The resume as a job-hunting device may be entirely displaced by the revolution in how companies define their core competencies. The downsizing of American and, to some extent, global corporations is more than shedding fat and unrelated divisions. It is a fundamentally different view of what constitutes a permanent need. Everything else can be outsourced. Two decades ago, outsourcing focused on personnel matters or data processing. Now it includes the CFO and the sales representatives. A person who is displaced by a revolution in philosophy will be handicapped in the job search by a resume written to obtain the job he is being displaced from and looking for a corporation organized the way his used to be.

A re-engineered strategy is to ditch the resume. Sign on immediately with a consulting, freelance, or executive temporary agency. They look for your next job for you. If it turns into a long-term job, and you've done well, there's a high probability it will be yours. If it's a short-term job, you move to the next one.

The message that needs to be communicated to the temporary agency is not one of achievement or skills. It's one of temperament — I'm flexible, will work for less, and will work hard.

New times. New vehicles. New routes. New messages.

MODEL MEMOS

"Just imagine being able to write a brief memo that jolts an often tardy employee into never being late for work." "Imagine writing a memo that inspires unprecedented effort and productivity in your people. Or one that spurs them to carry out a successful cost-cutting drive."

Just imagine? We would pay good money, big money for this. Business writing needs help. Seminars are booming, and where there's a need, there are self-help books. Prentice Hall's *Manager's Portfolio of Model Memos for Every Occasion* recently sent a flyer containing the quotes above.

It can be a useful book to get people to focus on what they want to say and how to get it across. But the "ready to use" memo (again quoting the book) that will "promptly put an end to the offensive behavior of a troublemaker" hasn't been written, or at least, it isn't in this particular book.

The memo that would "promptly put an end to the offensive behavior of a troublemaker" would have to go something like this: "Ed, mouth off at my staff again and you'll swim with the fishes. A tape of the *The Godfather* is attached to remind you of the details. Get the message before we get you. (Signed) Luigi 'the knife' Capello." A well-organized memo, of the sort in this and other books, can help communication, but it's not a guarantee.

Even if the claims are a little much, the need is great. Memos have a bad name because so many people write them poorly. They're too long, too boring, frequently pointless, badly organized, and there are just too many of them. But, happily, these are all problems which can be ameliorated, if not cured.

If you have too many memos, decree a reduction. It works wonders.

If memos are too long, make executives type their own. This is not a permanent or surefire solution. Many executives have mastered the typewriter or computer and discovered the joys of authorship.

Instill some basic reminders about communication. Who's the audience? What do I want them to remember? How many facts do they really need to know versus how many I can and would like to enumerate? Rewriting and editing are the best tools for good writing. If possible, get someone else to take a second look and react. If the person can't skim it, look up, and repeat it back to you, it's too confusing.

Some memos are bad because the writer never learned decent grammar. Run-on sentences, double negatives, and paragraph-long thoughts are really grammar problems as well as writing problems.

Some memos are horrible because the person is trying to use fancy words — "the committee was advised to congregate to take under consideration" — instead of simple ones: "the committee looked into."

There are some excellent books on writing, such as Barbara Minto's *The Pyramid Principle,* but they require that a person be able to read.

Many memos need to be broken up. That is, writing a memo is no different than a corporate newsletter. Today, a reader won't pore through columns of type appropriate in the 19th-century *New York Times.* Similarly, we won't wade through pages of single-spaced text. Shelaghmichael Lents, executive vice president and manager of Texas Commerce Bank's Retail Banking Department, needed to send a lengthy memo alerting her department's employees to discussions about the re-engineering planning. She came up with a four-page memo, which she knew people wouldn't take the time to read. She turned it into a two-page, back-to-back "Newsbrief," complete with quotes from departmental and corporate people.

I personally favor cartoons and headlines because they reproduce or scan easily and catch the eye.

Know What To Say To *Get Your Way!*

really gets my attention.

Notice that organizing memos doesn't assure results. It communicates well, which involves differentiation, affecting memory, and so on. Communication is a tool, often misused, which can help you be more effective. Miscommunication is frequently predictable and can be corrected. (For example, we have seen far too much material from human resource departments distributed in a way which ensures it will not be read or absorbed.)

There are many instances where memos are counterproductive or insufficient by themselves. Bad news or change should always be accompanied by a personal visit or by a group meeting so those affected have a chance to see and hear the executive responsible and to ask questions. (Even a televised meeting is preferable to just distributing memos, so those affected can see a few employees asking questions. Even if I can't ask a question, I can see that others can.)

Memos can be model communication, but model memos are only basic advice to learn from, not road maps or guarantees that you'll get to a desired destination.

> *"The next two big challenges for business are to enlist employees, via communication strategies, and to tap the networks of their own customers. Obviously, you have to have the right products and services to back up your claims, but communication training is the key that starts the engine."*
> — MERRIE SPAETH

COMMUNICATION TRAINING: I

Communication is one of the business buzzwords of the 1990s, but one of the most important ways to improve communication is frequently overlooked.

Communication training, which helps a company's employees understand how communication works, is in its infancy. It's where sales training was 40 years ago. Communication training can make a huge difference.

Here's an example from *Bank Marketing* magazine. A customer waited in a long line. A teller some distance off spotted her and offered to help. The woman was initially very favorably impressed. And the teller's actions reinforced the bank's advertising message about dedication to customer service. Unfortunately, when the customer asked for traveler's checks, the teller blurted out, "Oh no, just my luck. I hate doing traveler's checks." In this example, the good news — for the company's communication — was that the teller understood she was empowered and encouraged to approach the customer.

But the teller didn't understand the impact of an honest, offhand remark which undercut the advertising message. A little communication skills training would have prevented this problem.

Communication skills training can take as little as a few hours or as much as several days, depending on the level of the employee. Basically, sophisticated communication training today tries to accomplish several things.

First, it teaches the employee how to look at messages or information from the listener's point of view. That is, how to analyze what the listener will remember.

Second, training aims to give the employee the tools to monitor and improve his own skills over time. This is like the old joke, "How do you get to Carnegie Hall? Practice, practice, practice."

We believe communication should be driven by understanding how a person or audience *hears* certain things; what makes them *believe* certain things (and disbelieve others); and finally and most important, what makes that person or audience *remember* some things and not others.

This provides a method of analysis. We have seen many cost-cutting efforts flounder because senior management didn't understand communication. Oh, they were adept at saying "We really need to do this," and "This is important to the company." And those things were true. But top management wasn't willing to give up its bonuses, car allowance, or executive perks. The message to employees was that cost cutting was important but apparently not important enough to require cutting bonuses, etc. We are not arguing that executives cannot have bonuses and car allowances, but we are arguing that they need to understand how people receive and transmit information to make full use of communication as a strategic business tool.

Communication allows you to analyze other more traditional communication, such as advertising. We watched a positioning campaign fall flat because the producers didn't understand how people "hear." The ads used real quotes from the company's sales people talking about how they helped customers. The quotes were wonderful. But the ads were introduced by an announcer who sounded as if the last ad he recorded was for mattresses or used cars. The ad began and ended with music equally appropriate to a going-out-of-business sale. So it undercut the effectiveness of the agents.

With this as a foundation, communication training can go in many different directions. It can become crisis training. Using the media effectively during crises is very important. The reporter will want to ask all about the "fraud," "bankruptcy," "lawsuit," "layoff," or whatever. The spokesperson must be skilled enough to respond to the reporter's questions and to target his audience and reach them. For example, the reporter is likely to ask, "Were people killed?" and the short answer will be either "yes," "no," or "we don't know." The reporter needs to know when you might know. "We will be talking to the police in an hour." "We'll get back to you in a half hour." These are only the first level of communication. The spokesperson has to target the audience, probably employees, and communicate with them. "We are taking every precaution for our employees' safety." Or perhaps the audience is the general public. "We have an excellent safety record." Understanding how to deal with adverse situations where one must respond very quickly is a set of skills worth learning.

Communication can become negotiation skills, and these can have implications for sales training. For example, when a sales associate approaches you in a store and asks, "May I help you," you can answer "yes" or "no." "No" is not acceptable to the retailer, so we want to train the associate to reframe his or her questions to create a win-win situation. "I see you are looking at our new suits. I have some new blouses that look like silk. Would you like to see one now or would you like to look a little longer?" This gives the customer a "choice," but allows the sales associate to remain in control of the communication.

Training can help avoid problems. Physicians sit you down and say, "You're doing fine. Take three of these twice a day, two of these three times a day, and watch for symptoms of dizziness, nausea, and vomiting." Then, as you are trying to absorb it all, they ask, "Any questions?" Most of us say "no." We don't mean "no," but that's what we express. The busy physician thinks, "Good, no questions," and is out the door in a flash. You return home, still trying to absorb the instructions. Some people will actually experience dizziness, nausea, and vomiting just because the physician or nurse mentioned it.

As I mentioned above, communication helps us analyze the flow of information. In the scenario where you're a patient, you return home or to work and someone greets you, and you begin discussing how you feel. Somehow your friend or colleague mentions that his grandmother is taking the same medication but only once a day! You think — hmm, maybe if I took it only once a day, it might cost less, and I might have less chance of dizziness, nausea, and vomiting. The next day, you take the medicine only once, and it doesn't seem to make a difference. The next week, you see an article in the newspaper about how people taking this very medication are putting on large amounts of weight or experiencing impotence. So you cut it back to every other day. Again, to you there doesn't seem to be a difference. When you return for a checkup, the doctor discovers you aren't taking the medicine correctly, so he chides you in a patronizing tone of voice: "Now, Ms. Spaeth, we aren't doing what we're supposed to." You're angry, the doctor is angry, but this is really, in the phrase from *Cool Hand Luke*, a "failure to communicate."

Communication training looks at how messages travel between people and can be tapped to support the corporate strategic goal. For example, a company that can get its customers selling for it will be ahead of the competition. One step in this process is to enlist everyone in the company in the marketing effort. This is key from the company's point of view, and training is the platform or tool for getting you there.

When your employees are on board the program, they will enlist your customers. While training, Olympic bicyclist Lisa Fitch was hit by a truck, broke 26 bones, and fell into a fire-ant nest. When she was finally rescued and taken to a hospital, she was told she would never walk again. A year later, she was walking, bicycling, and competing. Today, she travels all across America to increase support for the country's bicycling teams and preaching safety messages. In the middle of one interview, the talk-show host asked her, "What was it like to be told you'd never walk again?" She began her reply saying, "I can't put it into words," and continued describing her state of mind at the hospital. But she didn't quit there; she said, "My physician brought me to Baylor, where they have a professional attitude and a team approach. They put me back together. I was just lucky to get to Baylor where there are real professionals." She then moved on to how much it meant to her to compete again.

The next two big challenges for business are to enlist employees, via communication strategies, and to tap the networks of their own customers. Obviously, you have to have the right products and services to back up your claims, but communication training is the key that starts the engine.

When a corporation devotes time and money to helping an employee improve, the company actually sends a strong message to the employee about his importance. You can't accomplish this in any memo from the chairman.

"No wonder this company was having trouble. They got what was basically a lecture and were left on their own." — STEVE HRONEC, ARTHUR ANDERSEN LLP, AUTHOR, VITAL SIGNS

Perceptions in the Workplace:
Reasons considered "very important" in deciding to take current job:

(Number 1) Open Communication	*65%*
(Number 2) Effect on Family/Personal Life	*60%*
(Number 15) Opportunity for Advancement	*37%*
(Number 16) Salary/Wage	*35%*

— FAMILIES AND WORK INSTITUTE

COMMUNICATION TRAINING: II

"Communication" risks becoming a word like "quality," a word everyone thinks they understand but which can divide rather than unite. A lesson from the quality movement is instructive.

Training can make the difference between wanting good communication and achieving good communication. Good communication is ranked as the number-one priority in a massive study done by the Families and Work Institute over a five-year period. "Open Communication" was cited by 65 percent of the respondents as "very important" in deciding to take their current job, scoring far ahead of traditional measures like salary, location, fringe benefits or even such hot, new topics as family supportive policies and quality of coworkers.

But there's no definition of communication. Many people think that just increasing the amount of information conveyed or interaction is increasing communication. But that's "communication" with no purpose or energizing philosophy. It's like eating without understanding nutrition. It goes down, but does it get you where you want to go?

Unfortunately, training is also a growth industry for people who can't find a job doing anything else. Although there are professional societies of training and development people, the quality of their services varies dramatically. Our advice on how to pick a firm or individual trainer is to try them on a trial basis and pay them. Companies that require a free session are really stealing the only thing a teacher has to offer — experience and time. (We do believe it's legitimate to arrange a special discounted fee for a pilot project when there is an honest intention to try to find an on-going fit with a service provider.)

Next, try two or three firms. There are a variety of approaches to communication training. Even specialty subsets of communication, such as sales training, have several different approaches. One company teaches traditional sales, including "how to close the sale" and "how to explain 'features' versus 'benefits.' " This works well in some fields, but for the professionals with whom we deal, it's out-of-date and can be counterproductive. Professionals are selling people, not Pontiacs, and the "sales" process is really one of creating and maintaining a relationship and differentiating yourself from the competition by using former clients, the press, your support material, and so on. Each company needs to find the right fit between approach and personality. (It's not "politically correct" to say it, but it's a fact of life that some top executives are not comfortable with minorities and women in counselling and training positions. One can work to change the world, but it's asking your training dollars to do two things if you're trying to get good training and change the world in the same session.)

Don't be impressed by a professor or an author. Professors and authors are wonderful. Almost any company operating in a global environment will find its money is well spent with Noel Tichy's program on global leadership at the University of Michigan. And Wharton's Ian MacMillan has a great deal to teach companies about entrepreneurship, creating entrepreneurial pockets within large corporations. But many companies hire professors or authors (or professors who are authors) and pay $10,000 or $15,000 a day without setting standards or understanding what they want for their money.

Steve Hronec, worldwide director of Arthur Andersen's Manufacturing Practice (and yes, it's true, also the author of *Vital Signs*), tells of leading a discussion in a major company about a quality initiative which was foundering. Hronec recalls that the group of high-level executives described a diagram drawn laboriously on a flip chart by a noted guru, but the executives couldn't recall what the diagram said or what they were supposed to do. "No wonder this company was having trouble," he observes. "They got what was basically a lecture and were left on their own."

Understand the difference between training and consciousness-raising or sessions designed to be thought provoking. Andrew Lebby, who lectures on why companies are "learning disabled" is a profound, entertaining, challenging speaker. Many companies need to hear his message. But it's a message, not a training session. It's up to the company to act on it.

Companies are trying to use technology to leverage talent and constrain costs, and there are indeed opportunities to do this. Video systems and television, when coupled with listener participation by audio, can reduce the barriers of distance. The benefits of technology are that it allows access for people who may not have had it before; well-designed interactive training allows people to work at their own speed and redo practice drills. But for "communication training," there's still no substitute for personal interaction and the ruthless critique that people give themselves when they see themselves on videotape. This is not just true for high-level executives, although it's a must for them because it allows them to begin to see themselves as others do. Poet Robert Burns' advice, now sadly forgotten along with many other aspects of Western Civilization, wrote, "O wad some Power the giftie gie us / To see oursels as ither see us!" Sales associates can use video and self-critique led by a gifted teacher to learn to critique themselves, incorporate a wide variety of skills, and model themselves on star performers.

Whether you call it sales training, presentation skills, showmanship or something else, when a corporation enlists every employee, it makes the whole corporation into a marketing and sales department. It is a key concept for the 1990s. Companies that articulate the importance of team players, empowered employees, and so on, but don't back it up with training, are placing their employees in a risky position. The employees *will* imitate someone, *will* pass on certain messages, and *will* communicate. But without training, the company will neither direct nor control it.

I AM NOT A CROOK

Some of the most famous quotes in history are negatives, such as "I am
not a crook." Reporters frequently quote negative replies, particularly
in an article that is hostile to the subject of that article. "The company
denied wrongdoing," is a favorite. It is self-defeating to pass along a
message that insists we are *not* something. Our listeners hear just the
opposite of what we're trying to communicate.

The "I am not a crook" comment was meant to be a ringing statement of the president's innocence. Instead, it sealed his fate.

Our speaking and communication instincts lead us to do exactly the
wrong thing. The hearing process has some peculiarities. Our ear frequently eliminates the word "not," so we frequently hear something
exactly opposite to what the speaker is trying to convey.

Part of this has to do with the importance of words in communication. Words are the levers that let us go back into memory and access
topics. So, although you are denying something, we seize on the word
anyway. What was Mr. Nixon's speech about? He talked about being a
crook. So, that's what we remember.

Another reason never to have a message of denial is that these phrases travel word for word. They are so memorable that one person repeats them, the next person repeats them, and so on. We see this frequently in companies. It's how rumors are spread. You say, "No, there are no layoffs planned." And before you can say "layoff" — poof, around the building is the rumor that there are layoffs.

Frequently, in these situations, someone else, like a reporter, has suggested the word. All you do is repeat it and deny it. My rule of thumb: When your first word is "no," stop and take a breath. Rather than falling into the trap of repeating the words someone else suggested, think about how to recast the question in a positive, affirmative light.

One reason for the problem is that we mimic the words of others. When a third party makes a charge against us — "They stole our secrets" — they have established the parameters of the debate by the choice of the word "stole." It is not enough to state, however emphatically, that "we did not steal their secrets," because it leaves the debate on the wrong topic and using the wrong words — "steal the secrets." In these cases, where the press is involved or in a courtroom where lawyers are involved, they are only passing along the charge that you "stole the secrets."

Lawyers and reporters frequently cause problems. Lawyers are trained to be meticulous in the wrong ways, at least for communication. They focus on narrowing the parameters of debate when one should be broadening them and substituting one image for another. Reporters are much more interested in bad news — fraud, complaints, layoffs, discrimination, failure — than in good news, so they eagerly arrive at your door with the questions on those topics.

The more untrue the charge, the more likely the respondent will get caught in the trap of denying it, thereby using the same words and unwittingly passing along the very terms he wished to erase. When something is indeed untrue, we become indignant, we resent the mere articulation of the words, and we want to stomp them out of existence. Unfortunately, we usually end up stomping them more into the listener's memory.

Each month brings some delicious examples, courtesy of the press. "I did not marry my husband for his money," insists 26-year-old model Anna Nicole Smith who married an 89-year-old Texas oil tycoon.

Deputy Treasury Secretary Roger Altman, dragged before a Congressional investigating committee says, "I did not lie to Congress."

National Security Advisor Anthony Lake defended a controversial deal for Haitian General Raoul Cedras. The United States offered to rent three houses owned by Cedras for $5,000 a month. Mr. Lake told reporters and the American people, "There is no bribe here; there is nothing hidden here; there are no hidden inducements." And to polish it off, he continued, "I am not apologetic in the slightest here."

The good news is that the technique of how to turn around evil words can be learned, and it's worth learning. Otherwise, you could end up like Jessica Hahn; she was "not a bimbo." And what word comes to mind to describe her?

A COMPANY'S GREATEST UNTAPPED RESOURCE — I

In the 1980s, companies went around selling off so-called hidden assets. Maybe in the second half of the l990s, businesses will discover a largely untapped asset — their employees. This discovery has particular relevance to companies that experience well-publicized problems.

Companies today are spouting the mantra that employees are their most important asset, but they do not take much time to enlist their employees as their prime communicators. Corporate America frequently acts as if communication is a one-shot, closed-end equation. You send a memo to an employee, do an article in the company publication, put an ad before the public, even do your annual report on video, but that's it. That approach neglects one of the most important aspects of communication — messages travel, that is, one person tells another person who tells another and so on.

A company's most important communicators *are* their own employees, but few companies realize this. Many do not provide the training to equip and motivate employees to see themselves as responsible for the company's communication. Getting the word out is not segregated in some box marked "advertising," "marketing," or "corporate communication."

Of course, each employee does communicate whether we like it or not. Sometimes their very silence communicates. For example, just after the scare about tainted meat sold by the fast-food chain Jack in the Box, I took my son, then five years old, into a Jack in the Box restaurant in Dallas. We wanted to see if the local employees would say anything about what happened in Seattle. The articles were still fresh in people's minds. Meat tainted with bacteria caused a rash of illnesses and at least one death. No one at the Dallas Jack in the Box made us feel particularly glad to be there. When I asked if business was down, the clerk just shrugged. When I asked if this store had taken any extra efforts to ensure its products were fresh, the clerk shrugged again.

She could have used verbal communication coupled with communication style. She should have *said*, "You bet. Besides reviewing our high standards for food quality and service, we want every customer like you to know we appreciate you letting us prove we deserve your business." Incidentally, they do. The curly fries are great, but stay away from the burgers. (Just kidding.)

She should have *looked* welcoming, with a smile.

As a rule of thumb in instances like these, the worse the situation and question, the more important to look friendly, animated, and even smile. It shows confidence, comfort with the material, and conveys honesty.

Food Lion, the supermarket accused of selling spoiled or outdated food, had a similar situation, that is, both these chains needed to respond to customers *locally* — not just through national spokesmen and the national press. Their employees needed to tell anyone who would listen that they had a great operation and needed a chance to prove how good they were.

This doesn't just apply to chains dealing with consumers on consumer goods. Price Waterhouse, one of the Big Six accounting and consulting firms, was savaged by Sam Donaldson on *Prime*TIME *Live* for allegedly charging the Resolution Trust Corporation (RTC) 67 cents a page for copying. Price Waterhouse subcontracted the copying work to another agency, which charged them a fraction of what Price Waterhouse charged the government. The implication was that Price Waterhouse dramatically overcharged the government and made millions of undeserved fees by finding a cheaper source. Price Waterhouse declined to be interviewed, so Donaldson reported, "Price Waterhouse declined to be interviewed by *Prime*TIME, but said in a statement that it has done nothing wrong."

Price Waterhouse should have participated in the story, but that's another issue. However, whatever their decision about the Sam Donaldson report, they should have enlisted all their people and equipped them to proactively talk to friends, family, clients, and prospective clients. The facts of the story had to be something like this: Price Waterhouse must have gotten the RTC job because they were the low bidder, or presented a low enough bid, coupled with their experience and reputation. *Their* story, delivered verbally, to target audiences should have been: "Whether you saw the awful story on Sam Donaldson's show recently, we want you to know the real story. We were hired by the RTC for a very large, complicated job that required careful attention to detail and security measures. Our bid was one of the most cost efficient (or the lowest), and we were chosen because of our bid and our extensive experience. We delivered on time and on budget despite significant cost overruns in some areas because we managed our costs in other areas. Our reputation is on the line with every job, and you know our clients come back to us because they find we can deliver in tough situations."

In other words, use the person-to-person networks of communication, whether the target audience saw the story or not. Why? Because someone at a client firm undoubtedly saw the story or heard about it. The best way to invalidate it is to use personal communication to present a competing, compelling image.

It takes courage and organization, but the old saying is correct. Every problem is actually an opportunity. Or, as Dale Carnegie put it, "Take the lemon, make lemonade."

To respond locally, a company needs a local communication strategy. A company needs to prepare its people and view them as a key link. A two-way system gets facts and talking points into the hands of the local spokesperson. Today's technology — the miracles of fax, voice mail, satellite, and Federal Express — make that easy.

Local contact with the local press is especially important because that's how the majority of Americans get information. And when something like the Jack in the Box scare happens, local press go right to a local outlet. When a local person talks to them, bad news can be contained, maybe even turned into positive news.

But local press needs to be reinforced by the verbal contact of local people. "Local" today means the people we talk to "in person," so "local" can mean talking to my suppliers or clients in distant cities.

The networks of communication are already there. They just aren't being used. Until companies truly regard employees as their most effective communication resource, they're wasting a valuable asset.

UNTAPPED RESOURCE: II

Putting crisis aside, a company demonstrates that it considers its employees its most important asset if it enlists them to promote the company — its mission, products, services, and place in the industry or community — no matter what their specific job. If a company doesn't do this, it is actually saying to its employees, "We trust you to process claims or weld doors, but we don't trust you to talk to anyone about what we do."

Creating what we call a *culture of communication* requires commitment from the top, absolute integrity from all stakeholders, and a willingness to invest for the long-term.

A culture of communication is not necessarily a selling culture, although companies exist to sell their products and services. Even not-for-profit organizations are selling something; they're selling their ideas or their abilities to perform a service or function. A culture of communication means that everyone in the company or organization feels a pride and responsibility for communicating something to some key audience without being told to. Employees are ultimately empowered to be the company's communicators, and they see themselves as a key part of an effort that includes advertising, marketing, collateral, the annual report, testimony before regulatory bodies, and any other "communication."

The world's businesses can learn something from the uniquely American direct-marketing companies. Mary Kay, Amway, Avon, and others have created a culture married to a system that generates enthusiastic participation from all employees.

There is no magic pill or consulting manual to automatically create a culture of communication, but there are some obvious steps for the communicating company to take. First, there is almost a constant stream of various kinds of communication flowing out to employees. Second,

193

the communication is varied, including financial information. The tone is personal. That is, the very organization of the material communicates accessibility to the employees.

Employees are encouraged to pass the information on to others. "Encouragement" methods are limited only by the creativity of individuals, which is to say, one important way to encourage employees is to ask them to represent the company. In most companies, the management never asks the employees to talk about the company. In fact, the informal but clearly heard message is "Don't talk about us." The reasons are, of course, that the company doesn't trust the employees to "get it right."

Two-way communication appears to be an important component of the communicating company. There are regular meetings, conferences, feedback mechanisms, and so on. And the management takes seriously what the employees tell them.

Status differences are not disabling in communicating companies. Sometimes this manifests itself by low-level employees calling the CEO by his first name. Sometimes it's detected by employees of a much lower level offering a critique or guidance to a higher level employee, and the critique is received respectfully. The higher level person responds to the comment or suggestion. This doesn't always mean the higher level person accepts the comment or acts on it. But reflection, respect, and reporting back create the ongoing loop that signals both parties are equals in communication contribution.

Recognition or reward — not by any means at the same time — identifies the culture of communication. The company newsletter or E-mail carries positive reinforcement of the deed or act. For example, a teller at one bank was taking a deposit from a customer. The teller saw the person had an exceptionally large amount of cash in a savings account that had a very low rate of interest, and the teller took it upon himself to tell the customer that the bank could be far more helpful. The teller asked if the customer would take just a few moments to chat with someone from the Capital Markets Department. As a result, the customer delivered almost a million dollars to the bank to invest. The teller didn't need to be an expert in asset allocation or know who's a candidate for small capital funds, which typically invest in smaller companies, but the teller did need to know enough to know that this much money in a savings account probably meant the customer wasn't paying attention to his investments. And, most important, the teller needed to be proud enough of the bank to tell the customer that the bank could help.

Punishment must be avoided in cases of failure or screwup. This teller also had to feel secure that if the customer bit his head off and complained, the bank would back him up and understand. The teller's reward here? A public handshake and letter of recognition. And that was enough.

Behavior like this on the part of a company sends the message to employees, customers, and others that the employees are indeed the most important asset. Then the employees behave in a way to live up to that standard.

Most of all, an outsider can spot a culture of communication when introduced to someone. An employee of Southwest Airlines is likely to say they work for Southwest Airlines and tell you something about it — their number-one market position, their on-time record, their unique culture as a place to work.

Other companies that want to be number one could learn a lot from communicating companies

DEALING WITH THE DIFFICULT EMPLOYEE

Every office has one. The person who is just hard to get along with. They never seem willing to help out; they're sour, always willing to blame someone else, and resist change. The temptation is to tell them to get with the program or get a grip. The temptation for a supervisor is to ignore them or try to work with others or unload the difficult person on someone else. It requires more work and mental effort to deal with these people, and we feel we just don't have time.

That's a risky strategy. The employee almost certainly has value, and human assets are so important that they should be salvaged whenever possible. In addition, the litigious nature of our society makes removing someone for something as subjective as being "difficult" risks a lawsuit charging discrimination or harassment.

There are some useful steps to take before throwing up one's hands. First, try to understand the reasons behind the difficult behavior. A person who is recalcitrant or rude because they have watched others being promoted needs communication help coupled with a career planning session. Someone else may have problems on the home front and need counseling. Many people have just gotten into bad habits of behavior around other people; these habits can frequently be broken or

196

changed. One study of more than 9,000 managers and professionals found many difficult people were perfectionists who held themselves and others around them to unreasonable standards.

Despite my dislike of attorneys and how they wreak havoc in the workplace, they usually advise documenting or recording your interaction and what you observe working with Hateful Harry on a day-to-day basis. This is useful, if for nothing else, to organize your own thoughts so discussions don't become opportunities to trade barbs.

At many large companies the personnel department can be extremely helpful. Smart companies use their personnel or human resource departments the way they regard their financial advisors, to develop their assets to the fullest, to protect against loss, and to have the right resources for the task needed. A shorthand way to assess if your personnel department is up to being an advisor and providing assistance is to look at how they communicate. Did they give you information about your new self-managed 401(k) plan in a three-inch-thick binder with multiple attachments? Are their memos and presentations laden with numbers, boring, and generally not helpful? If so, they aren't focused on good communication.

However, if the personnel department is the force pushing the humor seminars, if they're giving you the 401(k) information on single sheets (as Alcoa does) or with interactive videos, if they are the leader in figuring out how to recruit (as Arthur Andersen is), they are very likely to be the first place to stop for help in creating a plan to rescue the difficult employee. If the personnel head is viewed as a real leader whose own employees revere him, start here. (For example, the top employees in personnel at Federal Express produced an in-house videotape for a meeting showing their boss, Jim Perkins, in various scenes as a lion leading the pride, a elephant leading the herd, and an eagle soaring. Then they gave him a papier-mâché lion headdress to wear.)

A number of workshops and seminars can be extremely effective in changing the behavior of the difficult employee. Stephen Covey, who wrote *Seven Habits of Highly Effective People,* and Lance Lager, who teaches self-renewal, lead worthwhile seminars. One of the Big Six accounting and consulting firms keeps a full-time psychologist on staff to work individually with people so they reach their full potential and don't let unproductive personal habits derail promising careers.

On a very personal basis, a few things we frequently forget to do contribute to stresses and strains in the workforce and aggravate relationships. They include smiling at coworkers, thanking them, recognizing and acknowledging accomplishments, and stopping to take note of personal moments, such as birthdays and anniversaries. Although these sound trivial, they are the source of many employees' complaints that fellow workers don't care about them.

We mimic the behavior of those around us. A smile to the obnoxious person, even if he doesn't deserve it, can soften a demeanor over time.

A final tool that can prove useful is videotaping employees interacting in various settings within a training or skills improvement framework. We have witnessed dramatic changes in people's behavior when they see and critique themselves and their own communication abilities. This is because there is a huge gap between how we think we're behaving and what our actions look like to someone else. It's akin to listening to yourself on tape and feeling that couldn't possibly be you. This technique works best to cure bad habits that have built up over years but only if the individual in question is fundamentally honest because it requires a person to critique himself.

Videotape is coming into its own as a training tool, and our recommendation is very similar to the productivity improvement methods recommended by someone like Dave Miller, president of Lemco Miller. He videotapes tool setup processes at milling work centers to discover wasted motions. He lets management and workers look at the tape, which provides a much better way to learn than lectures or workbooks. Even though the viewers are watching themselves, they are watching objectively.

There are no simple answers, magic bullets, or one-shot, one-size-fits-all answers, but there are a variety of options that can make a big difference.

THE DIFFICULT BOSS

The only thing worse than the impossible employee is the impossible boss. We have all experienced them during our working lives. The boss who searches through our drawers or mail. The nasty, argumentative, verbally abusive boss who is smart enough not to be sexually abusive since there are laws against that but not laws against nastiness. Other bosses are known to scream and throw things. I had a boss who threw an ashtray at me once. (He missed.) And another, a news director for a New York City TV station, who got mad at a blurb on "Page Six," the gossip page of the *New York Post*. My boyfriend at the time worked for the *Post* in the circulation department, so the news director called to scream at me. He told me to tell the *Post* that this was in return for their unfair comments and he fired me.

How do you deal with them?

First, distinguish between difficult and evil. The screamers, throwers, and perennially nasty people — there's hope for them. The truly evil people — the abusive, the people who stick it to you behind your back, the ones who can't stand to see someone under them succeed, the ones who belong on Death Row — are the truly evil. Orchestrate your way out of their clutches as quickly as possible, but as you do so, keep a daily log of the outbursts, drawer rifling, threats, put-downs, and so on. You do not want to get in a verbal brawl, nor do you want to bring the lawyers in, despite your boss's unfairness and the moral truth of your position. In those cases, the victim is always hurt as badly or worse than the perpetrator. However, a day-by-day log will help organize your comments, and more important, it presents the picture of truth (frequently, much more important than truth itself). If you are lucky enough to work in a company where the personnel or human resources departments are

DILBERT reprinted by permission of United Feature Syndicate, Inc.

truly strategic players, they may be enlisted to help you remove yourself to safer ground.

"Isn't this giving in to the bad behavior?" asks "Marketplace's" morning anchor, Debra Baer. Yes, it is, but again, short-term self-preservation and advancement are usually the right course for the individual. It is true that in the case of the Sunbeam Corporation, it was reported that the board of directors was confronted by an ultimatum from a group of top managers detailing CEO Paul Kazarian's temper outbursts and behavior. The memo said, "It's us or him," and the board chose the managers. We can only imagine how long it took the executives in the company to reach the point of undertaking that strategy, and it's rare the board will not back the managers.

Before one gets to that point, there are ways of proceeding that may be helpful. There are actually many communication pitfalls which aggravate dealing with the difficult boss and which can be corrected. We tend to respond to nasty behavior with equally nasty behavior or by withdrawing into a protective shell of coolness. This is understandable but counterproductive. The best communication stance is to respond with pleasant facial expressions, enthusiasm (but not gushing), and warmth. This may loosen up the difficult person and will certainly shake him enough to break his rhythm.

Verbal communication techniques can be helpful, too. Approach him with comments like "*We* need to work together" rather than the *you* versus *me* syndrome. "You," the bad boss, are obnoxious whereas "I," the good employee, am perfect. This will not help. After establishing that this is "us" who are in it together, identify the "challenges" or "areas to improve" rather than the "problems" or "bad habits." The latter invariably provokes defensive reactions and explanations. One of the real virtues of a personal discussion is to send the signal that you are not accepting the person's behavior, will not ignore it, and will stand up for yourself. You'd be surprised how this can change someone's attitude about you.

There are a number of approaches for the difficult boss. Many organizations today offer seminars ranging from assertiveness training (for you) to team building, organizational dynamics, or executive coaching (for the boss). These can work miracles if the trainer or training organization is good, *if* the boss has some intellectual honesty, and if the corporate culture is generally more good than bad. Despite the three "ifs," this does happen frequently enough to keep the training business booming. The best reference for trainers, consultants, and seminars are previous clients. The best attitude is to remember the old "If at first you don't succeed, try, try again." It can take time to get through to someone and change old, bad habits.

Usually the first question is "Why can't I go to my boss's boss?" You can find experts to argue both sides of this, but the communication message of doing that is mixed. On one hand, one can argue that you show initiative and guts to do that, but on the other, the conclusion can be that you cannot manage the situation by yourself. Plus, it's one more thing for the boss's boss to handle. More people are likely to come to the negative conclusion than the positive one.

Again, as with employees, sometimes videotaping behavior can produce dramatic results. (Just as psychiatry today includes a group of practioners who produce quick results, we belong to the school of thought that champions the need for short-term gains. First, because it makes things better right away. Next, it produces positive value. Finally, short-term differences can actually affect the long-term effort and prognosis. However, we would be the first to admit this doesn't always work. It requires a fit between the trainer or coach and boss. Also, the executive needs to be honest enough to examine his own behavior as a third party.)

A few things not to do: Don't become difficult yourself. That is not a solution and sows the seeds of failure for you and your colleagues. However, you needn't suffer in silence or righteous isolation. The problem is widespread enough to be of concern to every organization and to generate books on the topic. *Coping with Difficult Bosses*, by Robert Bramsom, will give you hundreds of pages of instructive ideas and examples.

If none of this works or looks appealing, there's always the competition for the "Worst Boss" run by the 9to5, National Association of Working Women. There are many variations of the competition for the coveted award of the Worst Boss (coveted by the boss's employees). Some past winners include: a Cleveland boss who asked his secretary to deliver his stool sample to his doctor and a New York physician who demanded his nurse return to work after she had just found her children's babysitter dead at her house. Your boss could be next.

Part V

TIPS FOR THE
OUTSTANDING SPEAKER

THE INTRODUCTION

Most of us have been to speeches and cringed — not at the speech, but at the introduction of the speaker. It was boring, too long, or it was clear the person introducing the speaker didn't know much about him. The introduction is really a mini-speech.

We may not all be asked to give keynote speeches to large groups, but almost every executive has to introduce someone else. It's an art form, and most people don't spend the time to master it.

An introduction is a crucially important part of the overall program. At a conference where I was supposed to act as moderator of the plenary sessions with a special challenge of summarizing each speaker's main points, I was to be introduced by a top executive. He led off the program but wasn't prepared enough to know how long it would take him to cover his material. He ran 20 minutes over his time, suddenly looked at his watch and just stopped. He didn't wrap up his speech, and he didn't give his introduction explaining who I was and why I was there. He just said, "Here's Merrie Spaeth," and walked off. As I walked up to the podium, our program already way behind schedule, I faced 700 people who didn't know me or my purpose. I needed my introduction to set up my role for the next three days.

Besides not skipping the introduction entirely, here are some other things to avoid: Don't just recite the speaker's resume. Boring, boring, boring — and probably not relevant to why he's there or what he will discuss. Most people don't care where he went to college, how long he's been at the company, or which regional divisions he managed.

Don't gush about how wonderful the speaker is. Nothing is worse than hearing someone say, "This is the most exciting speaker I've ever heard." How can anyone live up to that?

Don't make other gratuitous comments: "I don't know our speaker very well," or "I can't stay for the speaker's speech" (then why should we?). These are both real examples.

Don't read from a prepared text without looking up and interacting with the audience just as you'd do if you were the speaker.

What to do: Get the speaker's resume or biography, and ask for copies of past speeches or clips where the speaker was interviewed. If he's a CEO, look at the annual report and read the CEO's letter to shareholders. (He probably didn't write it, unless you're lucky enough to be introducing Warren Buffet, but it will give you an idea of what the CEO thinks he sounds like.) Find out what organizations and charities he supports. Now you know more about him.

Use quotes, stories, and comments. For example, if your speaker is a real doer, remember Theodore Roosevelt's moving comment about the rare man of action who gets things done. You can quote someone recognizable, your next-door neighbor, the morning paper, or even the speaker. The function of a "quote" is to break up the speech (or in your case, the mini-speech) and to reenforce a point you are making. Those who say, "I never use quotes" might as well say, "I never read," or "I'm above learning anything from anyone else."

Relate directly to the speaker. I saw a banker introduce another banker who had a law degree. The introducer turned directly to the speaker and said, "John, I see you got a law degree before you decided to get a real job."

Comment on the topic. If the speaker is to address world trade, you can say it wasn't so long ago that long distance meant the next town or state.

Look for personalizing, humanizing nuggets. For example, one executive was responsible for an internal audit at a large company. This is never a popular function, although it's a necessary one. The executive was speaking to a group of top managers to admonish them about following the rules and the consequences of cutting corners. Again, not a popular topic. The person charged with introducing him reminded the audience that the executive raised show dogs and had a dozen four-legged residents inside his house. "How organized can someone be with 48 paws to wipe each time it rains?" he asked the group.

There is no set length of time for an introduction. Someone who is going to speak for five minutes should have a 30-second introduction; someone who's about to give a 50-minute address could have a four-minute buildup.

Finally, you must practice. Just like a speech or presentation, you're part of the program. You're on display and being judged. Consider it an opportunity and demonstrate your talent.

TELL AN ANECDOTE

Anyone with children knows the familiar plea, "Tell me a story." Businesses that want to communicate and that *should* communicate about important issues, need to learn to tell a lot of stories or anecdotes, often about the tribulations or successes of individual people.

Business clients frequently tell me, "We need to educate the public," or regulators or whomever about a particular issue. I applaud that because I believe business doesn't spend enough time making the case that a market-driven economic system provides the most benefits for everyone. Making this kind of argument to the public is very different from short-term lobbying of elected officials or regulators for this or that position.

However, it's a very tough job to actually educate people. People don't remember facts. They don't sift through all the alternatives and make the most *rational* choice. And they don't respond to discussions of market forces and regulatory costs. Do we really need to *educate* them? Or do we need to *motivate* them? If the latter is the case, it's key to remember that what affects people and what motivates them are the experiences of other people. The public policy debates that have a dramatic impact on business are fought that way — not by fact but by anecdote. A good example is the perennial debate on unemployment.

Politicians in favor of expanding benefits often tell a story about a man and his wife who lost their jobs. They had three kids. The kids had to drop out of little league baseball. The family had a dog; the dog was starving because the kids were eating the dog food. Those against extending benefits too frequently try to convince us with facts; it cost too much. Business couldn't afford it, and market forces would ultimately solve the problem. Guess who wins? Not market forces.

Virtually all consumer product safety regulation has come about through the publication of anecdotes about people who have been injured. The child whose hand has been severed by the lawn mower appeals to our compassionate natures. Businesses have tended to defend themselves by again arguing cost, or by pointing out that the machine has a label that says four-year-olds shouldn't use it or that the equipment should be turned off before one feels around for an obstruction under the blade. These are all true, but they can't compete with the image of the wounded child. We see ourselves in the one individual, so that's where our sympathy lies.

What's the answer? Business needs to present its case with anecdotes. National health insurance? Here's a small businessman with a print shop and 25 employees. Competition is fierce. Washington and the states kept expanding Medicaid, so his insurance premiums doubled, since insured patients subsidize Medicaid. He thinks his employees would rather have a job than health insurance, so he drops his health insurance. The result is 25 more uninsured people. And this is a real example. (Anecdotes need to be true, otherwise you need to admit they are composites or hypothetical.)

The *Wall Street Journal's* editorial page is particularly good at using anecdotes to illustrate its political philosophy. The *Journal* believes many regulations ostensibly designed to promote safety actually serve to keep new entrants out of a market and that minorities suffer most from such barriers. To illustrate this, the *Journal* found a young African-American resident of Washington, D.C., who had learned to braid hair. She had a thriving hair-braiding business in a very poor neighborhood. Her future looked bright. Along came the city's Board of Cosmetology, which decreed that she must have a license to "do" hair and a license is obtained only after a year at cosmetology school. The young hair braider protests that she doesn't have tuition for a year, and besides, she doesn't work with the chemicals that other hairdressers do. In fact, the hairdressing schools don't even teach hair braiding, and all she wants to do is braid hair! The board is immovable. Exit from the workforce one hair braider.

By this example, the *Journal* reveals the hypocrisy of the board's "safety" regulations.

Some people believe, as an article of faith, that numbers are information. In 1994 there was an excellent example of a company that tried to use numbers to argue its position, thereby providing me with a cautionary anecdote about the strategy of explaining via numbers.

As you will recall in "We Messed Up" (page 44), the Intel Corporation ("Intel Inside") Pentium chip had a characteristic that caused it to very rarely miscalculate. (The first hint of trouble for Intel should have been when the media started calling this a "flaw.") For months Intel denied it was a problem. Then they advanced the argument that this characteristic occurred only once in billions of calculations. In hindsight, they were correct in their facts and correct in their assessment that this was of no concern to the vast majority of business and individual users. Unfortunately, the debate really wasn't about the statistical calculation of how often the chip might produce incorrect calculations. It was about "dependability," and the concept of dependability is defined in the mind of the user. When your electricity goes off, you are not comforted by the thought that it has been on for months. The issue was also about trust, and Intel squandered the trust of the consumer by its denials and debates.

Bottom line: Business should bring issues alive. Forget the tables, graphs, and bar charts. Find the hair braider on your side of the issue, and tell us all about her.

BUT I CAN'T TALK WITHOUT OVERHEADS!

When IBM got a new chairman, the corporate community got an advocate for modern communication. Panic may sweep corporate America if IBM becomes a trendsetter.

The headline read "IBM's New Chairman Shuns Tradition." Not only did Lou Gerstner dispense with IBM's traditional decision-making committees, he asked managers to talk to him without slides or overheads. One IBM official lamented that this was "like asking Paderewski to give a concert without a piano." Was it really? No.

Mr. Gerstner asked people to develop new habits of communication. People persuade people. Overheads and slides frequently detract from the speaker rather than enhance his message. Overheads filled with numbers or words are especially damaging. The audience starts to read them or tries to figure them out — and stops listening to the speaker.

Overheads become a substitute for preparation and rehearsal. Our own brochure uses a quote from a client saying, "Of course I'm ready for my presentation. I have 100 overheads." If he had 200, would he be twice as ready?

Of course, overheads can be a very useful tool — *if used correctly.* Some kinds of overheads are especially clear, such as bar charts that show a trend. So when the speaker says, "Here are our sales for the last eight quarters," the bars show a clear up — or down — trend.

Other graphically comparative charts make a point. "Our pension fund was only 30 percent funded 10 years ago," so on the screen flashes a pie chart with three of 10 pieces colored to represent percent liability funded. "Today, our fund is almost 80 percent funded." The pie chart has eight of 10 slices colored. The visual impact will be significant.

211

By permission of Jerry Van Amerongen and Creators Syndicate

Mr. Gerstner may not like overheads (which IBM employees mysteriously refer to as "foils") because they are so frequently used incorrectly; that is, as a substitute for clear, personal communication. Too many speakers use overheads *hoping* the audience will look at the overheads rather than at them.

The speaker should put the slide up, and wait for the audience to absorb it. It takes several seconds for your listeners to look at it. The test is to sit in the audience and let someone else put up your overhead and time how long it takes you to grasp what it's telling you.

Overheads with only words work, although they tend to be overused. My own rule: Use only the words or phrases that you want listeners to remember. The overhead lets them hang in the air.

Anything that enhances a visual impression is also okay. I just saw a banker who wanted to point out that middle-market companies have a lot of business worth getting. So he said, "Recognize these companies?" Up came the logos — no one had a clue who the companies were. Then he showed a slide with the millions of dollars those companies had brought the bank.

Notice that in these examples the speaker uses the overheads almost as a partner, directing attention back and forth between him and the overheads. He is not just repeating what's on them. He's using them as a memory enhancer and to distinguish himself from other speakers.

To do that effectively, the speaker really needs to use other devices also — flip charts, props, video.

Overheads and slides offer an important opportunity to include humor, the element most lacking in communication today. Paul Dunn of Arthur Andersen frequently lectures on how to go about re-engineering projects. He has an overhead with a picture of a howling baby and the phrase "The only person who really likes change is a wet baby." Not only does it always get a laugh, but it says to the group or audience that it's all right to be nervous or suspicious about corporate change.

Overheads and slides also offer interactive capabilities but speakers rarely use them to their fullest capacity. For example, Len Podolin, head of Tax Quality and Standards for Arthur Andersen, began a speech saying, "I couldn't figure out what to call these remarks." The slide behind him said, "Who cares?" The audience laughed. Podolin turned around, ostensibly to see what had provoked the laughter. By that time, of course, the screen was blank again.

Jim D'Agostino, CEO and President of American General Life and Accident, was talking to sales managers about the changes in corporate practices and made a comment about different people wanting different kinds of rewards. The slide behind him said "MONEY." Again, the audience laughed. He turned. The screen went blank. The audience laughed again.

These techniques do require some minimal level of rehearsal. But who was it who said something about how to get to Carnegie Hall? Was it Paderewski? He could have.

We're interested to see how IBM officials interpret Mr. Gerstner's instructions. We bet the risk takers start using props, video, and even humor. Then Mr. Gerstner will be able to see if people get the message that the corporate traditions and culture need to change.

THE PERFECT SPEECH

"What would be the perfect speech?" asked one client. It depends on the circumstances, the target audience, and the objectives. Still, a model of the perfect speech might be the address given by Ann Rogers, executive vice president for human resources at Houston-based Texas Commerce Bank (TCB). "Perfect" in this case means all the elements of a fully integrated multimedia program are included; the speech differentiated the speaker and the speaker's organization; and the substantive material in the speech was advanced by the speaker's remarks and supported by the components.

TCB is recognized for its aggressive program of employee empowerment and satisfaction and for being the only Texas bank which survived the banking debacle (although TCB did merge with Chemical Bank). It is also recognized for handling a number of acquisitions while undertaking a major in-house re-engineering effort that resulted in millions of dollars of permanent cost savings.

Rogers is a private person. She accepted the invitation to address an industry group because it would tell TCB's success story. She was especially concerned because her presentation would only be one of many during a conference that took place over several days. (Conferences are death to memorable communication.)

She began by composing an outline of the topics she wanted to cover, which quickly expanded into a bare-bones outline of her remarks. She added the obvious slides depicting number, movement, or change. (Employee Satisfaction Overview of Results. TCB's quality customer service to clients rose 19 percentage points. TCB cares about the satisfaction of its employees; up 18 percentage points. TCB backs up its commitment with training; up 16 percentage points.)

She noted the comments or sections that she felt warranted pulling out, and then added a paragraph from the mission statement and words like "trust" to the slides.

Then she enlisted a team of advisors, internal and external, to help her. They suggested ways to start the speech: a picture of the bank when it first started — predictably, a group of primarily white, male executives, which would contrast dramatically with her point of how the work force and clients had changed and how the bank had to change to serve them. What about some recognizable movie clips showing "old" banking? The scene from *It's a Wonderful Life*, where Jimmy Stewart pleads for his customers and the banker retorts, "What is this? A charity?" She also liked the scene from *Mary Poppins* where Mr. Banks brings his children into the bank and the stiff, unapproachable executives come around the corner and confront them. A few seconds of both clips were written into the draft. (Neither studio would give permission to use the clips, despite the nonprofit status of the convention, so the clips were dropped.)

A variety of other illustrative material flowed out. Cartoons and articles with headlines like "Banking in Crisis" were found to illustrate other points about the major changes in the overall banking and work environment referred to in the speech. Additional quotes and comments from experts, customers, and others added third party validation. Some of those found their way onto slides.

The next review of the slide tray showed that it was growing too quickly, so some of the quotes came out and went on poster board, which would be displayed on easels around the room.

Video was the next target. A short clip illustrating "Commercial Blitz" days shows TCB employees paying calls on customers and target customers, which supported the section about how marketing is everyone's job. It also supported the contention that humor is an important part of team building. Some team leaders shed their bankers suits on stage (revealing the "team" clothes underneath).

Anecdotes and personal illustrations followed naturally. Rogers had called on a company that makes holes. Holes, Inc. drills large holes in concrete for office buildings and other large projects. Holes, Inc. needed letters of credit and other banking services. Rogers found that they also had major concerns about safety and worker training, concerns she dealt with every day. She had an excellent visit, and felt she could make a contribution to the company personnel's knowledge, and that she added real value to TCB's claim that it is a business advisor to its clients. Holes, Inc., became one of her anecdotes, and the Holes, Inc., business card became a slide.

She was still searching for more video components; the bank's television ads were the natural addition. They were already done. They supported her point about the importance of being customer focused, since the ads use real bankers and real customers discussing real needs.

Her concern now was to demonstrate how challenging change is, and how it starts with a fundamental examination of a value system, so she excerpted part of a self-administered test designed to determine values. During the actual speech, she handed out the test. She also decided to bring in one of her vice presidents to do the introduction and summary. They allotted 10 minutes for audience members to do the test, and five for the summary. This introduced audience interaction, audience participation, and a second person in the presentation. It also introduced a series of props, since she held up, the various tools TCB was using to help its own employees change their views and improve their skills.

Props also included the bright red ribbons handed out for superior work or attitude. These supported her comments about reward systems and also about cultural change, since one of the comments was that the support staff initially received and displayed the ribbons while the executives viewed them as gimmicks. Over the months, however, executives started to receive, display, and then covet the awards, which now are widely seen at all levels.

Props also included bank credit cards, one of which was cut up and taped back together, illustrating her point about the employees' ability to spot areas of improvement. The bank had routinely issued PULSE cards (automatic money cards) to all customers. But customers of the international division rarely needed or used them, so the secretaries cut them up, but then taped them back together so they could account for them in internal audits. This senseless but time-consuming procedure actually cost the bank $100,000 a year. The secretaries pointed it out, recommended the elimination, and benefited from the savings.

Rogers now had a truly multimedia speech, in which she and her vice president were part of the overall presentation. Her final steps were to rehearse several times with all the components, pack them all into a suitcase, and climb on the plane. She reported after the conference that numerous people stopped her to tell her how much they enjoyed her comments, got good ideas from them, and how welcome they were after a long series of decent speakers who blended into each other after a few hours. She didn't feel perfect, but she was perfectly effective. And that's the goal today.

> *"The listener will tolerate a great many flaws in 'presentation' if a message is clear, concise, and tailored to a specific audience."* — MERRIE SPAETH

YOU DON'T HAVE TO BE PERFECT

A client recently said, "Merrie, you'll never make me into a good communicator." He was wrong. The idea isn't to be perfect. The test should be *"Did you get the right message to the right person? Was it remembered? Was it acted upon?"* The listener will tolerate a great many flaws in "presentation" if a message is clear, concise, and tailored to a specific audience, and if it includes anecdotes and information pertinent to the listener.

Conversely, a speaker can be "perfect" — great eye contact, confident body language, expansive hand gestures, smiling face, resonant voice, twinkly eyes — and be a disaster. If all you remember is the person looked and sounded good, then you had an entertainment session. Being a good entertainer can be part of communicating; in some circumstances, it can be an important part. But it's not *what* you are communicating.

We did a two-day seminar for one of the Big Six accounting and consulting firms. Our job was to acquaint them with the importance of communication as a strategic tool, to work with their presentations, reports to clients, and so on based on our research about what a listener remembers. I was taken aback when the head of the worldwide practice asked me at the last minute, "Can you do something about the way they look?"

This is, in negotiating training, an "A or B" question, where the speaker offers you two choices and clearly expects you to pick one. This is the "yes or no" version of the "A or B" question, and the speaker (or the listener, if there is a third-party listener like a jury or a reporter) expects to hear "yes" or "no." The speaker in this case expects to hear "yes." The actual answer, alas, is "no." How to meet both our needs? I answered "Yes. I can add someone to the session who can."

That someone turned out to be a manager from the Jos. A. Bank company. Finding him took a half dozen phone calls and produced turndowns from five other men's retail clothing stores. Apparently, they'll talk to you if you come into their stores, but it's not worth their time to come to you. On the appointed day and hour, a nice looking man arrived with a slide tray and a script.

The script was quite good, but it was single-spaced and stapled together, and he read from it, forcing his head down. Any text which is read loses its spontaneity. The slides were also quite good and the presentation, apparently available for any Jos. A. Bank manager, had some humor, but any slide presentation which goes on and on will become monotonous. So far, so bad.

But this story has a happy ending. After about a minute, the Jos. A. Bank manager glanced at a slide and said, "This reminds me of a story" and told of an experience helping a customer update his image slightly. A few slides later, the manager said, "Let me describe whether these shirts would be appropriate for a few of you," and he picked out people in the group. A few slides later he said, "Shoes! I'm not going to embarrass anyone, but I want you to look at your shoes and look at your belt while you're at it. Ask yourself what you would think of someone wearing those shoes and that belt? Does it look as if he dresses with care?" Every single partner stared intently at his shoes, then hooked a finger under his belt and studied it.

When their eyes returned to the screen, the manager resumed reading the script until he had another thought triggered by a slide.

A presentation skills class would give this speaker bad marks, but he was very good. My test is that the next day, I asked the group what they learned, and they all had several things they found valuable to them. I asked if they planned to stop at Jos. A. Bank, and they all said they did. One reported that he had talked to his wife in the evening, and in describing the day, he had mentioned the Jos. A. Bank presentation. His wife told him they received catalogs from the company and that she would mark things for him.

The group was pleased, and the company should be pleased with its investment of time. I asked the group if they would like to hear from Jos. A. Bank again or recommend to their colleagues that they invite a speaker from the store, and the endorsement was unanimous.

A physician for a major hospital was asked to speak to one of the country's largest Rotary Clubs. The doctor, a nationally known specialist, agreed and the public relations staff agreed to help him redo and update his slides and presentations. The PR staff wanted to encourage the doctor to do more speeches to general or business groups as a way of promoting the hospital's prominence and experts.

The physician agreed to "update" and "tailor" his presentation for nonmedical groups, but then refused to change a single slide. The PR staff had lobbied to take advantage of technologies like PowerPoint which can make slides more colorful, appear to be animated, and add a wide variety of possibilities to a presentation. This sounded fine in the beginning, but the end product was the same, crowded slides done in color on PowerPoint.

The physician went off with his slide tray and his 80 slides. (He had also been introduced to a laser pointer with the result that many of the slides looked as if lightning bugs were inexplicably attracted to them.) Again, a presentation skills review would give the doctor low marks. The slides were too crowded and too much information was presented.

But the audience felt he was a success. He was not pretentious; he was conversational; he was relevant to them; he clearly liked being with them; and he had — under all the verbiage — a clear message: "Change your eating and lifestyle or die."

A final caution: This is not an excuse for those who will not try to improve their presentations, who will not rehearse, who resist multimedia, or who are deadly boring. These things make everyone a *better* speaker and communicator. As H.L. Menken said, "The race may not always be to the swift and sure, but that's the way to bet." Improve your chances by rehearsing, using modern techniques, and looking critically at your skills. But don't compare yourself to someone else, particularly not to professional speakers and certainly not to politicians, who have polished the art of presentation while neglecting or ignoring the substance. My client became a very *effective* communicator, and that's the goal.

LET A SMILE BE YOUR UMBRELLA

My mother always used to say, "Laugh and the world laughs with you, cry and you cry alone." This is another time when mother did know best.

Recently, I was reminded of the importance of the very first rule of communication. Look pleasant and smile. I was in a store and the clerk looked sour; I spoke up and asked if she was in pain or if I was imposing on her. She looked very surprised and said she was just concentrating on the transaction.

A smile or pleasant expression is a key to controlling communication. The first things we subconsciously ask ourselves when dealing with someone is, "Do they like me?" "Do they want me here?" If you smile naturally, it's a gift from God. If God hasn't given you the gift, don't worry; it can be learned. Look in the mirror and see what it feels like to move the muscles of the face so the cheeks or cheek bones AND your mouth look pleasant and animated. We have two separate faces, the face we wear when talking and the way we look when we are listening. It's particularly important to learn how to monitor and maintain a pleasant expression of animation when listening. Many people "go grim" when listening. The mouth turns down, and the eyes narrow and squinch up. They look fierce and hostile. They're really just concentrating, but have fallen into bad muscle habits.

A smile is an important selling tool. If what you're selling is information, or you're trying to get someone to buy something, you want them on your side. If you can get someone to smile back at you, it actually means they are listening more closely.

We mimic the behavior and gestures of the person we are listening or talking to, so a smile will usually elicit a smile in return.

Smiling also changes the tone of your voice. Customer service representatives who deal with people over the phone need to smile. Though the customer doesn't see them, they actually feel the smile in the tone of voice.

221

Some people believe that to be a professional or an expert they should be aloof, or that when addressing serious topics, they should look serious. Actually, it's just the opposite. Real professionals, those who are truly self-confident, look warm and animated.

While generalizations can get an expert into trouble, there do seem to be some groups which have trouble smiling: women and minorities, probably because they try to look like senior professionals. They don't want to be dismissed as "nonprofessional" or not serious enough. And CEOs, who are still overwhelmingly older white males, allow the corners of the mouth to point down and the cheeks to sag. This may be more a problem of age than unfriendliness. My physician pointed out that when you get to your mid-forties, "Everything starts to sag." That's true of the facial muscles as well.

When addressing a serious topic, animation conveys concern and empathy. People frequently say, "But it's a serious topic, shouldn't I look serious?" Usually, the answer is "no." One can smile or look pleasant without a Jimmy Carter-style grin or without looking like movie star Jim Carrey, of *Dumb and Dumber*. Looking "serious" too often looks hostile and forbidding.

One of my favorite quote books, *Good Advice*, by William Safire lists an old Jewish saying: "If you can't smile, don't open a store." Today we're all selling something. And, as the old song goes, pack up your troubles in an old kit bag, and smile, smile, smile.

> *"Entertainment is an important part of making people* want *to listen to you, but entertainment without substance is the Chinese food of public speaking. It leaves the audience laughing but empty."* — MERRIE SPAETH

INTERACTION: TODAY'S KEY SPEAKER'S TOOL

Many, if not most, executives understand and accept that good communication skills are a crucial tool. Many understand the demands of "public speaking," the ability to get up on one's feet and offer a cogent presentation, argument, or set of remarks. Despite the annual surveys saying things like "10 percent of business people fear death, but 90 percent fear public speaking," many businessmen and women have discovered that they can perform decently, even well. Training and practice are, not surprisingly, key elements in developing and improving these skills; as a result, organizations like Communispond, SPEAKEASY, and Dale Carnegie are flourishing.

They're not good; they're just flourishing. Perhaps I should modify my criticism to say that these courses are "not all that good" or that they have significant drawbacks. It is absolutely true that any attempt to improve one's skills in communication should be applauded and pursued, and all these seminars definitely have something to offer. My concern is that they have a prepackaged list of dos and don'ts while truly superior communication skills are highly individual. The goal should not be to insist that everyone has "broad, expansive hand gestures indicating confidence" (as one course advises), but that the speaker understand and leverage his strengths and minimize his weaknesses. Following rules can lead to rigid behavior. One of my clients has an Effective Presentations in-house course, which advises, "Plant your feet firmly on the ground." No doubt the origins of this advice stems from watching new hires twist and wiggle. However, some people interpret and internalize this advice, so that they rise in front of a group, plant their feet on the ground (firmly), and never move them. They contort their bodies to reach a flip chart or overhead machine, rather than disturb those firmly planted feet.

The real test of good communication in public speaking is: *did the desired or target audience hear the desired message, believe it, and remember it?* Actually, unless the speaker drools overtly, an audience will put up with a lot of infractions of style if they feel the message or information is interesting and relevant *to them.*

Entertainment is an important part of making people *want* to listen to you, but entertainment without substance is the Chinese food of public speaking. It leaves the audience laughing but empty.

Most speakers, even most good speakers, overlook a useful tool: choreographed interaction with the audience.

The first level of interaction with the audience comes naturally to many speakers. It involves asking such questions as, "How many of you are owner-operators of a business?" Some people raise their hands; others look to see whose hands are raised. The exercise only lasts seconds, but it gets the blood flowing in some of those arms, stimulates interest, and — most important — alerts a target subgroup of the audience (the owner-operators) that you're about to reach out to them. Thus, it enhances their listening.

These back and forth Q&As should be used throughout the speech, not just at the start.

A slightly more aggressive variation is to move from the "speech" mode, where the speaker ploughs through prepared remarks, to what my professors used to call the Socratic style, where the material is heavily laced with questions to the audience. For example, to illustrate how these principles of memory work, I play a taped report about a story on banking. The story actually reports that banking is healthier, but the reporter uses the word "fail" three times, and the report is full of confusing numbers. So when I ask the audience, "If you were to summarize this story, what would you tell the next person? That you heard a story about . . . ?" The audience will murmur "failure." This adds verbal expression to audience interaction.

Here is an example of very aggressive, impressive, and effective audience interaction. At a conference of the National Association of Former United States Attorneys, one speaker was asked to discuss Alternative

Dispute Resolution (ADR). First, you should know that ADR is a hard sell to most attorneys because they are not schooled in it and because their education, careers, and mind-set is that if you are really serious, you sue. U.S. Attorneys personify the hard-nosed, tough-guy approach to legal issues. The speaker was not impressive physically. He was dressed in a blazer and slacks. He did not have a commanding voice, and he certainly didn't have a snappy opening. However, he began by handing out a scenario about a manufacturer of gambling tickets who had fired an employee.

He asked the audience to divide itself into threesomes, with someone playing the employer, the fired employee, and the mediator. The groups had five minutes to find a resolution. The exercise woke everyone up and convinced us that dispute resolution was as promising as he claimed.

This exercise combined a number of elements. First, he asked the audience to form themselves into groups. People had to turn to their neighbors and divide themselves into teams. Second, the speaker had to stand quietly on the dais for almost 10 minutes while the audience completed the discussions. Next, he had to call them back to order. Then he had to query the audience and ask for a show of hands: "How many groups arrived at a solution? How many feel confident you could arrive at a satisfactory solution?" After that, the speaker called on a few people to explain how they worked things out. Occasionally, the audience couldn't hear the explanation, so the speaker had to be sensitive to this and translate for the greater audience.

This speaker allocated approximately 15 minutes of his allotted hour to this exercise. It was extraordinarily effective.

Two other examples are drawn from management consultant and thought leader, Dr. Andrew Lebby, who preaches that companies have become "learning disabled" because they learn the wrong lessons from past successes. Dr. Lebby draws a diagram on the board and asks the audience to connect A to A, B to B, and C to C using only three lines without intersecting any of the lines. The audience immediately copies the boxes and starts drawing lines.

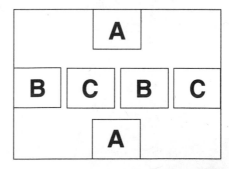

Dr. Lebby walks around the room and looks at how people are experimenting. Some people try to break the rules by going outside the boxes. Others cross over the lines. He looks to see who gets the correct solution and what it requires. (See page 292 for the solution.)

In a second interactive drill Dr. Lebby asks the audience to break into pairs. One person tries to bend the outstretched arm of the other. The arm bends easily. Then Dr. Lebby explains and illustrates how to look beyond the partner, to a point beyond, and by extending his point of reference to a distant point, the arm becomes much harder to bend.

Both exercises require the speaker to stand without speaking for significant periods of time, and both illustrate his points far better than mere verbiage or even compelling language with visual aids. In my class on communication and teamwork at the Cox School of Business at Southern Methodist University, I begin by handing out a sheet that says, "You have just recommended to your CEO that the company consider using teams as a way of improving quality, which is declining, and maintaining market share. Your CEO says, 'What exactly is a team?' What do you tell him?" The graduate students have about three lines to jot down a definition. I collect and read them. They always vary enormously: "a group of people working on a common problem," "a separate group of employees whose work will be judged collectively," and so on. My point is that the word "team" means different things to different people and many teaming efforts and projects fail because there is not an established and common meaning at the outset.

Ideas for interaction with the audience are unlimited. Successful interaction gets the audience up, stimulates attention, creates a shared bond, is generally fun, and is a powerful tool to affect memory and differentiate a speaker.

HOW NUMBERS LIE

Is the media losing credibility? Many business executives say that when it comes to business matters, the press has a long way to go. It's particularly irksome to the business community to see how numbers — statistics — are misused by reporters who don't understand them. "Number of Uninsured Stirs Much Confusion in Health Care Debate," notes the *Wall Street Journal* (June 9, 1993).

There are, of course, many funny comments about statistics, most often quoted, "There are lies, damn lies, and statistics." Another favorite, less used in this day of the politically correct, is Mark Twain's comment, "Statistics are like ladies of the night. Once you get them down, you can do anything you want with them."

One of the most annoying habits of the press is reporting "big" numbers — "big" being anything beyond our own weekly paycheck. This "big" number is set up as a strawman for the virtuous reporter to knock down. Even CBS's Charles Osgood falls prey to misusing and misinterpreting numbers. Mr. Osgood is one of the nation's favorite commentators, well known for his wonderful reports in rhyme. (One of our favorites was "Yuch versus slime.")

However, in one commentary he said, "The IRS says that there were still, in spite of all the tax reforms and loophole removals of the past, 779 couples and individuals who made more than $200,000 in 1990, and paid no federal income tax whatsoever."

First, the IRS's statement said no such thing about "loopholes." The agency did reveal, as required by Congress, the number of people paying no tax whatsoever. But that doesn't mean the press has to play into Congress's hands. Mr. Osgood wondered how these earners managed not to pay taxes. Well, most of them got their entire income from tax-free interest on investments in municipal government bonds, which is perfectly legal — even vital to local government. Municipal bonds are tax-exempt because they're riskier than U.S.-guaranteed securities.

Unlike the U.S. government, which can print money, or a corporation, which actually makes and sells something, cities can only pay back their debts if the tax base stays secure. And this doesn't always happen. New York City, the center of finance and industry, effectively did go bankrupt in the 1970s.

Some of the 779 paid no taxes according to Mr. Osgood because they lost money as part of "Subchapter S Corporations, whatever they are." These are small businesses, particularly family-owned businesses, or new businesses where the entrepreneur makes little or nothing. Because virtually *all* new jobs come from businesses like these, even Congress encourages their formation.

Mr. Osgood did give us more information in the form of "the numbers," noting, "These magic 779 represent one out of 1,000 tax returns at that level. The other 798,000 paid some tax, the IRS says."

This is another example of how numbers are not real information. These are meaningless statistics. True, a careful reading reveals that only a tiny percentage pay no taxes, but we get the impression of fat-cat rich guys evading taxes the rest of us pay.

In a final slam, Mr. Osgood noted legislation in Congress will not change the situation. "These other folks who use legal deductions and credits would escape again."

"Escape?" The use of the word "escape" infers they've pulled a fast one and ignores why municipal bonds are tax-free. The press shouldn't take cheap shots at taxpayers who have accepted greater risk for their money and receive tax-exempt investments or who are trying to start companies. They are contributing to America's future. By implying that they are evading taxes the rest of us dumb clucks have to pay, Mr. Osgood is misleading the public, fanning the flames of envy, and encouraging people to believe that risk and profit are bad instead of the foundation of our economic well-being.

I love Charles Osgood, but with a tax statistic, he makes a striving business owner go totally ballistic!

MORE ON HOW NUMBERS LIE

Most people think numbers are information; they are, however, only proxies for information. It's the context or comparison with other numbers or a greater whole that provides the information. The number without the context can become a lie.

A teacher wins an award for $6,000. Sounds nice. But when you know that the teacher won the largest award ever given by a corporation because her teaching was so unusual, the dollar amount tells us something.

Some of the most important debates of our time have been distorted by the picture created by numbers. Before 1992, those who favored replacing the nation's health care system with a massive, government-run effort began to say that "37 million Americans are uninsured."

The National Center for Policy Analysis (NCPA), a Dallas-based think tank, looked behind the numbers and found a different picture. Whatever the actual number of Americans without health insurance, nearly two-thirds are without coverage for less than a year. Of the actual figure, about 17 percent are without health care insurance for longer than two years. Beneath these figures, NCPA found that some children and older people were without coverage for much longer periods.

The figure and catch phrase "37 million uninsured" creates the impression of a massive disaster waiting to happen. (This is illustrated and "proved" by the individual anecdotes such as Mary Bigamon, 38, who had to separate from her husband so she could legally qualify for Medicaid and afford the $500 a month for needed medication. See "Tell an Anecdote" for how atypical anecdotes "prove" a larger issue.)

Our daily reading is replete with inaccurate figures that are used as a basis for public policy debates. For years, groups representing the homosexual community claimed that 10 percent of the population is homosexual. The Family Research Council analyzed the data gathered by the U.S. Census Bureau and discovered that "the general population estimate for homosexuality would fall below 1.5 percent."

Redbook magazine asked demographer Cheryl Russell to look at 15 numbers which have been enshrined in popular discussion. She found that they were all wildly inaccurate. The statistic: "Women have a one in nine chance of getting cancer." The reality: This represents all women from birth to age 95. Women in their thirties, a high-risk period, have about a one-in-100 chance of getting cancer during that time frame.

"The average person's free time is declining." While I might personally testify to the truth of this statement, we have a lot *more* free time, but we have many more *choices*. Women, in particular, are working more in the job market for pay but doing a lot less housework. We're allocating our time differently.

"Single women in their thirties and forties have little chance (five percent and one percent respectively) of marrying." In fact, this titillating statistic added that "older, college-educated women had a better chance of being killed by a terrorist than of marrying." The truth is a Census Bureau statistician showed that 32 percent of women in their thirties and 17 percent of women in their forties will marry.

"Rich people increased their income almost 100 percent while the poor got poorer." The truth is the Urban Institute found that in the 1970s and 1980s, those in the bottom 20 percent of income earners increased their earnings about 75 percent. Income for those in the top 20 percent grew about five percent over the same years. (Relative to the fairness issue of income distribution, the top one percent of income earners pay 27 percent of all federal income taxes, and that percentage rose almost 20 percent during the Reagan years of supposed greed. By contrast, the entire bottom or lower 50 percent of income earners paid only five percent of all income tax collected, and that figure shrank by seven percent over the same years.)

Misleading or selective statistics are used by those who want to advance a certain cause. That's understandable but dangerous. For example, the "one-in-nine" breast cancer statistic did impel many women to see their doctors. However, many women who should have seen their doctors were so frightened by the statistic that they decided not to go. How many of these contracted breast cancer? We'll never know. But we do know that however well intentioned the scare tactic, it also caused harm.

Those who inflate numbers to increase attention to a cause in which they believe can hurt their credibility. The O.J. Simpson trial highlighted the issue of battered women. The National Coalition Against Domestic Violence reports that half of all women, more than 27 million, will experience violence during their marriage. Secretary of Health and Human Services Donna Shalala reported in a speech that four million women are battered each year; that's as many as give birth. Is there a war on women, as these advocacy groups would have us believe? No. The National Family Violence Survey, which has tracked family behavior for two decades, finds that 16 percent of families experience violence against the spouse, predominantly the woman. Running their numbers produces a figure of 188,000 (according to the *Washington Post*) of women injured severely enough to require medical attention. That's too many, that's bad, but it's a long way from 27 million.

The danger is how men perceive these figures. If half of all males batter their partners, a man might think, why shouldn't I? It's apparently pretty common, almost the norm. Another danger is how the public perceives a figure. We might be able to do something about a problem that affects 188,000 women — about the number affected by a few earthquakes and floods — but 27 million is beyond me.

The press feeds this phenomenon, usually willingly, by repeating the proffered number without pointing out the bias of the group, and frequently without probing and looking for verification. *Working Woman* magazine, an admitted advocate for feminist goals, did the unusual but right thing by challenging "Work Force 2000," an often-quoted study from the Labor Department. The study purported to find that by the year 2000, the white male would be an endangered species. *Working Woman* pointed out that the Labor study "misinterpreted" the findings and made "one whopping mistake" by omitting the word "net" from the discussion of newcomers to the workforce. Without repeating their paragraphs of exploration and discussion, the effect is as dramatic as giving your family's income as "$100,000" or "a *net* $100,000." The first figure means you made $100,000, but tells us nothing about you; the second, tells us you had $100,000 left over after taxes, etc. Many small businesses make $100,000 but find that after taxes and expenses, their net earnings drop all the way down to zero. The difference between "15 percent of entrants to the workforce will be white males" and "15 percent of *net* entrants" is the same difference. Actually, the workforce in 2005 will be mostly white, 73 percent down from 78 percent today;

African-American women, instead of making dramatic gains, will increase only from 5.4 percent to 5.6 percent. Not exactly a revolution.

Working Woman, which had originally reported "Work Force 2000" as proof of women's dominance in the workforce and therefore a mandate for radical change by employers, maintained its credibility by reporting on the correct implications, once they became known.

More typical is the unquestioned reporting of a poll sponsored by the National Conference of Christians and Jews that African-Americans, Hispanics, and Asians are "united by a collective sense of discrimination" while whites are insensitive to the issue. The poll created headlines across the country. Finally, an Hispanic columnist for King Features, Roger Hernandez, got the entire poll and analyzed it in *National Minority Politics.* Reported Hernandez: "What the survey actually found, contrary to what its sponsors claim, is that Hispanics and Asians view life in America, at least in terms of opportunities available, in much the same way Anglos do." Hernandez exposed that the National Conference on Christians and Jews first withheld this from its report and then had a second question asked about whether Hispanics and Asians felt victimized only after the regular survey was completed and Hispanics and Asians had not provided the expected response. This sort of manipulation destroys the faith of the public, not just in numbers but in the integrity of our public debate.

THE PANEL

For business executives, panel presentations are frequently the most neglected communication opportunity. Few of us are invited to give major speeches, but everyone participates on a panel from time to time.

Our "panel nightmare" is a whole conference of panels, with as many as five speakers on each panel, and each speaker has 45 minutes. By the end, the audience is comatose. The next day, they remember nothing. Companies should banish panels, or they should insist that their executives and the staff who organize these conferences make them productive and memorable experiences.

A panel is not a series of separate mini-speeches. It's a "joint appearance." If you're a panelist, you need to prepare your remarks and be prepared to differentiate yourself and your message.

First ask yourself, "What do I want people to remember?" (If you haven't done that, why not? The probable reason is that when you were asked to participate on a panel, you either couldn't decline or the event seemed far in the distant future.)

Here are the basics of panel manners:

➤ Panel size should be limited to three with a moderator. This is the maximum an audience can understand.
➤ Panelists should be chosen for the total message, never because "so-and-so had to be added."
➤ Each set of remarks should be limited to 10 minutes followed by Q&A. Fifteen minutes is the maximum. The Q&A period is the opportunity to make important points again and to add material that didn't fit in your presentation.
➤ Visual supports must be varied between panelists. It's death for every speaker to roll out his slide tray. If one speaker is planning to use overheads, another should use video, poster, props, or blackboard techniques. One speaker should speak without visual aids.
➤ Never turn down the lights. You are the message, not the slides. You may reduce the lighting for brief periods of time if you are

playing a short video, such as a new commercial the company is about to start running. If you use slides or overheads, they should not be dreary recantations of boring words or lines of numbers. They should be key phrases you want to hammer home, charts where the visual comparison emphasizes or headlines a point that something is changing (up or down, bigger or smaller, better or worse), visual counterparts — such as the picture of the building you're going to buy, a map of a designated area, or components complementing other material.

➤ Make sure visual material can be seen by people at the back of the room. Otherwise, people are struggling to see the slide, not concentrating on you. I recently saw the managing partner of a major company talk for 40 minutes in semidarkness just reading text and numbers projected on slides. It was invisible to those in the back and boring to all.

➤ Don't be afraid to use props. They can differentiate you from the other panel members. One of our clients participated in a two-day conference. To make the point that the industry was at a crossroads, he took a miniature street crossing sign with tiny lights, put it on the podium, turned it on, and let it flash for several seconds. It was the highlight of the conference.

➤ As a panelist, look at the person speaking. Panelists are just as much a part of the total communication as if they were at the podium. The other people on a panel are usually looking at their own notes, into the air (waiting for divine messages), or at the audience. We have seen them scratching themselves, chewing on ice from their water glass, doodling, or napping. The audience sees the entire panel. If other members send the message "This is boring," why should the audience be interested?

If you are presenting with a colleague from your company, you should look rapt with interest no matter how many times you've heard it.

Since panels also present opposing sides, you may be with someone with whom you disagree. Be attentive. The audience thinks you're being contemptuous if you act bored. But you must register disagreement on a key point, again by a subtle frown and shake of the head. If you don't indicate where you two are at odds, you appear to be endorsing what your opponent is saying.

➤ Orchestrate, but do not read, interchanges with the moderator or another panel member. Ask him a question or tell a short anecdote. This emphasizes the working relationship from a communication point of view; it is a gimmick to reinforce a point and break up the presentation.

➤ Take all material out of coats or pants pockets before you head to the dais. Get rid of all wallets, checkbooks, diaries, change, etc.; they only weigh you down and disfigure the jacket line. Fiddling with keys or change is an annoying and noisy nervous habit. Take a pen or pencil with your notes.

➤ Write your own introduction. Don't just send the moderator a resume or biography. Send a paragraph of "suggested highlights" with it. Nine times out of 10, that's what he'll read. That paragraph should have your current position, why you're uniquely qualified to address this point, what made your career special, and a summary line about your involvement in the company, community, industry, or civic area.

➤ Try to go first or last, but if the order has been set by other factors, make sure you have "one last point" at the very end so yours is the last comment the audience hears.

➤ Enforce time limits. Start the questioning by indicating the procedure to be followed and asking the first question if necessary.

➤ The moderator should conclude the session and thank the panelists. Make a short, summary statement about what the session found or accomplished. Thank the audience for attending and repeat any instructions about picking up handouts or turning in feedback mechanisms.

Don't forget that the conference or panel organizer needs support. Frequently the moderator's staff person or secretary is designated to ensure the event runs smoothly. Be prepared for this person to encounter annoyance from panelists being pressed for details, assigned one sort of visual over another, or being reminded of time limits and communication tips. Higher-ups need to back up the staff person and remind people that this will make everyone look good. The staff organizer sets deadlines for material, tracks down biographies, schedules rooms for rehearsal, and lines up people to critique presentations. Good panels, like anything else, take preparation. But good "panel manners" turn dreary meetings into memorable experiences.

Part VI

WHEN YOU HAVE
TO SAY IT YOURSELF

I'M SORRY

You bump into someone in front of you and say, "Oops, I'm sorry." The client says you're not getting the point of something, and you respond, "Sorry, let me try again." The weather forecast isn't good, and your child is disappointed, so Mom says, "I'm sorry."

Why? Why should we be "sorry" for these things? It isn't our fault or anything we could change. We say we're "sorry" lots of times when we really don't mean much by it, and we fail to say, "I'm sorry" many times when we should.

I recently dialed Washington, D.C., telephone information from my car phone to get the number of the Hotel Washington. I dialed the number given to me by the operator, and it was the wrong number. I reached the Washington Hilton. I asked the Hilton's operator if she had the other hotel's number, and she said, "I'm sorry. I can't help you" and hung up. I dialed information back and explained. The information operator on the phone didn't sound the least bit sorry. She didn't say she was sorry. She sounded bored and she gave the correct number. It left me with a sour taste in my mouth.

Last week, our morning paper, the *Dallas Morning News,* didn't arrive. I called the circulation delivery number to complain. The woman took the information and said, "I'm so sorry for the inconvenience, and we'll get that paper right out to you." And she did. She delivered the words with feeling as if it were her paper.

When I had to tell one of our young staff people that our training and consulting business wasn't the place for her, I said, "I'm sorry. This isn't the right place for you, but we'll help you find the right place." I *was* sorry, and we did help her. We gave her three months' salary, a year of health insurance, and helped her look for her next job.

Good customer service and good business demands that you recognize that things won't always work; there will be problems; you won't do things right; and the customer won't be satisfied. Say, "I'm sorry" and mean it, like the woman at the paper. The acknowledgment that the paper had messed up made me feel better.

Saying "I'm sorry" is very important for service people when they can't get to you right away, when a job's actual cost veers from the estimate, or when they don't do it right the first time. They might say, "I thought I fixed all the problems with the sprinkler, and I'm sorry I missed those heads around the driveway. I'm sure sorry they went off, too, just as you got into the car to go to church."

Retail associates who keep you waiting a long time usually announce the fact that they are busy by saying, "I'll be with you in a moment," signaling that they know you're there. That's fine, but when they do get around to you, they should share their feelings by saying, "I'm sorry to keep you waiting so long." Then, add the explanation, "I always want to make sure my customers are fully satisfied." Now, move to the new customer: "How may I help you?"

For a company, the question is how to get people to behave this way? This is another one of those things that can't be dictated by a memo.

MEMO
From: The Boss
To: All Employees
Subject: Say You're Sorry

It won't be very effective. The person at the top sets the tone. Too many CEOs today give the impression that they aren't sorry about anything (except that their salary isn't higher). One CEO argued that it showed "weakness" to say he was sorry for something. To the contrary, it shows good common sense and concern.

Today, there are instances where something goes wrong and litigation results. (Actually, litigation results from things that don't go wrong. People imagine they were wronged.) Deny an insurance claim incorrectly, perform a surgical procedure which goes awry, or mess up a deal, and there's a lawsuit. The lawyers don't want you to admit anything to anyone at anytime. Certainly don't take the extra step of saying, "I'm sorry." Again, I disagree. When something goes wrong or doesn't work out, even if both parties had a role in it, saying "*I'm sorry*" is important.

Of course, you have to say it as if you mean it, and it's important to move to the next point very quickly: "I tried as hard as I could." "Let's see what we can do together to work it out correctly." "You're right, we should have moved faster."

It may not be love, but in business, good relations do mean occasionally saying, "I'm sorry."

> *"The executive, who was unavailable for comment,
> announced he was leaving to pursue other interests."* —
> PRESS RELEASE QUOTED IN THE NEW YORK TIMES

I WAS FIRED

We've all heard the catch phrases. Usually, the press release says the executive left "to pursue other interests." We understand what happened. The guy was fired. Traditional wisdom has been that when you're about to be fired, you resign or pretend to resign, and never, never admit it. Maybe it's time to rethink that old advice.

For decades it's been humiliating to be fired. No one wants to admit it. The problem with not admitting it is that no one is fooled. In communication, when you say one thing, and people know it's not true, it hurts your credibility.

Getting fired is no longer a disgrace. As management changes become more common, and business changes faster and becomes more volatile, it's typical for people whose only sin was they were there to lose their jobs. I was just solicited for recommendations for the chief of communication for a *Fortune* 500 company. The headhunter told me that the new person will get to hire 12 people. Why? Because the new CEO had bounced everyone hired by the old CEO.

Several years ago, Ed Harper, executive vice president and CFO of Campbell's Soup, surprised people by insisting that the press release announcing his departure candidly explain that he had been recruited and groomed to succeed the CEO. When the board picked someone else — despite his stellar performance — he felt it was a matter of principle to leave. Harper, who had been head of the Domestic Policy Counsel under President Reagan and who is a Ph.D., continued to move up in his career, heading the American Association of Railways with a six-figure compensation.

Other similar incidents include the columnist and compensation specialist Graef Crystal, who was fired by *Financial World*. The magazine

242

had tried to get him to revise a story and analysis. He refused; they canned him. The magazine tried to say he was leaving "For personal reasons," but Crystal reported the true reason. His integrity was enhanced, the magazine's diminished. Nick Nicholas, a Time Warner executive, also refused to resign and was fired for his differences of opinions over the company's future.

A very public, badly handled firing was the parting of Jimmy Johnson, former coach of the Super Bowl-winning Dallas Cowboys football team. The background: Following the second Super Bowl win all participants were "celebrating." The celebration included alcohol. Grousing and imagined slights were magnified, fed, and fanned by the media. Within hours, what was probably a bellyaching, late-night remark by Jones about how "I'm going to fire that S.O.B." became a gauntlet thrown down. Both parties — owner Jerry Jones and coach Johnson — had their heels dug in, the hair on their necks up, and wouldn't budge.

Trying to clean up the image of big egos squabbling without regard for other players and fans, a press conference was called where they announced it was a "mutual agreement" to part ways. A poll by the *Dallas Morning News* the next morning found that 71 percent of readers did not believe it was a mutual agreement and 24 percent did. Despite the insistence that they were "still friends," 71 percent didn't believe it. Despite the insistence that Johnson's departure would have no impact on the team's performance, 80 percent felt it would have a negative effect. (They were right.)

What could they have said? Strange as it seems, what about the truth? What about saying, "We have had a great few years together. Jimmy has coached this team to back-to-back Super Bowl wins and, over that time, frictions build up. The tensions have reached the point where I, as the owner responsible for this team, think this is the time to make clean break and start with someone else. Jimmy Johnson was a great coach, is a great coach, and I will remember the good things he did for the team."

The problem with saying things you don't believe is the audience knows it isn't true. It severely compromises your credibility, and people, like elephants, don't forget. Once people know you'll say things that aren't true, they remember the next time.

For the person being fired, being able to speak your mind and tell the truth allows you the opportunity to say why you're leaving. People may disagree with your analysis, but you have communicated that you stand for what you believe and that you're honest. If it turns out they should have had more consumer focus, or whatever the reason, you are vindicated. In addition, there will almost certainly be people within your industry who agree with you. And now, they know you're available and that you're in tune with their philosophy.

This approach may not be for everyone. But it can be very successful, and is clearly no longer an automatic black mark to be shown the door.

I QUIT

You got the new job. The dream has come true. You can walk into the boss's office and quit. Communicating you are leaving one job for another is actually a stressful, difficult task. Most people don't do it well. There may be gender differences in how men and women announce they are quitting. What should be a great moment often becomes a miserable one.

Over the last 12 months, our small business has seen several talented employees leave. As we've developed, we have become known for our talented people and unique approach. One employee was even recruited by one of our clients. One moved to a senior position in government. Another joined her father's fast-growing business as head of marketing, and another wanted a job with much shorter, more predictable hours. Each found announcing the decision worse than interviewing for a job.

Most people dream about being able to quit and move up, and they imagine the opportunity to tell the current boss or company all the things they did wrong. One author, Evan Harris, who edits *Quitter Quarterly*, calls these fantasies the "Burn a Bridge and Make a Scene" scenarios. In "Burn a Bridge," he writes, "You will be fearless. Tell your boss he or she is a pig, has bad taste in suits, and couldn't manage the contents of a grocery bag. Slam the door when you leave. Never look back." In "Make a Scene," you "Lie in wait for your boss to enrage you one too many times and respond by tearing up important documents. Or choose a location with high visibility to execute the quit. Be loud. Then leave, shouting insults or worse." He also describes the Bobby Fischer technique of quitting, named after the chess grandmaster who quit playing for 17 years, returned to win the world championship, then vanished.

Quitting is actually an act of growth that requires you to take charge. Despite the psychic satisfaction, don't make a scene, scream, tell the boss everything that's wrong, or lord it over the boss. Like all communication, quitting should be customer focused; in this case, the "customer" is your about-to-be-former boss. He or she can still be a reference in the future (when you quit your next job, or when you need someone to tell the newspaper reporter why you were the clear choice to be recruited as CEO of Amalgamated Global after spending only eight months as CEO of a rival firm). He or she can send you business and give advice. Life may look different to you when you're the boss yourself in the next position.

Look at it from the boss's point of view. When you arrive in the office to announce your move, you are also saying that you've been looking for work without telling him and that the company and job weren't sufficiently challenging or rewarding enough to keep you. In those cases where the boss was a personal mentor, you are rejecting that relationship, growing up, and heading out on your own. This is disconcerting, if not a slap in the face.

Approach the situation as the first step in your new job. If this were a prospective customer, you'd check up first on what might affect your ability to do business, such as the policies and procedures that affect the situation; you'd have something positive to say about what the boss or company has done for you; and you'd use a combination of verbal and written communication. You'd think through your strategy first.

This translates into knowing your company's policies and being sensitive to the demands of your immediate colleagues. For example, you may be required to give two weeks' notice, but two weeks' notice just as a major project is starting can create a real problem for your boss and colleagues. I have personal experience with this. One of our talented associates took another job just as we began working on a major bankruptcy. She gave the proper notice but it included Thanksgiving week. We were glad about her opportunity but in a real bind ourselves.

Hand your boss a letter that communicates in writing what you are about to say in person. Include comments about what you've learned and thanks for some specific assistance or advice. Even if you've worked for a candidate for the World's Worst Boss Competition, you'll be able to say truthfully, "I learned a lot from you." You do not have to add that what you learned was what not to do.

This assumes that you have thought through the strategy and are not going in to bargain, threaten, or waffle. These will change the session's tone dramatically. Frequently, your announcement will prompt the boss to advance propositions of more money, quicker advancement, more responsibility, or something to keep you. Reject these firmly and politely.

If you are in a position where, because of existing contract or special skills, you anticipate the company may try to bring legal pressure to bear, consult your own attorney first. Then be prepared to say, firmly and politely, that you have checked this aspect and the lawyers' involvement would only complicate everything and add expense. You might also mention that life is long, and you expect to have future relations with the boss or company that should not be complicated or poisoned by the squabbling attorneys.

Finally, like all speeches, this is a presentation and should be thought through, outlined, and practiced. Quitting is a memorable event for you and the boss, and today it's mandatory to take full advantage of all those instances where you are virtually guaranteed to be remembered.

Are there gender differences in quitting? I am always reluctant to comment on gender differences because generalizations are "proved" by anecdotes, yet the range of behavior of men and women is broad. A characterization can damage other individuals. Yet there are undeniably more instances of women getting teary or bursting into tears when they have to deliver the message that they are leaving.

Whatever you do, remember that this is the first step into the next part of your career and should be handled accordingly.

Part VII

DEALING WITH THE MEDIA

NO COMMENT

Recently, there seem to have been a number of critical stories about business — poor decisions, investigations of fraud, or angry stockholders filing lawsuits — where the company's response is "no comment." Some business people complain that in complicated situations, reporters won't take time to understand the situation. Reporters put executives in a difficult position when they seek a last-minute comment, but the executive can still make it an opportunity for a positive story or just grumble and allow it to be a disaster. Here are some examples:

A *Business Week* article appeared on bad investments made by a company named Hedged Investments Associates, which lost people millions in computer-driven options. The individual investors tearfully commented that this represented their life savings. The story suggested that the fund manager was incompetent, ill advised, and may have profited personally; but we don't hear directly from him. The magazine explained that "He declined to be interviewed."

The *New York Times* reported money manager and investor Fred Carr may have the distinction as the person who believed in junk bonds the longest. When First Executive, a California insurance company, went bust, Carr tried to shore up his own investments by questionable and complicated methods. The implication is those magazines have been illegal, too. For those who take the trouble to read all the way through, this article actually tells us that Carr's "Ethical standards were higher than others in the junk-bond market." Alas, we don't hear from Carr directly as he "didn't return telephone calls."

It's true, reporters frequently get all the bad news, the charges of wrongdoing, and so on, then call you at the eleventh hour for a comment. And it's true, it's usually not possible to really explain or to rebut it at all. But you can't be quoted saying "no comment" or that "you couldn't be reached." "No comment" is a comment; it's a confirmation of all the bad stuff. It says you have something to hide.

Executives duck even when it's not a crisis or hostile story. Early in 1995, two senior executives resigned from IBM, reputedly when it was clear they were not getting promotions. The news made, well, the news. The reports weren't hostile or damaging to IBM or to either individual, yet both executives "were not available for comment." This is an automatic response. These executives can still say, "It seemed like the right thing at this time," or "I plan to use this as an opportunity to examine different industries and new challenges." Those are plain vanilla, but they show the executive isn't afraid.

It used to be that getting fired or being shunted aside implied humiliation of the executive. Today, it's so common, it only means change continues. It's a shame that the "no comment" tradition hangs on.

In those more difficult situations, particularly where the reporter is writing about damaging issues, what do you say? Understand, you can't say enough to educate the reader. But you can tell the reader or listener something else — what you stand for and what you've accomplished. Fred Carr could have said, "Over the years, I've made a lot of money for my investors." But what about those cases where litigation is involved and your lawyers tell you not to talk? Don't say, "Our lawyers have advised us not to comment." Instead try, "It's not fair or appropriate to discuss this while it's in litigation." Then you have established your concern for fairness, something the American people value.

Over the years, I have personally observed a change in reporting, perhaps paralleling a change that has occasioned comment in the political world. A number of political figures including former Congressman Tony Coehlo and former U.S. Senator John Danforth, have been quoted for their concern that a mean spiritedness and vindictiveness is far more prevalent in politics today than when they began. It's true, our memories of "years past" usually reinforce the positive and mitigate the negative. (Women who have been pregnant understand this. Even though a trouble-free pregnancy is difficult and tiring, years later only the positive memories remain.) One cause of that increasing vindictiveness is clearly the role of the press. An example early in 1995 was the interview by Connie Chung of Speaker Gingrich's mother where, after hours of "just chatting," Ms. Chung suggested in a whisper that Mrs. Gingrich could just "whisper" what the Speaker thought of Mrs. Clinton, and that it would just be "between you and me." CBS then sat on the interview, done in mid-December, and released it the day of the Speaker's triumphant swearing in.

This "gotcha" journalism colors business reporting, too. A disturbing number of journalists believe that just placing a call to someone — at 5:05 p.m. — means they were fair. They weren't.

For the executive who receives the late-in-the-day call asking for "comment," the first step is to request more time. If this is a story only for the local paper, can it be covered tomorrow? The company needs to have a good reason, such as consulting with legal counsel, a chairman of the board, notifying financial interests, employees, and so on. The reporter will probably give the knee-jerk "can't wait" response. The reporter is correct from his or her point of view. Daily reporting means just that — daily. If you ask him or her not to write the story that day, he has some explaining to do to his editor. Help him. Call the editor and make a compelling case that being clued into the story this late isn't fair. (The word "fair" is the crucial word. Reporters' self-image is that they are "fair" even if they are not and have no intention of being so.)

If a story is of interest to more than one media outlet, it will be a story for tonight's news or tomorrow's headlines. In that case, asking a reporter to give you until tomorrow won't work because it isn't fair. But it is fair to ask the reporter for time to think about one or two decent quotes, and perhaps to ask the reporter to call one other person who might have an opinion on what kinds of service or products the person or company has provided over the years. Only a few reporters want to be seen as vipers, and most will try to extend themselves to get a more complete story. (Don't hope for objectivity. That isn't the reporter's job.)

Declining to comment can also color how a publication sees your side of the story. *Business Week* wrote a full-page, thoughtful piece on the troubles facing Kidder Peabody & Co. after the disclosure that trader Joseph Jett's practices had cost the firm hundreds of millions of dollars. Kidder's response was to say that Mr. Jett, a highly regarded and recognized employee, had pulled the wool over their eyes. Mr. Jett's boss, Edward Cerullo, with a decade and a half of experience himself didn't detect the problem. The magazine could have slammed Kidder. They didn't, but they were clearly skeptical. The subhead for the article was "Wall Street is skeptical of the 'We wuz robbed' explanation." Kidder's CEO is photographed and defends Mr. Cerullo, but "Cerullo declined comment."

Marketplace Communication

No matter how bad the problem or how late the hour, never refuse the reporters phone calls. Never decline, refuse, or avoid comment. The reporter is offering you one chance to stand up for yourself. Take it.

"It is possible to comply with the rules and still speak English, but many lawyers don't know that." — MERRIE SPAETH

CONFIRM OR DENY

"We can neither confirm nor deny," says the company press release. The phrase is a staple in corporate communication or rather, non-communication. It fits right in with saying "no comment."

The problem is that usually "no comment" is a comment when the reporter asks the question a certain way. "I hear rumors that you are acquiring the Mega Gadget Corporation. Is this true?" asks the reporter. "No comment," says the company, leaving the impression that Mega Gadget is about to be gobbled up.

To avoid that impression, corporate communication people and lawyers borrowed the "neither confirm nor deny" line from law enforcement. If the local paper picks up the rumor that the FBI is nosing around asking questions about the Mayor's remarkably prescient purchase of land in the path of the expressway, the FBI will tell you it, "Can neither confirm nor deny an investigation."

I'm concerned that "neither confirm nor deny" has become a proxy for "no comment," which the public hears as confirmation, not as a legitimate refusal to comment. After all, if they weren't considering it they'd tell us.

The Coca-Cola Company's comment on a report by CNBC reporter Dan Dorfman is a notable departure from the bland, uninformative nature of most corporate communication in these situations. After he reported that Coca-Cola wanted to acquire the Quaker Oats Company and pay $60 a share, Coca-Cola issued a release which said, "It is the policy of the Coca-Cola Company not to comment on rumors about acquisitions or divestitures. That remains our policy. However, today we would like to elaborate on our statement and observe that Dan Dorfman does not have a clue."

Is this a good idea? Yes.

255

DILBERT reprinted by permission of United Feature Syndicate, Inc.

First, a reminder of why companies use the "neither confirm nor deny" phrase. Public companies are under very strict rules from the SEC about what they can and can't do that might influence the price of the stock. We might think some of these rules might not make a lot of sense, but the SEC is very picky about observing them. When it comes to matters involving the SEC, the corporate lawyers call the shots. (It is possible to comply with the rules and still speak English, but many lawyers don't know that.)

Next, when companies are in the midst of doing something, public scrutiny can change the equation and destroy the deal; that is, discussions have to be conducted in private so the parties can adapt their position as appropriate. (This is, of course, true of government — something the proponents of the so-called "Sunshine" laws never understood. However, that's another topic.) Even if workers and others have a real interest in what's happening to their company, the right to talk privately must remain with the management or nothing will ever get done. In other words, we relinquish some claim on openness and "right to know" in order to facilitate business with an end goal of employment for all and market efficiency, even if that means some unfairness or that some people are shut out of the discussion.

Coca-Cola's response was appropriate and added needed humor and realism to the world of work. It was a reminder that real people working on problems very real to them are trying to do a good job for all the people who depend on them. It put a human face on a very large company. It was also appropriate because the Coca-Cola Company makes a lot of products, many of which are associated with having fun. The statement fit the image of a company that understands the consumer wants to have fun with its products.

The Dorfman-Coca-Cola exchange points out one problem with the media today. There is less trust between business and the media.

Reporters used to be extremely concerned with getting a correct story. Increasingly, they are only concerned with getting a story. Company officials could develop a relationship with a reporter interested in correct facts, and it is frequently possible to privately warn a reporter off a story that isn't true — without seeing it in print. True, business sometimes abused this relationship, but it has a real role in communication. Even though it rarely admits it, the FBI will try to see that reporters don't go with wrong stories. It is not only highly placed political figures that concern them. All agencies survive because the public trusts them. Nothing breaks down trust more than being unjustly accused, so a report of an FBI investigation has serious implications for a business's lenders, employees, suppliers, and customers. The FBI is primarily concerned about carrying out its law enforcement mission, but it is not insensible to the damage done by incorrect reporting. Where possible, the FBI tries to have both.

This doesn't work as well in today's world, however, where reporters feel justified in saying anything they can claim they heard somewhere. The Coca-Cola story may have started with an overheard discussion between analysts about what would make sense for Coca-Cola to do to broaden its base still more, or perhaps marketing experts were tossing around ideas about what company would reinvigorate Quaker Oats. Someone mentioned that the Coca-Cola Company had a good track record for that. Another person passed along to someone else who told another person who told Dorfman that Coke was thinking of buying Quaker. Presto! The rumor becomes public.

One more observation about why Coca-Cola was the big winner in this exchange. The *New York Times* reported the exchange and noted that the "normally courteous" Coca-Cola Company had responded. What an endorsement from the *Times*. The paper would usually be caught dead rather than let you know that a certain company had good manners. So Coca-Cola got its point across and also got the *New York Times*, the paper of record, to attest to its professionalism in handling corporate communication. Now, if we could only write that *Times* reporters were equally concerned about being correct, let alone courteous.

WHAT DID YOU REALLY SAY?

I am glad I'm what's called an electronic journalist, because when I, and my colleagues in radio and television, come to interview you and pick out the quote or the infamous sound bite that will illustrate your interview with us, we use your actual words. We know you really said it. In print, you may no longer have that same assurance.

In today's media-savvy world, most businessmen know they will be interviewed about things they want to talk about and things they don't — plant closings, litigation, consumer complaints. Most business people are sophisticated enough to know that the reporter will select certain quotes to illustrate the story.

We have surveyed business executives over the past eight years, and overwhelmingly they are concerned about being misquoted. Approximately 87 percent of executives in our survey say they are concerned that they will be misquoted. While many believe the press "Just picks quotes to illustrate a point they want to make," many executives believe they are misquoted because "I could have been clearer."

The print medium recently went through one of those esoteric disputes that make reporters look foolish to the rest of us. The issue is: Can the reporter totally invent a quote for you? You may say "no way"; some reporters say "yes."

The background is this: Reporters have always felt it was fine to "clean up" quotes, to take out the "uhs" or times when you start the same sentence over. It's also okay to condense a quote or make it clearer. For example, the CEO's comment "We think it's appropriate and consistent with industry standards and important to our shareholders to reduce the number of separate job classifications" becomes "The company announced it was reducing job classifications to fit 'industry standards.' " The reporter can even impute motive, so now the quote reads "After years of disputes, the company unilaterally announced it was reducing job classifications arbitrarily, claiming the need to be 'consistent with industry standards.' "

It's a little more controversial to put words in the subject's mouth, although every reporter knows it's done. Example: "Mr. Jones, are Mega Bank's capital adequacy ratios out of line?" He says, "No, they're not out-of-line." He actually used the words, but the reporter suggested them. This happened to the J.C. Penney Company, where, after a number of straight quarters of increased earnings, company officials were justifiably pleased with themselves. Preparing for an even better holiday season, they increased inventories. Analysts and the reporters who listen to analysts and analysts' meetings, noticed the jump. "Are inventories excessive?" they asked on a conference call. Company officials said, "No, they are not excessive." The headlines read "Earnings Up — Concern Inventory is Excessive." They did discuss whether inventory was "excessive." The notion was planted by a third party, not the reporter. It was overblown by the reporter and headline writer.

Suppose the person being interviewed just says "No" to a question like this, but the reporter writes John Smith denied "that Mega Bank's capital adequacy ratios are out-of-line." It makes us uncomfortable, but everyone knows it's a frequently used device.

A reporter for the *New Yorker* (yes, the *New Yorker*) was sued by a subject whom she interviewed for 40 hours on tape. She quoted him as saying he was an "intellectual gigolo," yet those words are nowhere on the tapes. Another quote that was on the tape, "There would have been parties and laughter and fun," looks suspiciously like a quote in the book, "It would have been a place of sex, women, and fun," which is nowhere on the tape.

What's appalling about this dispute is that any journalist would defend it. Some people actually say that inventing directly attributed quotes is not a violation of ethics as long as the writer fairly represents the speaker's character. I think that's a hard sell, and I am advising my clients to have their own tapes of interviews. There is simply no other way to ensure that you're quoted fairly. It's sad that relations with the media have come to this. The dictionary defines "to quote" as "to reproduce the words." Journalists who want to keep the respect of the public should leave it at that. And you can quote me on it.

REPORTING — JUST THE FACTS

"Everything you read in the press is true . . . except the rare event of which you have personal knowledge," says Erwin Knoll writing in *The Progressive* magazine. The saying is now known as Knoll's Law of Accuracy in Media.

But what if you read something in the press that appears to be directly contradicted by something else in the press? What if it's contradicted by a report about the very same event in another paper? A major study by the Families and Work Institute serves as an illustration. In our local paper, the *Dallas Morning News*, the headline read "Workers Stressed Out but Committed." The article reported that the Institute surveyed thousands of workers on their attitudes toward their jobs, discovering that employees were stressed out but nevertheless committed to doing a good job. So much for the idea that the worker of the 1990s has little attachment to his employer.

The *Wall Street Journal* also read the same study. Their headline read "Workforce Study Finds Loyalty is Weak, Divisions of Race and Gender are Deep." The first paragraph read: "A brand new survey of American workers depicts a workforce that has little loyalty to employers and is deeply divided by race and gender."

A major radio station interviewed Ellen Galinsky, one of the study's authors. The thrust of the interview was about how her research showed significant differences in attitudes about work between people with children and those without.

How could these all be the *same* study? Some of the headlines and findings in one report appear to directly contradict what's reported elsewhere. This, of course, happens frequently. It's frustrating to many businesses and industries, and they say, correctly in my view, that reporters pick out unimportant facts and miss important ones.

Some business people truly believe that reporters will always, and only, choose negative or sensational material.

These opinions are all true and can occur at the same time. The reporting on the workforce study is an illustration of why reporting is reporting and not like a college research project or discovery in litigation. First, it was a big study and it covered a lot. After all, if you interview 3,000 people over five years, you pile up a lot of material. A reporter's job is not really to report *everything*, it's to report *something*. And that means making choices about what to report and what to omit.

All these stories were accurate. Our *local* reporter was taken by the conclusion that workers were conscientious but overwhelmed by work and family demands. The *Journal* reporter, with a business perspective, looked at another aspect of the findings which showed employees were fearful and distrustful, with downsizing and firing on their minds. The *Journal* reporter also thought the discoveries on racial and ethnic attitudes were important, noting that the study challenged the widely held idea that younger workers will be more open and more comfortable with diversity. Our local paper didn't mention this at all.

The radio interview mentioned none of these because the host began with a question about child care and the line of questions and answers went down *that* path.

Numbers, or statistics, were included in all the reports. That's because numbers have a comforting solidity for reporters. "Twenty percent fear losing their job." "Fifty-seven percent say they try to do their jobs well, whatever it takes." Numbers, of course, can be exceptionally misleading, but they appear to be so factual. But what does "47 percent reported their company recently cut their workforce" really tell us? Have almost half of American companies downsized? Are we talking 30 jobs (which made headlines when Steak & Ale did that in Dallas) or 5,000 jobs for American Airlines (which made national headlines).

Our local paper selected numbers supporting the "stressed out" findings, noting that 14 percent felt frustrated very often, 15 percent often, and 31 percent less often, but everyone feels stressed out at some point. These figures didn't make it into the *Journal* article, but they reported that only 28 percent of employees said they were willing to work harder to help the employer succeed and that slightly more than half of 50 percent of people say they prefer working with people of the same race and sex.

All these numbers were in the study. After several pages of them, are we getting a better picture of the workforce, or are we just drowning in numbers?

The point here is that there are lots of ways to report the news. A consumer, and we are all consumers of news and information, needs to have a well-rounded information diet, just like the food we eat.

My favorite advice is a combination of comments, one by the founder of Burlington Coat Factory, Sy Symms, who said, "An educated consumer is our best customer," and one by a nutritionist at Baylor University Medical Center in Dallas, who said, "Balance is important." And that's true in the news and information business, too. Comparison shopping and several sources yield the fullest picture.

There's a cautionary note for journalists, too. I've personally seen too many damaging facts pulled out and reported as the representation of the whole picture. The media's defense is always that the fact or statistic was in the study or did happen. That may well be the case, but the real question should be, Does the journalist do justice to the real story or the whole picture?

The reporter and the reader have responsibilities: the reporter to report the "facts," and the reader to have a variety of news sources.

NO FAIR

Business people wonder what a reporter considers fair. Fundamental fairness is a concern of most reporters, but it's up to the individual and the company to stand up for themselves and for what's right.

"Just between you and me," murmurs Connie Chung to Newt Gingrich's mother. Between Connie, Mrs. Gingrich, and millions of viewers. This is not fair. This shows the importance of understanding the competitive element of journalism today. Say something stupid? It's fair game. Want something not to be quoted? Better make that clear *before* you say it.

Sometimes reporters go too far in trying to produce the story they want. In the aftermath of the scandal over very high salaries and perks at the United Way headquarters, a paper in West Virginia decided to do the local version and investigate executive salaries of charitable organizations, including the local chapter of the American Heart Association. The Association came off clean, with high devotion to service, very moderate salaries, and no fancy perks like country club memberships or private planes. What a disappointment for the reporter who had invested a lot of time. So the reporter refocused the story on how executives plan a career track in nonprofit organizations, and made it sound as if the nonprofit field is just as high powered and political as General Motors. The final article even noted that the subject, the executive director, in question, "Declined to be photographed." Raise your eyebrow? Make you think there's something more there?

What really happened was that the reporter wanted a picture of the Association's West Virginia director in front of a big desk, in a suit and tie. But the executive doesn't have a big desk, and although he may wear a tie, he is just as likely to be out leading a 10-K run — as he was that day. "Come along," he invited the reporter.

The *reporter* declined. He wanted a picture of the executive looking, well, like an executive. Wearing a jogging outfit for a 10-K run didn't fit the reporter's story. But the American Heart Association puts darn near every penny into research and programs to further their mission to improve American health and save lives. That's why their executive was out with the 10-K run.

Before the paper published the story and before the reporter wrote it, at the first hint the reporter was pushing for something artificial, the Association should have contacted the paper's editor and explained the situation. Reporters do sometimes get overly focused on one aspect of a story. Fortunately, many of these disagreements can be worked out so everyone is happy, but you have to stand up for yourself first. Make your case to the editor — nicely.

How should the association have divined that this story was going to slam them? Where do we purchase that crystal ball? The sophisticated company can sense when the media thinks it has a story or has discovered something inconsistent between what a company says and what it actually does. I admit that it's a real stretch for a small affiliate of a not-for-profit organization, which does actually have a nice clean record, to figure out that this reporter was writing a story designed to take him to a larger market.

So the question is how one should behave *after* the damage is done. In this case, the association should have sent a note to the editor saying the reference left an incorrect and unfair impression. They should have also sent an official "letter to the editor" for publication. The tone of that letter shouldn't be defensive. It should say: "Any of your readers who saw the article on executives' salaries may have noticed that there was no picture. Participants at our 10-K run that day knew why: Our executive director was there!"

Reporters can also be unfair because they're lazy or sloppy. A small plane owned by a service chartered by FedEx to deliver express packages crashed in a rural area in California. The local TV station reported the story correctly — that a small, single engine plane crashed resulting in the death of the only on-board individual, the pilot. A TV station in Memphis reported that a jumbo jet had crashed. They did not call FedEx to check the report, so the company was deluged by calls from crew members' spouses. The company called the station while the newscast was still on. They offered the correct information and asked for a correction, but it was hours later and after a great deal of emotional turmoil that the station corrected the report. The station claimed that the original story had come from the affiliate where the small plane went down, although in this case, the company already knew that wasn't true.

When this happens, a company needs to write the station manager and the network. Again, the tone should be respectful but firm "You messed up, and it caused real problems."

A company need not and should not suffer in silence. Too many companies grumble privately and say, "That's just the press being sensational." They take the abuse. Memphis-based Baptist Memorial Health Care System was asked to take over a municipal hospital in Columbus, Mississippi, a town of 30,000 in the bustling Golden Triangle area of the state. The owner of the only newspaper in town made a bid for the hospital, too, but was rebuffed by the town supervisors. There's an old saying, never argue with someone who buys ink by the barrel. The newspaper owner waged a year-long vendetta by printing every letter critical of the hospital and ignoring any letter that praised them, burying or ignoring good news such as obtaining permission from regulators for a new cardiac cath lab (so residents wouldn't have to travel to other cities). Finally, employees and patients started their own letter-writing campaign to protest when they saw the paper's unfair treatment. After a couple hundred letters descended on the paper describing the hospital's accomplishments, the publisher moderated his editorial tone. It's important to do this for the sake of the company and the press. In the first example here, the association needs to assure the public of its commitment to be open and responsive. Reporters and editors want us to read their stories and believe they tried to be fair. We need to occasionally remind reporters that what seems like a minor detail or throwaway line to them can have important implications for the people or institutions about whom they write. Paying attention to the spirit, not just the letter, is what's really fair.

> *"Don't send me the PR person. Send me someone who knows something."* — REPORTER FOR THE DALLAS MORNING NEWS

WHAT DO REPORTERS THINK OF PR?

EXECUTIVE SUITE reprinted by permission of Newspaper Enterprise Association, Inc.

The words we use convey what we think of an individual or the work he does. If you were a surgeon, how would you feel if someone described you as a "slicer and dicer," or a lawyer and they called you a "vulture," or a teacher and discovered you were being referred to as a "baby-sitter" — you get the picture that the person talking about you has a low opinion of your profession and your integrity.

In an article about business schools more aggressively recruiting students, *Business Week* wrote that the University of Chicago had hired someone to "flack" for them. The word "flack" implies a mouth for hire, someone who will say anything, who ignores bad news, and mindlessly promotes puffery. This out-of-date picture of public relations, if it were ever true, is unfortunate and dangerous.

Communication today is, or should be, a strategic tool for business. The Public Relations Society of America has tried very hard, for the most part successfully, to increase the professional criteria and skills of its practitioners. They want public relations professionals to help their clients, both internal and external.

You do not help your client by being dishonest, either by refusing to give your client honest feedback and criticism or by painting a misleading picture to the outside. Honesty is the first and best policy. Companies that expect their communication people to "flack" are disappointed. They also underutilize a sophisticated resource.

The *Business Week* implication is also dangerous for reporters. In today's complicated, volatile world, company communication people are a prime resource for reporters. I've dealt with business reporters who didn't know what a basis point was and who didn't understand derivative products.

Many people may not know immediately what those are either, but in our society, one way the company communicates to its employees, customers, the public, regulators, and investors is through the press. When reporters don't understand, refuse to learn, and refuse to use an important resource, then everyone loses. A reporter's automatic conclusion — the communication person is a dupe, a dodo, and a front — is insulting and not warranted.

It is certainly true that some public relations people are barriers between the reporter and management, and there are some who are incompetent or dangerous; that is, they hurt the strategic corporate goal.

Sandoz Pharmaceuticals was in the news when its drug, Clozapine, was featured in Diana Ross's TV movie, *Out of Darkness*. The movie depicts Ross as someone who wrestled for years with the devastating illness of schizophrenia until the powerful drug comes to her rescue. Sandoz stood to reap millions in free publicity from the movie. Experts like Dr. William Reid, chairman of the National Clozapine Task Force, wrote in the *Washington Post* that the movie "focuses attention on a powerful new drug, Clozapine, and its impact on people." He added that the drug "has opened the door to a more normal and productive lifestyle for many people with schizophrenia." For good measure, he added that it was "highly effective" and would benefit most of the people currently in other kinds of therapy. Sandoz, however, also came in for some bad publicity when reporters noticed that the company was sending press releases touting the movie but had their outside PR company mail them on the PR company's stationery. Sandoz's spokesman was quoted as saying, "I don't want to make it seem as if we're trying to exploit this," and that the outside PR company "ran out of [our] letterhead."

Behavior like this gives companies and PR people a bad name with reporters. First, he clearly wants to "exploit" the movie. He should, and he should be honest about it. Second, in this day of desktop publishing, it's not credible that the PR firm put the releases on their stationery because they "ran out" of the client's letterhead. In the *Journal* article, another expert, Richard Rothstein, president of Edelson Medical Communications, comments on the situation. Part of his quote deals with the importance of handling communication so people don't wonder, "What is Sandoz up to?" Unfortunately, their actions make it clear that they are not behaving in a straightforward manner, and they have no respect for the public relations function. They may have a great product, but their communication strategy and skills don't match it.

At the nation's largest jewelry retailer, the director of corporate communications reported to the corporate treasurer, who was unfamiliar with sophisticated, aggressive communication. The company abandoned its program of talking to editors of women's publications, to the daily fashion press, or to the business press but spent hours in meetings deciding how to announce a corporate contribution of $5,000 to a United Way campaign, a minimal sum by corporate standards.

These examples of incompetent communication people, strategies, and efforts are examples of the exception, not the rule.

Part of a good communication program, but only part, is to promote the company's products or services or to argue a point of view. Good communication frequently tries to influence a target audience. For example, human resource departments need to convince a company's own employees to pay more attention to their retirement needs.

Business Week undertakes these same efforts. They want you to think their publication is worth reading and has something to offer that others don't. Good PR understands the parameters of how people perceive things. The $5,000 United Way contribution was worthwhile, but the company's expectation that the press would make a fuss over it made the company look foolish.

In both these examples, the problem wasn't the product, Clozapine, which is top-notch, or even the $5,000 contribution, which shows participation. The problem was the communication strategy, which was unrealistic.

Despite examples like these, there are dozens where a well-informed, talented public relations person literally made it possible for a reporter to write a story. Reporters covering the unprecedented filing of Chapter 9 bankruptcy by Orange County, California, found the complexity and uncertainty of the story overwhelming. In the absence of specific news events, the media looks for "angles." One major publication's reporter was assigned to write a story on how long the bankruptcy would last. Of course, there was no answer. One of the PR people representing one of the professional advisors found several prestigious individuals — a lawyer, a former CEO, and a partner in a Big Six accounting firm — who had been through complex corporate bankruptcies. The PR person persuaded them to speculate for the reporter and worked out a reasonable, if hypothetical, time line. The reporter would not have otherwise had the credible contacts to complete the story.

PR people save reporters frequently from mistakes or from being manipulated by others with a vested interest, such as lawyers. Incorrect information about the appointment of a new CEO for a *Fortune* 500 company was leaked to a reporter at 5:15 one afternoon. The PR person's relationship with the reporter was good enough that she was able to tell the reporter that the information wasn't reliable.

When Zale Corporation, the nation's largest retail jeweler, went through bankruptcy, lawyers for the various feuding creditor committees routinely fed retail reporters incorrect information. Lisette McSoud, Zale's PR counsel, became a regular checkpoint who would objectively respond to every question and explain the context for why a certain committee took a particular position. The complex issues, including recapitalization and financial structure, required quick, complete, truthful — more to the point, useful — information and quotes. Pat Baldwin, retail reporter for the *Dallas Morning News,* said she was helped enormously through the Zale bankruptcy by McSoud's open line.

Name calling serves no good purpose except to allow reporters to think that they are the purveyors of truth and justice while the rest of us are artful manipulators. For example, Vice President Gore announced cuts in the federal workforce, including public affairs officials. Reporters at KRLD radio in Dallas, reporting the news, commented that this was a good place to start since their jobs were "only to say good things about their agencies." The people at the Federal Trade Commission, who worked long and hard to get the public to understand the so-called "Lemon Laws" governing used-car sales, the Care Labeling Rules (the little tags in the back of your clothes), and the nutritionists at the Agriculture Department, justifiably took umbrage at this thoughtless, supercilious remark.

It's right in line with a reporter for one of the morning shows at Disney World interviewing the actors playing Ken and Barbie, the famous dolls. The reporter asks Ken, "When are you going to pop the question?" Ken tactfully responds that the kids who own them like to marry them off. The reporter comments, "Oh, you've got a great future in PR. Someone who doesn't answer the question."

This is no more true than business people who dismiss reporters as sensation seeking, superficial slobs who drink heavily and ignore, if they are not too dumb to understand, the real story. "Oh, a reporter, we can't expect him or her to get the story right," would be the comment.

Let's be a little more careful how we describe our colleagues across the aisle. We'll all benefit.

Part VIII

BEGINNING THOUGHTS ON COMMUNICATION, GOVERNMENT, AND PUBLIC POLICY ISSUES

USE GOOD JUDGMENT

Have you ever read one of those wacky stories in the paper and thought, "Now there's an example of someone with not enough to do"? These incidents are not really funny; in fact, they're damaging because they affect what we think about a company or organization.

Ripley's Believe It or Not doesn't have a competition for stupidity. If they did, the U.S. Fish and Wildlife Service would be listed. Here's the story: An artist in a small town paints outside. Over a decade, she collected feathers that had fallen on the ground, and put them in a box. When the box was full, she was going to throw it out, but she just happened to be painting a picture of a phoenix, so she decided to use the feathers to make a collage. The artwork attracted attention from the Feds. They arrested the artist and confiscated the painting. Her crime? It is illegal to sell migratory birds or "their parts." The penalty is up to two years in prison and a $25,000 fine. The wildlife agency has informed the artist's lawyer that they will prosecute on behalf of each and every species they identify.

Now really. There's a trillion-dollar deficit. Murderers walk out of prison after 10 years; convicted rapists are sentenced to a dozen years and serve an average of 13 months. And they're going to throw the book at an artist for collecting feathers?

Of course, this is funny and ridiculous. And all of us can understand why this act got passed. I'm a little young to remember when women wore hats with whole birds on them, but I gather fashions at the turn of the century just about wiped out whooping cranes. But, can't we distinguish between that sort of trade and what this artist did?

The problem is that the federal official is probably right. We can't because laws and regulations have been reduced to such ridiculous minutiae that no one is allowed to use good judgment. And the problem, in communication terms, is that we read a story like this, and it makes us think the government doesn't have enough to do and can't spend taxpayer dollars prudently. In other words, it calls the work of the entire agency, if not the government, into question.

People need to be allowed to use good judgment. But when they do, they will occasionally err or make mistakes. That's the price of trying. However, when you try to hem people in so closely with pages and pages of regulations, you get this kind of ridiculousness.

Bird feathers probably aren't that exciting, but imagine this principle applied to how employers comply with the Americans with Disabilities Act, the issue of sexual harassment in the workplace, and a hundred other issues, and you've got one explanation of why our country is in trouble. Too many lawyers writing laws and not enough "good judgment."

Incidentally, the birds were duck, blue jay, cardinal, possibly owl, and yellow-shafted flicker. I don't think the flicker was the only one shafted.

SHOULD BUSINESS COMMUNICATION INVOLVE ECONOMICS?

Many of us who struggled through Economics 101 wonder if "business" has anything to do with "economics." Businessmen and women need to take a broader view of their responsibilities to educate the public.

Most of what companies talk about is related to specific events in the life of their company — earnings up (or down), new president hired (or fired), plant closed (or opened). Occasionally, a company relates its own news to broader economic conditions. For example, when the Zale Corporation entered Chapter 11 bankruptcy, it noted that two back-to-back disastrous Christmas seasons played a major role in the company's problems.

But comments about economic matters in general seem to be totally missing from corporate communication. This deafening silence does nothing to help get a generation of Americans out of economic illiteracy.

Here are some examples of the danger. Scott Burns, personal finance columnist for the *Dallas Morning News*, found few people knew that entitlements make up more than *half* the federal budget. Entitlements, defense, interest, and mandated programs make up almost all the budget — making it very hard to cut. A University of Nebraska professor found that only 20 percent of the public came close to guessing the unemployment rate. It was seven percent at the time, but the professor reported that people estimated much higher figure because they read all the stories about layoffs, and they hear all the politicians moaning and groaning.

The public is woefully unaware of how much profit American business makes. The Nebraska professor found only one person in eight had a true picture of corporate profits, which have been about 13 percent for the past decade. The public wildly overestimates profits at more than 30 percent. Columnist William Raspberry says he routinely asks high school students the same question. They have similarly unrealistic estimates.

American business should care about this level of ignorance because American business has the most to gain or lose. Public perception drives Washington's policy initiatives. For instance, if the public believes "waste" and "fraud" are the problem in the budget, they'll resist cutting entitlements. And if the public thinks business racks up a 30-percent profit, why not tax them a bit more?

The Clinton Administration routinely says that the tax increase only hits "wealthy" Americans. Their definition of "wealthy" includes a lot of two-income families with $30,000 or $35,000 salaries.

Similarly, they claim that the "rich" don't pay their fair share. Actually, the top one percent of earners paid 27.4 percent of federal income taxes, and that figure has increased from 19 percent in the previous decade. By contrast, the entire lower 50 percent of income earners paid 5.1 percent and that was down from 7.3 percent a decade earlier.

Although there are several groups, such as Citizens for a Sound Economy and the Taxpayers Union, trying to get the message across, they don't get much, if any, help from the business community.

CEOs should use their positions to shed light on this ignorance. They should talk candidly and frequently to employees, customers, and the community about the economic facts of life. The women's movement advocates economic empowerment and independence, emphasizing that women must understand how to manage money in order to be truly independent. I'd carry the premise a step farther: *Americans* need to be far more savvy about economics. Once that happens, we'll make better decisions, not only about our household budgets, but about our city, state, and federal governments. If you don't know the facts, you're not deciding — you're guessing.

BANKERS' CONFUSION

Despite historically reasonable interest rates, many businesses report problems getting credit and loans from their banks. Everyone says they wants to solve the problem, but points a finger at someone else. Bankers say they have money to lend. The politicians and Congress blame the bankers. Off the record, bankers say it's the fault of overly zealous regulators who swoop down on them for imagined future problems. Off the record, regulators say Congress is just looking for another excuse to have hearings and look for scapegoats and take attention off its own role in the regulatory difficulties.

We know the problem is real, at least from the point of view of business. You've seen the newspaper stories about the "credit crunch," and we probably all have anecdotes to confirm it — friends or acquaintances with excellent payment or credit records who can't get money from their bank. The prime rate goes up and down but is nowhere near the inflationary 1970s, so what's the problem?

The Administration and its bank regulators deny they are tightening standards, but this is a classic example where the authorities are sending mixed messages. For example, they are forcing banks to list some loans as bad (called classifying a loan) even when the business has never missed a payment. Regulators are trying to anticipate if a business *might* default on a loan. Examiners are insisting that bankers begin a discussion about financial products. They should start with a grim statement saying that certain products are not insured and risky.

So who can blame the bank officers that deal with business people like me for being confused? They are responding by trying not to make mistakes. You know that old saying "You get good judgment from those

277

times when you used bad judgment." Business is about judgments — some good, some bad. When you try not to make any mistakes, you end up not making any decisions at all. Business slows down or grinds to a halt. We have a credit crunch.

Historically, bank loan officers looked to lots of things to decide if you were creditworthy, including indicators within a business such as your receivables or contracts signed for future delivery. But they also looked to what kind of person you were: Did you take your commitments seriously, and did they *think* you would pay your debts.

The culprit is Congress. The old rules that governed how banks and thrifts lent money were radically changed in the 1980s in response to the escalation of interest rates in the 1970s. Congress sent the clear message that it was okay for the thrifts to dive into new areas, that go-go-go was the order of the day. Of course, many of those bankers, both the high-flying thrift operators and ostensibly conservative bankers were only too happy to help their pals in Congress raise campaign funds.

In 1986, Congress enacted a major rewrite of the tax laws, sweeping away decades of tax breaks, many of which had benefited industries like real estate. Some estimate that billions of dollars in assets were wiped out overnight because of the immediate revaluation of what real estate was worth. Not surprising, this industry tsunami caused widespread havoc. It revolutionized banking in states like Texas; as late as 1994 real estate had still not returned to 1986 values in many areas. Congress howled and looked for wrongdoers — but not in the mirror, of course. And when regulators did find evidence of actual wrongdoing, not just bad business judgment, members of Congress hastened to step in to protect their pals (witness the Keating Five). So Congress said to the regulators, in effect, bring me someone's head on a silver platter, any head, anywhere. And don't be too picky.

Lest you think this is too harsh, consider this: The FDIC Chairman, Bill Seidman, visited with the officers of First Republic Bank Holding Company in Texas and asked them to stay and help rebuild the new bank. He said they were not a target of any litigation by the FDIC. Thus assured, the bank used up its insurance fund to settle shareholder suits. One day before the three-year statute of limitations expired, the government brought suit against more than 60 directors and officers. The suit was finally settled after years of wrangling, and the directors paid millions from their own pockets. One had to sell his house, and another eliminated an IRA.

Congress and the regulators scare banks because they are unpredictable. You face endless hearings looking for a fall guy — for the S&L crisis, for the so-called "credit crunch," for alleged redlining and discrimination.

Imagine you are a bank examiner and you got the following memo entitled "Examining for Residential Lending Discrimination." The set of procedures involve looking at whether groups are treated differently, whether the result of a seemingly neutral policy is that groups end up being treated differently in terms of actually getting loans or if the examiner has "reason to believe" that discrimination existed. What's "reason to believe"?

The procedures state: Reason to believe exists when "a reasonable person might conclude from credible information in hand (or from additional information that appears likely to be obtained through further investigation) that illegal discrimination occurred." Not bad, but don't stop there. The memo continues, "The examiner who believes personally that there was *not* (emphasis added by me) discrimination should consider whether a reasonable person *might* (emphasis added by me) reach the opposite conclusion." If so, reason to believe exists. Now, just in case you miss the point, the badly written memo continues, "In other words, it is not necessary that the evidence to compel the conclusion that illegal discrimination occurred. Reason to believe may exist when the evidence is not yet developed." Translation: Bring back bodies and don't worry about the fine print.

This is not a Republican or Democratic problem. Members of Congress from both parties were guilty of creating this situation. They should fund the required regulators; let them commit to writing clear, limited regulations, and Congress should leave them alone. The reason some people have trouble getting credit and loans isn't because the banks aren't listening; it's because they are hearing too many contradictory messages.

"Society's values have a stronger influence on people's actions than do laws and regulations, so elected officials and regulators should focus on other ways besides more laws or 'tougher enforcement' to achieve the desired result."
— MERRIE SPAETH

LAW ABIDING

What makes us obey the law? Do we assess the chances of being caught and prosecuted? The first question we should ask is why we behave in certain ways, and why we do certain things and not others. Society's values have a stronger influence on people's actions than do laws and regulations, so elected officials and regulators should focus on other ways besides more laws or "tougher enforcement" to achieve the desired result.

A Florida court case got my attention because of an announcement that this case was being prosecuted "to send a message" to the rest of us. The facts: A couple was driving a few blocks from a store to their home. Their three-year-old child was ill, so the wife held her instead of placing her in a safety seat or seat belt as required by law. They were hit by an oncoming car, and the child died. The father is being prosecuted for murder.

The case demonstrates how lawyers have dominated our thinking. Lawyers can only think of laws to affect behavior: Write a law, look for lawbreakers, and prosecute them. Does this really work?

Will that make parents drive safely? Or get businessmen to put the correct information in advertising? Did that stop insider trading, junk bonds, or the excesses of the S&L crisis? There were already laws against those things, and I think the people involved had at least a passing awareness of them.

Most of us learn what's legal through a more informal process, not because we follow every move our legislatures make. We talk to our colleagues. We see media coverage. More than anything else, we are affected by what others do and think, and by the general values of our society and community.

Look at drunk driving. Tougher law enforcement was indeed important, but society's view of what was acceptable changed dramatically. It changed because groups like Mothers Against Drunk Driving went on talk shows, visited neighborhood groups, and rallied others. As a result, the vast majority of people think it's *not* okay to have a few beers in the buggy.

Actually, seat-belt use has increased dramatically over time as a result of many public service announcements and messages. As an example, 71 percent of Texans wear seat belts. It's also a result of how the media reports the news. Frequently, when an accident is reported, the reporter will tell you that a passenger was or wasn't wearing his seat belt. When someone survives a bad accident, the reporter will frequently ask if the seat belt helped him survive. Over time, the listener absorbs these messages.

Is prosecuting this father for murder going to make mothers in Memphis or dads in Detroit buckle up? People are more likely to comply with any law, whether designed for our own good or for society's, only if we make the long-term effort to stress that values do matter and that we disapprove of people who disregard standards of ethical behavior.

Outreach campaigns and neighborhood discussions about values aren't nice and crisp. You must "pass a law and now it's done." Lawyers like things nice and crisp. But they'll save more children, improve business practices, and ultimately draft laws that do what they're supposed to, which is getting us on the side of the line labeled "law abiding" rather than the side labeled "lawbreaker."

THE BUDGET AGREEMENTS

Every year produces a new budget agreement in Washington, and Congressmen and women head out on the campaign trail with the message that they will cut federal spending. They are sending you a message all right, but you need to listen carefully.

To describe the so-called "budget agreement" that supposedly cuts spending, I think of Alfred E. Smith's comment, "No matter how you slice it, it's still baloney."

Folks, over the years, we've been had. Most readers know that there has been a significant increase in their taxes. But you've probably read the comments about cuts in federal spending. Many people think billions have been cut. That's what press reports lead us to believe; for example, the *New York Times* says $60 billion will be cut from Medicaid.

Samuel Butler said, "I don't mind lying, but I hate inaccuracy." There has not been a penny of actual reduction in federal spending. Here's why. You're a bureaucrat with a $100-million program. You want $120 million next year and Congress wants to give you $120 million so they can brag to a special interest group that they got them more money. After all this negotiation, you, Mr. Bureaucrat, end up with $110 million. Most of us think that's an increase. Not our pals in the Capitol. They've counted that program as cut by $10 million. That's why the debate on Capitol Hill under Speaker of the House Newt Gingrich is important. If true, it will reverse decades of misleading the public, at least in how the budget is figured and reported.

The importance is not just semantic. The previous way of budgeting meant that total federal spending continued to increase in 1992 by about $100 billion, or eight percent, well above inflation in 1993 and 1994.

Had this book been written in July 1994, I would have noted that Congressmen and women of both parties and the President are indeed sending you a message. When they say "this made progress," that it "cut spending," they are really communicating to you that they think you are economically ignorant and believe everything you hear.

If they had any respect for you, they would explain that these so-called "cuts" come from the "current services budget." This is a wish list which includes every program's largest possible increase and greatest expansion if every group's wildest dreams were granted; that is, it's inflated spending levels which would never actually happen.

Our elected officials sent us a message that they think we're easily misled, and that when we read headlines saying that "Tax rates hit rich," we won't realize that we're footing the bill.

But in November 1994, the voters sent Congress a message. "Just because we don't understand the specifics doesn't mean we don't know what's going on," they said. The leadership of Congress was turned over to a new party for the first time in 40 years.

This is a fascinating example of Abraham Lincoln's often quoted comment, "You can fool all the people some of the time, and some of the people all of the time, but you can't fool all of the people all of the time." The percentages in that equation shifted dramatically in the November 1994 election.

The current party in power now has a challenge of its own. The public is looking for some specific things. My bet is that the "must-have" list includes truth-in-budgeting and making Congress live under the same rules as the rest of us. (Do you pay just $25 a month for your comprehensive health insurance? Does your business have to pay attention to the EEOC and OSHA, or can it just ignore them the way Congress can?) The real test, however, will be term limits, which *Wall Street Journal* writer John Fund calls the most important reform today because it will clearly tell us whether Republicans believe in less government, more accountability, and more openness, or whether they just want to be the ones handing out the goodies and enjoying the perks.

In my earlier years, my family drank much more alcohol than we do now. We particularly liked champagne. My father used to say that when he drank champagne, a little birdie came and sat on his shoulder and said, "Drink it all now. There will never be any more." Washington has its own little birdies, and they very quickly sit on the shoulders of members of Congress. They say, "You're so bright. You're so smart. We need you. Only you can solve these problems." And the bubbles dance around the brain.

The messages for members of Congress, voters, and politicos from the 1994 elections are clear. But American business can learn something, too. Not just that this is the moment to jump on tort reform, but that the status quo can quickly evaporate.

In the early 1970s, I was a researcher for a New York foundation months before the city went bankrupt. People were denying the problem would ever become that extreme. It just couldn't happen. But it did. Twenty years later, Orange County, California, went bankrupt. Before it happened, the prevailing mood was it can't happen. Someone would prevent it from happening. But it happened.

The American business system, despite the welter of confusing regulations and a government that sometimes seems determined to prevent business from growing and providing jobs, is really about confidence and shared trust. When that shared trust breaks down, the worst can happen.

> *"Is there anyone who really reads the inserts in prescription drug packages?"* — MERRIE SPAETH

DISCLOSURE? DISCLOSING WHAT?

Truth-in-advertising laws mandate that advertising must be truthful. There are many other laws and regulations that specify just what must go into material for the public. The intentions of the regulators may be good, but they end up hindering, rather than helping us sort out information.

Years ago, the *New York Times* wrote an editorial calling the Federal Trade Commission the "national nanny," saying it was time for the regulatory agency to stop thinking we were all morons and trying to protect us all.

It's time for another crusade against national nannyism. My dictionary tells me that to "disclose" means "to reveal or to make clear." When regulators specify what an advertiser actually puts in an ad, what a drug manufacturer puts in the insert, or what the finance company includes in a brochure, they make it harder for a company to communicate. What is "communication" and how do you achieve it? Disclosures in their many forms today (no pun intended) are how not to achieve communication.

Here's a disclosure from a 60-second ad for Toyota. The spot tells you that they are offering $1,000 cash back and 4.9 percent financing. The disclosure requires that the announcer read the following in about 12 seconds: "$1,000 cash back applies only to Tercels and two-wheel drive trucks, 4.9 percent APR applies only to Camrys and Corollas on 36 months and with 25 percent down plus TT&L, dealer participation may affect final price."

This is ludicrous. It isn't helping us understand. It's hurting our ability to understand what Toyota has to offer. Taking 12 seconds from 60 is like stealing 20 percent of the company's advertising budget.

Of course, there are ads that are not truthful communication, just

285

the old bait-and-switch technique or downright fraudulent. But the so-called solution — to specify what goes into so-called disclosure — hurts communication. It doesn't help, it adversely affects, impairs ability, causes pain.

Most of us know that advertising is the company telling us certain things (buy a certain car, get $1000 cash back) or putting its best foot forward. It's up to us to learn a little more and make a decision.

The problems with mandated disclosures are most evident in the electronic media, but they are just as relevant in print ads or in other printed "informational" material. For example, sweepstakes ads have paragraphs of text in print so tiny that many people need a magnifying glass to read it. The way the print is set off actually encourages the eye not to read it. Similarly, in many ads with financial information, the print and numbers are in tiny text and jumbled together. The eye wants to skip over it.

While we're discussing tiny text: Is there anyone who really reads the inserts in prescription drug packages? How do they get the print so small? Who writes these things? Answer: the lawyers. Why? Answer: for future litigation, so they can say they told you the product caused two percent of people to develop green spots on their skin while suffering nausea and vomiting. None of us read this, and even if we did, we don't "hear" it as applicable to us.

Pharmacists have made progress in understanding how to get through to consumers. When I pick up a prescription, it may say in bold letters "DON'T DRINK ALCOHOL WITH THIS MEDICATION." This message is reinforced verbally by the pharmacist.

Like the drug inserts, there is meaningless disclosure language in such legal documents as title searches, lease forms, and the like. The language is written by lawyers for purposes other than truly explaining to you, the consumer, what's inside.

One interesting approach with great promise comes from American General Life and Accident. Their CEO, James D'Agostino, said to his top people, "If there are nutrition labels on Twinkies, why aren't there fact labels on our insurance products?" Now that's a novel idea. Put labels, which consumers are used to seeing, on traditionally dense, legalistic, insurance policies.

There is a difference between a disclosure and a signal. A disclosure tells you that the pool leaks, which you might not know or be able to find out by looking at it. A signal tells you that there's more to find out.

Some of the most effective disclosures, such as the warning labels on cigarettes, have actually been signals. "Cigarettes can be hazardous to your health." It doesn't tell you how or why, it signals that you might want to find out more. Signals recognize that we get information from multiple sources, so they work in conjunction with other cultural influences. The words on the cigarette packs don't explain the enormous shift in public opinion about smoking, which produced all kinds of laws and regulations. News articles, talk shows, movies, lectures, and a host of other influences are involved.

There is only one area where line-by-line regulation is needed and appropriate: political advertising. But the unholy alliance of regulators and lawyers has resulted in disclosures disclosing nothing, which hurts the consumer it's designed to help and steals from American companies.

DISCLOSURE, DISCLOSING NOTHING

Read this as fast as you can. "Tax-and-title-extra-APR-nine-percent-warranties limited-dealer-and-destination-charges-not-included-offer-ends-May-17th." If you're good, you did it in three seconds. Do you think your listener learned anything?

Next, imagine you're opening a drug product. Inside is a small piece of paper with densely packed information printed in this type size and going on for paragraph after paragraph. Do you whip out the magnifying glass and read it? Most of us don't.

These are "disclosures," and they are examples of regulations gone amuck, where simply cramming words into air copy or onto a page is supposed to convey information. It's time to recognize how consumers process information and to have some faith in consumers.

Disclosures get started because someone somewhere didn't understand something. Frequently, the person got hurt. Regulatory agencies — too numerous to mention but including the Federal Trade Commission and every state attorney general or state commissioner of consumer affairs who seeks higher office — get into the picture and decree that the risks or conditions be "disclosed." They interpret disclosure as the inclusion of certain information. Almost always, it's not the information that helps to promote the product so it's squeezed into the smallest space possible to meet the legal requirements.

Has the regulator accomplished the disclosure of anything? Of course not. His audience is not the consumer; it is consumer groups and members of Congress or other legislative bodies who are wedded to the idea that people can be educated and protected by governmental bodies without any responsibility or effort on the individual's part.

The worst disclosures on radio and television involve financial terms that the ear has a hard time hearing, that needs to be repeated, and may not be terms in common use. Again, they are usually said so quickly that the ear simply waits for the next recognizable word.

There are other categories of disclosures, including the lengthy paragraphs of legal language accompanying large consumer products. The consumer has time to read them, and the vehicle (the mortgage or title document or the understanding between buyer and seller) has space to include them. The problem is that they are written by lawyers for future litigation. "You never told me the pool leaked," says the buyer, and the seller replies, "The agreement disclosed that the buyer was responsible for future repairs." This is a lose-lose situation with only the lawyers gaining.

Disclosures on drug products present a special challenge. Again, they are written by lawyers with an eye to future litigation. Since many products require watching for side effects or limiting the use under certain conditions — "Don't use this product with alcohol," "Don't drive while taking this" — the information *is* important. A simple, densely written flyer is insufficient. An example of a helpful vehicle to increase understanding is the sheet used by Eckerd's Pharmacies. It's simple to read, comes in large type, and is stapled to the prescription bag when it's handed to you. Since the next thing that happens is that the clerk rings up the sale and processes your payment, you are likely to look at it at that moment. In the Eckerd's near our house, the pharmacists know us by name and will mention anything new or important.

Some mass media disclosures can work, but they are either very simple or are repeated over long periods of time ("Smoking can be hazardous to your health"), or they are signals; that is, the ad signals to you, the reader or listener, that you have to make an investment of your time to find out more. Phrases like "conditions apply" or "not available everywhere" let you know there are some strings attached.

Too many slogans are jargon. "Nine percent APR compounded quarterly" means absolutely nothing to most readers and listeners. The "nine percent" is all that can be remembered, which is very misleading when compared to "eight percent compounded daily" or "three percent APR first three months." The eye compares nine, eight and three. Which is lower? You don't know.

There are some bright spots. Some ads for sales and specials for cars are starting to contain an 800 number. "Call this number for the details." Again, this requires that the consumer make an investment of time; it offers the seller the chance to take more time to give the specifics, and also separates potential buyers from disinterested people.

Disclosures frequently are required because someone abused the public's trust. That's unfortunate and to be condemned and pursued if possible, but disclosures don't rebuild the public's trust. They only encourage the listener to tune out.

ABOUT THE AUTHOR

The *Dallas Morning News* wrote, "No one can accuse Merrie Spaeth of living a boring existence." A former teenage movie star who appeared in *The World of Henry Orient* with Peter Sellers and Angela Lansbury, Ms. Spaeth went on to found a company that teaches innovative techniques in communication. Her clients include Federal Express, Citicorp, the J.C. Penney Company, and many others. One CEO who is a client calls her "a pioneer," and another says flatly, "I've taken many courses, and yours is the best."

Former President Ronald Reagan appointed her director of media relations and the *Washington Times* said she took the White House "into the Space Age." A former White House Fellow, she has also worked in every area of the media as a print reporter and writer for the *Philadelphia Inquirer* and *New York Daily News*, in radio and television and is currently featured regularly on "Marketplace," the national public radio show heard on hundreds of stations across the country.

A graduate of Smith College, with a Masters Degree from Columbia Business School, she lectures now at the Cox School of Business at Southern Methodist University. Her awards include *Glamour* magazine's "10 Outstanding Women of America," as well as the "Young Poet of New York" (back when she was young)

When not traveling to lecture and teach, she lives in Dallas with her family.

Marketplace Communication

Answer to exercise on page 225.

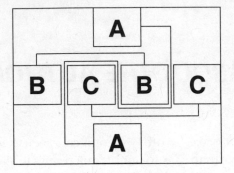

MasterMedia Limited
17 East 89th Street
New York, NY 10128
(800) 334-8232 *please use Mastercard or Visa on 1-800 orders*
(212) 546-7638 (fax)

OTHER MASTERMEDIA BUSINESS BOOKS

POSITIVELY OUTRAGEOUS SERVICE: New and Easy Ways to Win Customers for Life, by T. Scott Gross, identifies what the consumers of the nineties really want and how businesses can develop effective marketing strategies to answer those needs. ($14.95 paper)

POSITIVELY OUTRAGEOUS SERVICE AND SHOWMANSHIP: Industrial Strength Fun Makes Sales Sizzle!!!!, by T. Scott Gross, reveals the secrets of adding personality to any product or service. ($12.95 paper)

HOW TO GET WHAT YOU WANT FROM ALMOST ANYBODY, by T. Scott Gross, shows how to get great service, negotiate better prices, and always get what you pay for. ($9.95 paper)

OUT THE ORGANIZATION: New Career Opportunities for the 1990's, by Robert and Madeleine Swain, is written for the millions of Americans whose jobs are no longer safe, whose companies are not loyal, and who face futures of uncertainty. It gives advice on finding a new job or starting your own business. ($12.95 paper)

CRITICISM IN YOUR LIFE: How to Give It, How to Take It, How to Make It Work for You, by Dr. Deborah Bright, offers practical advice, in an upbeat, readable, and realistic fashion, for turning criticism into control. Charts and diagrams guide the reader into managing criticism from bosses, spouses, children, friends, neighbors, in-laws, and business relations. ($17.95 cloth)

BEYOND SUCCESS: How Volunteer Service Can Help You Begin Making a Life Instead of Just a Living, by John F. Reynolds III and Eleanor Raynolds, C.B.E., is a unique how-to book targeted at business and professional people considering volunteer work, senior citizens who wish to fill leisure time meaningfully, and students trying out various career options. The book is filled with interviews with celebrities, CEOs, and average citizens who talk about the benefits of service work. ($19.95 cloth)

MANAGING IT ALL: Time-Saving Ideas for Career, Family, Relationships, and Self, by Beverly Benz Treuille and Susan Schiffer Stautberg, is written for women who are juggling careers and families. Over two hundred career women (ranging from a TV anchorwoman to an investment banker) were interviewed. The book contains many humorous anecdotes on saving time and improving the quality of life for self and family. ($9.95 paper)

THE CONFIDENCE FACTOR: How Self-Esteem Can Change Your Life, by Dr. Judith Briles, is based on a nationwide survey of six thousand men and women. Briles explores why women so often feel a lack of self-confidence and have a poor opinion of themselves. She offers step-by-step advice on becoming the person you want to be. ($9.95 paper, $18.95 cloth)

TAKING CONTROL OF YOUR LIFE: The Secrets of Successful Enterprising Women, by Gail Blanke and Kathleen Walas, is based on the authors' professional experience with Avon Products' Women of Enterprise Awards, given each year to outstanding women entrepreneurs. The authors offer a specific plan to help you gain control over your life, and include business tips and quizzes as well as beauty and lifestyle information. ($17.95 cloth)

SIDE-BY-SIDE STRATEGIES: How Two-Career Couples Can Thrive in the Nineties, by Jane Hershey Cuozzo and S. Diane Graham, describes how two-career couples can learn the difference between competing with a spouse and becoming a supportive power partner. Published in hardcover as *Power Partners.* ($10.95 paper, $19.95 cloth)

WORK WITH ME! How to Make the Most of Office Support Staff, by Betsy Lazary, shows you how to find, train, and nurture the "perfect" assistant and how to best utilize your support staff professionals. ($9.95 paper)

THE LOYALTY FACTOR: Building Trust in Today's Workplace, by Carol Kinsey Goman, Ph.D., offers techniques for restoring commitment and loyalty in the workplace. ($9.95 paper)

DARE TO CHANGE YOUR JOB—AND YOUR LIFE, by Carole Kanchier, Ph.D., provides a look at career growth and development throughout the life cycle. ($9.95 paper)

BREATHING SPACE: Living and Working at a Comfortable Pace in a Sped-Up Society, by Jeff Davidson, helps readers to handle information and activity overload, and gain greater control over their lives. ($10.95 paper)

TWENTYSOMETHING: Managing and Motivating Today's New Work Force, by Lawrence J. Bradford, Ph.D., and Claire Raines, M.A., examines the work orientation of the younger generation, offering managers in businesses of all kinds a practical guide to better understand and supervise their young employees. ($22.95 cloth)

BALANCING ACTS! Juggling Love, Work, Family, and Recreation, by Susan Schiffer Stautberg and Marcia L. Worthing, provides strategies to achieve a balanced life by reordering priorities and setting realistic goals. ($12.95 paper)

STEP FORWARD: Sexual Harassment in the Workplace, What You Need to Know, by Susan L. Webb, presents the facts for identifying the tell-tale signs of sexual harassment on the job, and how to deal with it. ($9.95 paper)

A TEEN'S GUIDE TO BUSINESS: The Secrets to a Successful Enterprise, by Linda Menzies, Oren S. Jenkins, and Rickell R. Fisher, provides solid information about starting your own business or working for one. ($7.95 paper)

TEAMBUILT: Making Teamwork Work, by Mark Sanborn, teaches business how to improve productivity, without increasing resources or expenses, by building teamwork among employers. ($19.95 cloth)